INTRODUCTORY HEBREW
METHOD AND MANUAL

WILLIAM R. HARPER'S

Introductory Hebrew
METHOD AND MANUAL

REVISED BY

J. M. POWIS SMITH

THE UNIVERSITY OF CHICAGO PRESS

CHICAGO & LONDON

The University of Chicago Press, Chicago 60637
The University of Chicago Press, Ltd., London

Second Edition published 1885. Reissued 1959 by
The University of Chicago Press. Midway Reprint 1974
Printed in the United States of America

International Standard Book Number: 0-226-31683-1
Library of Congress Catalog Card Number: 59-7624

FOREWORD

At last students can again obtain William Rainey Harper's *Introductory Hebrew Method and Manual* and *Elements of Hebrew*, textbooks which for generations have been used with great success in the teaching of biblical Hebrew. It was with regret that we saw them withdrawn and it is with enthusiasm that we welcome their return. No other textbooks have been able to win the respect and popularity that the Harper books have always had. Pupils and teachers alike can testify that they furnish an excellent and enduring means for gaining a knowledge of Hebrew.

The inductive method employed by Professor Harper is based on sound educational principles. From the very first lesson the student has the incentive of a feeling of definite accomplishment. The constant repetition of the biblical material both establishes and fortifies the student's knowledge of the Hebrew language.

The grammar, as presented in the *Elements of Hebrew*, is neither oversimplified nor belabored with involved and wordy complexity. Essential principles are enunciated briefly, clearly, and soundly, with ample illustration. They can be grasped and retained easily.

The aids to instruction incorporated in the *Introductory Hebrew Method and Manual*, used in conjunction with the *Elements*, are a teacher's delight. In addition to the discussion of the biblical words in the reading lesson, there are exercises that are distinctive for establishing a real appreciation of Hebrew style and syntax. The volume also contains the vocalized text of Genesis I–VIII for reading purposes, the unvocalized text of Genesis I–IV for practice in vocalizing, and the transliterated text of Genesis I to afford the

v

student a check on his work during the early lessons. In addition to the usual vocabularies necessary for the lessons, the *Manual* also contains the frequency lists developed by Professor Harper to help the student master vocabulary rapidly and efficiently by learning first the words most frequently used in the Bible. Such accessories are valuable aids to the teacher, for they make possible greater flexibility in method so that materials can be adapted to the needs of the class.

These books were written long ago by Professor Harper, the first president of the University of Chicago, on the basis of his successful experience both with classes and with his famous correspondence courses. They have met the test of time and are surprisingly modern. As his employment of the educationally sound inductive method and his development of frequency lists in vocabulary demonstrate, Professor Harper could be said to be ahead of his time. Judiciously and carefully revised by Professor J. M. P. Smith, these books are regarded by many as still the best tools for the learning and teaching of biblical Hebrew. While it is true that Hebrew studies have progressed in the interim and that consequently at some points minor improvements might be made if and when a revision is undertaken, there is no serious obstacle to the use of these volumes as now reproduced.

With the present increasing interest in biblical Hebrew, the reintroduction of these fine textbooks will afford an opportunity for increasing numbers of students to learn Hebrew quickly and well, whether in class or privately.

RAYMOND A. BOWMAN

UNIVERSITY OF CHICAGO

PREFACE

The *Method and Manual* of the late President William Rainey Harper first appeared as *A Hebrew Manual* in 1883. Since the 2nd edition in 1885, several reprints have been made, but the text of that edition has stood practically without change. The Inductive approach to the study of Hebrew represented by the Harper text-books has commended itself to a wide circle of teachers and has yielded satisfactory results in arousing and maintaining the interest of large numbers of students. The fact that since its first presentation more American students have studied Hebrew by this method than by all other methods combined, and that notwithstanding the need of revision in the text-books, the method has held its own in a field where competition is keen, warrants the effort to bring the *Method and Manual* into line with advancing knowledge. The scope of the revision has been determined by the New Edition of the *Elements of Hebrew* (1921) with which the *Method and Manual* should be used.

The student mind is confronted by an ever-increasing variety of subjects, each with its own special appeal and many of them offering an apparently short and easy route to a desired goal. It is inevitable that Hebrew should suffer some loss of adherents; and it is well that such as have no special aptitude for linguistic study should expend their energies in fields that are for them more productive. But as long as the Old Testament remains one of the great historical documents of the Jewish and Christian faiths, there will ever be many who will seek to obtain a scholar's control of the literary sources of their historic beliefs. As the prologue to the Wisdom of Sirach says, "When things spoken in Hebrew are translated into another tongue they have not quite the same meaning; and not only these things (i. e. the following chapters), but the Law itself and the

Prophecies and the rest of the books, convey a different meaning when spoken in their original [language]." All who would enter into the inner sanctuary of the Hebrew spirit must first equip themselves with the linguistic key. The chambers to which it furnishes access are spacious and splendid to a degree that can never be appreciated by one who has not seen them. The Hebrew mind must remain largely *terra incognita* to him who does not know its native language. That the first steps in the learning of that language may be made simple and may represent actual progress in the mastery of the Old Testament in its own idiom is sufficient reason for sending out the Harper *Method and Manual* in a new edition.

To my colleague Professor Ira Maurice Price who guided me in my first journey through the *Introductory Hebrew Method and Manual*, and has aided in the making of this edition by reading both copy and proof, I gratefully acknowledge my indebtedness. To teachers long familiar with this book in its old form, I offer no apologies for changes. Every true teacher rejoices in the progress of knowledge, even when that progress is at his cost. New editions teach new duties. The best teachers are always themselves eager learners.

J. M. POWIS SMITH

THE UNIVERSITY OF CHICAGO

PREFACE TO THE SECOND EDITION

The student of a language must acquire three things: (1) a working vocabulary of the language, (2) a knowledge of the grammatical principles of the language, (3) an ability to use this vocabulary and to apply these principles, so as to gain the best results, whether for a literary or an exegetical purpose.

While all agree as to the end desired, the method of attaining this end is a question in dispute. According to one view, the student is first to learn the principles as they are laid down in the grammars, and then apply them to selected words, or short sentences. And after a short preliminary training of this sort, he is plunged headlong into a text without notes of any kind, and expected to make progress, and to enjoy the study. His vocabulary is to be learned by looking up the words in the Lexicon, until they become familiar. Different phases of this method are in use among teachers of Hebrew; but all follow practically the same order, (1) study of grammar, (2) application of grammar.

It is the purpose of this volume to furnish a text-book, which shall assist in acquiring the Hebrew language by a different method. The method employed may be called an inductive one. The order of work which it advocates is, *first*, to gain an accurate and thorough knowledge of some of the "facts" of the language; *secondly*, to learn from these facts the principles which they illustrate, and by which they are regulated; *thirdly*, to apply these principles in the further progress of the work. A few words of explanation are needed at this point:—

(1) The method is *an* inductive, not *the* inductive method; and while, upon the whole, it is rigidly employed throughout the course, a slight departure is made at times, in order to make more complete the treatment of a subject, for some detail of which an example has not occurred.

(2) The term "facts," as used, includes data from whatever source gathered; not merely the grammatical forms found in the passages studied, but also the paradigms which contain these and other forms systematically arranged.

(3) It is not to be supposed that a long time must elapse before

ix

the beginner is ready to take hold of principles. On the contrary,
he is taught important principles, and that, too, inductively, during the first hour's work. The three processes are all the while
going on together. He is increasing the store of "facts" at his
command, and, at the same time, learning from the facts thus
acquired new principles, and applying these principles to the new
forms continually coming to his notice. Great care must be exer-
cised, however, that the correct order be followed. Let him at-
tempt to learn no principle of which he has not had several illus-
trations. Let him be required to apply no principle the application
of which he has not already learned from familiar cases.

(4) The memorizing of the "facts" of a language, before a
knowledge of the principles has been acquired is, indeed, a piece
of drudgery; yet not so great as is the memorizing of grammar
without a knowledge of the "facts." Nor will it long remain
drudgery; for very soon, the student will begin to see analogies, to
compare this word with that, and, in short, to make his own
grammar. From this time, there will be developed such an interest in the work, that all thought of drudgery will pass away.

The question is frequently asked, How is the first lesson given?
A brief statement must suffice:—

The first word of Genesis I. 1 is written on the board, and the
English equivalent of each consonant and vowel-sound indicated
to the student. The word, as a whole, is then pronounced, and its
meaning given. The student is called upon to pronounce it, and
to give its meaning. The second word is taken up and treated in
the same manner. Then the two words are pronounced together,
and their meaning given. After this, each remaining word is
considered, and with each new word a review of all the preceding
words is made. When he has learned thus to pronounce the entire
verse, and to give a Hebrew word when its English equivalent is
named, the student is shown the "Notes" (see pages 3–4) of the
"METHOD," where, for his private study, he will find, for substance, the aid already given orally. His attention is also directed
to the "Observations," with most of which he has been made
familiar by the previous work. He is now informed that at the
following recitation he will be expected (1) to pronounce the
verse without hesitation from the pointed Hebrew (2) to pronounce
it, and write it on the board, from the English translation; (3) to
pronounce it, and write it on the board from the unpointed text; (4)
to write the transliteration of it, as given in the "Notes" or in the
Manual. The absolute mastery of the verse is, therefore, the
first thing. There will remain to be taken up, (1) the "Notes,"
for all of which the student is held responsible; (2) the "Observations," which he is expected to recall, at the suggestion of the
word on which the observation is based; (3) the "Word-Lesson,"

which, at first, includes few words not contained in the verse or
verses of the Lesson, and which is to be learned in such a manner
that when the English word is pronounced, the Hebrew equivalent will be given; (4) the "Exercises," which are to be written
on paper beforehand, copied on the board in the class-room,
criticised by instructor and class, and corrected by each student on
his paper.

The "Topics for Study" are intended to furnish a resume of
the more important points touched upon in the Lesson. By
their use, a rapid and helpful review of the hour's work is accom-
plished.

In subsequent "Lessons," a "Grammar-Lesson" is assigned.
In every case, however, the instructor should read and explain
each reference to the class before asking them to prepare it.

The "Lessons" cover chapters I-VIII. of Genesis, and include
a formal study of almost every important portion of the grammar,
except the Accents, the Euphony of Vowels, the Euphony of Consonants, the Verb with Suffixes, the Irregular Nouns, and the
Inflection of Feminine Nouns, to all of which, however, numer-
ous allusions and references are made in the "Notes."

All the help possible is given the student in the first fifteen
"Lessons." But from this point he is led gradually to rely more
and more upon himself. The "Lessons" will be found to contain
more, perhaps, than some classes can prepare for a single recitation, although this will depend largely upon the character of the
class and the number of recitations during a week. It was deemed
best, however, to make them thus, since it is an easy matter for
the instructor to indicate that a certain portion of the exercises
may be omitted. The author himself will feel inclined to require
everything in the "Lessons."

Special attention is invited to the "Review-Lessons," in the
study of each of which two or more recitations may profitably be
spent.

The "Method" is understood to include also the "MANUAL,"
although the latter, for a sufficient reason, is paged separately, and
given a title-page and preface of its own.

For the material contained in these Lessons, and for its
arrangement, the author is indebted to no one. The book, as it
now appears, presents the results of five years' experience, during
which it has been his privilege to teach not less than five hundred
men their first lesson in Hebrew.

Many valuable hints have been received from Mr. Frederick J.
Gurney, by whom great assistance has been received in the work
of the Correspondence School of Hebrew. He has also kindly
helped in the preparation of manuscript for the printer, and in
revising the proof-sheets. For similar service the author is in-

debted to Mr. C. E. Crandall, and to Rev. John W. Payne. To the
latter credit is also due for his painstaking care in the typograph-
ical work of the book.

With a faith in the Inductive Method, which grows stronger
every year, and with the hope that the time may soon come when
many others shall have an equally strong faith in it, the author
commits the "METHOD" to its friends.

W. R. H.

MORGAN PARK, September 1, 1885.

TABLE OF CONTENTS

INTRODUCTORY METHOD.

TABLE OF CONTENTS.

MANUAL.

INTRODUCTORY HEBREW METHOD

LESSON I.—GENESIS I. 1.[1]

[*To the student* :—Let it be understood from the outset that nothing short of complete mastery, and that, of everything in the Lesson, will accomplish the end in view. Not a needless word or statement has been inserted. Let it be a matter of principle to do just what is assigned,—no more, no less.]

1. NOTES

1. **בְּרֵאשִׁית**—b'rē'-šîθ (two syllables)—*In-beginning:*

a. *Six letters:*—בּ (b); ר (r); א, called 'ålēf,[2] not pronounced, but represented by ' ; שׁ (š =sh); י (y), here silent after ‐‐; ת (θ= th, as in *thin*).

b. *Three vowel-sounds:*— ‐ː (ˈ) under בּ , pron. like e in *below*, see § 5. 6. a;[3] ‐‐ (ē), like ey in *they;* י_‐ (î), like i in *machine.*

2. **בָּרָא**—bå-rå' (two syllables)—(he)-*created:*

a. *Three letters:*— בּ (b); ר (r); א (') called 'ålēf,[2] see 1 a.[4]

b. *Two vowel-sounds:*—Both ‐ː (å), like d in *all.*

3. **אֱלֹהִים**—'ĕlô-hîm (two syllables)— *God* (literally *Gods*):

a. *Five letters:*—א ('); ל (l); ה (h); י (y), silent after ‐‐; ם (m).

b. *Three-vowel-sounds:*—‐ː (ˈ), like e in *met*, quickly uttered, § 5. 6. c; _‐ (ô), like ô in *note;* י_‐ (î), see 1. b.

c. The accent ‐ˆ with ‐‐, marks this word as the middle of the verse.

4. **אֵת**—'ēθ—not translated, but represented in translation by)(.

5. **הַשָּׁמַיִם**—håš-šå-mä'-yim (four syllables)—*the-heavens:*

a. *Five letters:*—ה (h); שׁ (š =sh), but שׁ (with a dot in its bosom) is š doubled; מ (m), written so at beginning or in the middle of a word; י (y), not silent as before but like y in *year;* ם (m), written so at end of a word, § 3. 2.

3

b. *Four vowel-sounds:*—⟋ (ă), like *a* in *hatter*, § 5. 1; ⟋, **see** 2 *b;* ⟋ (ă); ⟋ (ĭ), like *i* in *pin*, § 5. 2

c. The sign ⟋ under מ is used arbitrarily in these Lessons to indicate the position of the accent when as in this word, it is not on the last vowel.

d. The ĭ of the last syllable is only of secondary importance.

6. וְאֵת—wᵉ'ēθ (one syllable)—*and-*)(, see 4:

a. *Three letters:*—ו (w), like *w* in *water;* א (');ת (θ).

b. *Two vowel-sounds:*—⟋ ('), see 1. *b;* ⟋ (ē), **see 1. *b.***

7. הָאָרֶץ:—hā-'ā'-rĕṣ (three syllables)—*the-earth:*

a. *Four letters:*—ה (h); א (') ;ר (r); ץ (ṣ), a sharp hissing sound, § 2. 7.

b. *Three vowel-sounds:*—⟋ (å) ; ⟋ (å) ;⟋ (ĕ), like *e* in *met.*

c. The last vowel is of secondary character, as in 5 *d.*

d. The accent ⟋, under א, marks this word as the end of the **verse**; the **:** is equivalent to a period.

2. OBSERVATIONS.

1. The letters in this verse are:—(1) א, (2) ב, (3) ה, (4) ו, (5)', (6) ל, (7) מ, (8) ם, (9) ץ, (10) ר, (11) שׁ, (12) שׂ, (13) ת.

2. The vowel sounds:—(1)⟋, (2) ⟋, (3) ⟋, (4) ⟋, (5), ⟋, (6) ⟋, (7) '⟋, (8) ⟋, (9) ⟋.

3. To be carefully distinguished in pronunciation are:—

(1) ⟋ ('), ⟋ ('), ⟋ (ĕ), ⟋ (ē) ; (2) ⟋ (ă), ⟋ (å) ; (3) ⟋ (ĭ), '⟋ (ĭ).

4. *Above* the line, a dot is ō (as in *note*); *below* the line, it is ĭ

5. The Hebrew is written from right to left.   [(as in *pin*).

6. The plural ending of masc. nouns is ם'⟋ (îm), as in אֱלֹהִים (lit., *Gods*); cf. the Hebrew words that have been Anglicized, *cherub*-im, and *seraph*-im.

7. אֵת ('ēθ), not translatable, is a sign placed before the **object** of a verb, when that object is both direct and *definite.*

8. The preposition *in*, בְּ, and the conjunction *and*, וְ, are never written separately, being always *prefixed to the* following *word*.

9. When it is desired to pronounce a letter *twice in succession*, that letter is written but *once*, and a dot inserted (see שּׁ) in its bosom.

10. The letter of the Definite Article (*the*) is הַ (h).

11. Most words are accented on the last vowel; those which are accented elsewhere mark the place of the accent in this book, by the sign ־ֹ.

12. Every syllable begins with a consonant. The vowel-sounds ־ and ־ֱ cannot alone carry a syllable.

3. WORD-LESSON.

(1) אֱלֹהִים *God* (5) בְּ *in* (9) מָשַׁל[1] *he-ruled*

(2) אָמַר[1] *he-said* (6) בָּרָא[1] *he-created* (10) רֵאשִׁית *beginning*

(3) הָאָרֶץ *the-earth* (7) הַ, הָ *the* (11) שָׁמַיִם *heavens*

(4) אֵת)((8) וְ *and* (12) שָׁמַר[1] *he-kept*

4. EXERCISES

1. To be translated into Hebrew:—(1) *And-beginning;* (2) *And-heavens;* (3) *He-created*)(*the-earth and-)(the-heavens;* (4) *God kept* (Hebrew order: *kept God*))(*the-heavens;* (5) *God (is)[2] in-heavens;* (6) *God ruled* (Hebrew order: *ruled God);* (7) *In-beginning God said;* (8) *The* (הָ)*-beginning;* (9) *the* (הָ*-God;* (10) *And-the-earth.*

2. To be translated into English:— (1) וְהַשָּׁמַיִם; (2) שָׁמַר (3) אֱלֹהִים בְּשָׁמַיִם; (4) מָשַׁל אֱלֹהִים; אֱלֹהִים אֵת הָאָרֶץ וְהָרֵאשִׁית; (5) אָמַר הָאֱלֹהִים.

---

[1] A verb in the past tense 3d person singular masculine.
[2] Parentheses ( ) enclose words which are not to be rendered into Hebrew.

3. To be written in English letters: — (1) שָׁמַר‎, (2) אָמַר‎, (3) אֱלֹהִים‎; (9) וְאֵת‎, (8) בָּרָא‎, (7) הַשָּׁמַיִם‎, (6) וְ‎, (5) בְּ‎, (4) מִשַׁל‎ (10) הָאָרֶץ‎.

4. To be written in Hebrew letters:—(1) lå, (2) låš, (3) hîl, (4) bĕ, (5) rå, (6) yĭm, (7) îm, (8) lᵉ, (9) hᵉ, (10) lē.

5. TOPICS FOR STUDY.

(1) The sounds represented by the letter e as variously printed.

(2) The plural ending; the preposition in; the conjunction and.

(3) The sign אֵת‎; the method employed to indicate the doubling of a letter.

(4) The article; the usual place of the accent; the difference between מ‎ and ם‎.

LESSON II.—GENESIS I. 2a.

1. NOTES.

8. וְהָאָרֶץ‎—wᵉhå-'å'-rĕṣ—and-the-earth: see 7, preceding Lesson.

9. הָיְתָה‎—hå-yᵉθå(h) (two syllables)—(she) was:

a. 1st syllable, הָ‎ (hå), ends in a vowel and is said to be open, § 26. 1.

b. 2d syllable, יְתָה‎ yᵉθå(h); the final ה‎ is silent, as always at the end of a word; the ◌ָ is not a full vowel, and goes with what follows.

c. The sign ◌ֽ with ◌ָ indicates a secondary accent, § 18.

10. תֹהוּ‎—θō'-hû (two syllables)—(a)-desolation:

a. 1st syl., תֹ‎ (θ), ◌ֹ ō, (not ô), ends in a vowel i. e. is open § 26. 1.

b. 2d syl., ה‎ (h), וּ‎ (û), like oo in tool, is open, § 26. 1.

11. וָבֹהוּ‎—wå-vō'hû (three syllables)—and-(a)-waste:

a. ב‎ is not b (בּ‎), but v as in vote.

b. Each syllable is open, § **26**. 1.

12. וְחֹשֶׁךְ—w⁰hō'-šĕχ (two syllables)—*and-darkness:*

a. וֹ (w); ח (ḥ), a harsh *h*-sound, § **2**. 3; שׁ (š =*sh*); ךְ (χ), like German ḏ͡j (weak).

b. ⟶ (ᵒ); the ⟶ over שׁ serves also for the vowel ō; ⟶ (ĕ).

c. The ⟶ in ךְ must be written, when final, but it has no sound.

d. The final vowel here is of secondary character; see 5.*d* and 7.*c*.

13. עַל-פְּנֵי—'äl+p⁰nê (two syllables)—*upon+faces-of:*

a. עַ ('), practically unpronounceable for us, called 'ä'-yĭn, § **2**. 2; לֹ (1); פּ (p); נ (n).

b. The י after ⟶ (ê) is silent, as was that after ⟶ (î), see 1. *b.*

c. The sign ▪ is the Hebrew hyphen, represented in transliteration by +.

d. These two words, *upon* and *faces-of*, are pronounced as if one.

14. תְהוֹם—θ⁰hôm (one syllable)—*abyss:*

a. A syllable beginning with two consonants, but between them is the short *e*-sound described in § **5**. 6.*a*.

b. Tne syllable ends in a consonant,—it is *closed*, § **26**. 2.

c. As י is silent after ⟶ or ⟶, so ו is silent under ⟶ (ô).

d. ⟶, see 3.*c*, preceding Lesson.

2. LETTERS AND VOWELS PROMISCUOUSLY ARRANGED.

י	ה	בּ	ח	⟶	⟶	—
ה	ךְ	ם	נ	⟶	⟶	⟶
ב	נ	א	י	⟶	⟶	⟶
ע	ר	ץ	פּ	⟶	⟶	⟶
שׁ	ת	ו	בּ	⟶	⟶	ו
ל	פּ	מ	ה	ו	—	⟶

Suggestion.—Study this table until every sign has been mastered. It contains sixteen out of the twenty-two letters, and eleven out of the fifteen vowel-signs in Hebrew.

3. OBSERVATIONS.

13. New letters: (1) בּ, (2) ח, (3) ך, (4) עֲ, (5) פ, (6) ג.

14. New vowels: (1) ִי, (2) ֹ‎‏__, (3) ִי; but ֹ‎__ and ִי (ê and ô) are pronounced just like ‾‾ and ‒ (ē and ō), the former having what is termed a *fuller* writing.

15. ‐, called Šᵉwâ, is the least vowel-sound and cannot carry a syllable.

16. While the conjunction *and* (ו) is usually written with Šᵉwâ (thus: וְ), it is once written in this lesson וּ (wǎ).

17. Syllables ending in a vowel are called *open;* ending in a consonant, they are called *closed.*

18. Observe the difference between בּ (b) and ב (v); ח (ḥ) and ה (h); א (') and עֲ ('); ו (w) and (û).

19. Observe that י is silent after ‾‾ or ‾‾ ; ו, under ‒ or with a dot in it (וּ); ה, at the end of a word.

20. The Hebrew verbal inflection distinguishes *gender.*

21. While most Hebrew words are accented on the last vowel, see Obs. 11, *four* words in this Lesson, out of *seven,* have the accent elsewhere, as shown by the position of the sign ‾.

22. The Hebrew says: *faces-of abyss,* not *faces of-abyss;* that is, the *first* of two words in the genitive relation suffers change; this order is never changed.

4. GRAMMAR-LESSON.

Learn in the "Elements of Hebrew" the following sections:—

1. § **2.** 1—3,6,8,   The pronunciation of א, ה, עֲ, ח, שׁ, ו.
2. § **3.** 1,   Order of writing; extended letters.
3. § **9.** 1, and § **5.** 6.*a,*   Šᵉwâ, its representation and pronunciation.

4. § **26**. 1, 2,   Open and Closed Syllables.

5. § **49**. 1,   The ordinary writing of the conjunction *and* (וְ).

5. WORD-LESSON.

(13) בֹּהוּ *waste*   (16) חֹשֶׁךְ *darkness*   (19) פָּנִים *faces*

(14) הָיָה *he-was*   (17) עַל *upon*   (20) תֹּהוּ *desolation*

(15) הָיְתָה *she-was*   (18) פְּנֵי *faces-of*   (21) תְהוֹם *abyss*

Note.—The word for *waste*, when it stands by itself, is בֹּהוּ (bō'-hû), not בְהוּ (vō'-hû); so we say תֹּהוּ (tō'-hû) *desolation*. not תְהוּ (θō'-hû), and תְהוֹם not תהום.

6. EXERCISES.

1. To be translated into Hebrew:—(1) *In-beginning was* (f.) *the-earth;* (2) *Darkness was upon+the-earth;* (3) *Desolation* (תֹּהוּ, not תְהוּ) *was* (m.) *upon+faces-of the-heavens;* (4) *Faces;* (5) *Faces-of abyss;* (6) *God ruled in-*(= *over*)- *darkness;* (7) *God-of* (אֱלֹהֵי) *the-heavens;* (8) *God was in-beginning;* (9) *He-created*)(*the-earth and-*)(*the-heavens;* (10) *The-earth was* (f.).

2. To be translated into English:—

(1) חֹשֶׁךְ הָיָה עַל־פְּנֵי הָאָרֶץ וְעַל־פְּנֵי הַשָּׁמַיִם

(2) הָיְתָה הָאָרֶץ בְּחֹשֶׁךְ וְחֹשֶׁךְ הָיָה עַל־פְּנֵי תְהוֹם

3. To be written in English letters:—(1) פָּנִים, (2) הָיָה, (3) אֱלֹהֵי, (4) הָיְתָה, (5) תְהוֹם, (6) תהום, (7) תְהוּ, (8) תֹּהוּ, (9) בְהוּ, (10) בֹּהוּ.

4. To be written in Hebrew letters:—(1) hâ, (2) hû, (3) hă, (4) hō, (5) hî, (6) ḥō, (7) ḥâ, (8) nîm, (9) 'ăl. (10) šĕx, (11) pâ, (12) šâ.

7. *TOPICS FOR STUDY.*

(1) Two ways of writing *and*. (2) The circumstances under which **ו** and **י** are silent. (3) New letters and vowels. (4) Open and closed syllables. (5) The sign ־ ; its representation and pronunciation. (6) Extended letters. (7) Words in the genitive relation.

LESSON III.—GENESIS I. 2b, 3.

1. *NOTES.*

15. וְרוּחַ—wᵉrû(ă)ḥ (one syllable)—*and-spirit-of:*

a. *Three consonants:*— **ו** (w), **ר** (r), **ח** (ḥ) the harsh *h*-sound.

b. The conjunction *and* (**ו**) written with Šᵉwâ, §49. 1; **ו** = û, as *oo* in *fool;* the ־ (ă) to be pronounced *before* the **ח**, and not after it.

c. This word is treated as having but one syllable, the ᵉ and ă not counting as full vowels.

d. The ־ is slipped in between the û and the ḥ in order to form a transition sound between these two sounds of such different physiological formation.

16. מְרַחֶפֶת—mᵉrā(ḥ)-ḥĕʹ-fĕθ (three syllables)—*brooding:*

a. **פ** = *f*, while **פּ** is *p;* cf. **ב** = *v* and **בּ** *b*, § 12. 1. N. 1.

b. The final unaccented vowel is of secondary origin, cf. 5.*d*, 7.*c*, and 12.*d*.

c. **מ** indicates that the form is a participle; **ת**, that it is feminine.

17. הַמָּיִם :—hăm-mâʹ-yīm (three syllables)—*the-waters:*

a. **מ** = m, **מּ** = mm: a point in a letter preceded by a full vowel indicates doubling, and is called Dâḡēš-fōrtē, § 13. 1, cf **שׁ** (5. *a*).

b. The **י** here precedes ־ and so is sounded (as *y* in *year*).

c. The article *the* is **ה**, with ־ under it and Dâḡēš-fōrtē in the following consonant; cf. **הַשָּׁמַיִם** (5), § 45. 1.

d. The ī is an unaccented secondary vowel; cf. 5.*d*, 7.*c*, 12.*d*, and 16.*b*.

e. The accent ־ָ indicates the end of the verse; ׃ always follows this accent.

18. וַיֹּאמֶר—wăy-yô''-mĕr—(three syllables)—*and*-(he)-*said*, §§ **26.** 1, 2, Note 1; **13.** 1:

a. The perf. 3rd. p. masc. is אָמַר ('ă-măr) *he-said*.

b. The prefixed י indicates the imperfect, יֹאמֶר

c. The conjunction (וַ) connects this sentence with the preceding, and also makes the imperfect equivalent to a *perfect* (*and-he-said*). This seeming anomaly will be taken up later; it is sufficient here to learn that אָמַר = *he said;* וַיֹּאמֶר = *and-he-said.*

19. יְהִי־ — yᵉhî+—*shall-be* (or *let-be*), §§ **10.** 1; **26.** 1; **17.** 1:

a. The first י indicates the imperfect as in יֹאמֶר.

b. The ־ְ being a šᵉwâ vowel, this word has but one syllable, § **27.** 1.

c. הָיָה *he-was; cf.* הָיְתָה (9) *she-was.*

20. אוֹר—'ôr—*light*, §§ **5.** 5; **26.** 2:

a. א has no sound, but is represented by ', § **2.** 1.

b. ו , with a point over it, unites with the point, as in תְּהוֹם (14).

21. וַיְהִי־—wăy-hî+—*and*-(there)-*was*, § **17.** 1:

a. The conjunction here, as in וַיֹּאמֶר (18), not merely *connects*, but *converts* the imperfect (*shall be*) into a perfect (*was*).

b. The conjunction in וַיֹּאמֶר was וַ, but here it is וַ, the Dăgēš-fōrtē having been rejected.

c. The sign (ֵ) with ־ indicates a secondary accent, cf. 9. *c*, § **18.** 1.

d. י forms a diphthong with preceding ă; cf. § **10.** 2 *a.*

2. *WORDS ARRANGED PROMISCUOUSLY FOR EXAMINATION.*[1]

הָיְתָה	וַיְהִי־	תְּהוֹם	בֹּהוּ	אֱלֹהִים	מַיִם
יֹאמֶר	בָּרָא	אוֹר	רוּחַ	הַשָּׁמַיִם	הַמַּיִם
וַיֹּאמֶר	עַל	תֹהוּ	פְּנֵי	מְרַחֶפֶת	בְּרֵאשִׁית
יְהִי	אֵת	חֹשֶׁךְ	וְהָאָרֶץ	בְּרֵאשִׁית	

[1] Examine, pronounce aloud, translate, and *master* these words.

3. OBSERVATIONS.

23. A sign of the feminine gender is the letter ת.

24. פ = p, but פ = f; ב = b, but ב = v.

25. A syllable closing with Dåḡēš-fŏrtē is called *sharpened*. All *sharpened* syllables are, of course, *closed* syllables.

26. The prefix י marks the *imperfect* (3 masc. sing.).

27. וְ connects, but וָ, a stronger form, connects and *converts*.

28. Roots have *three* letters (see אָמַר *he said*, בָּרָא *he created*), all other letters are prefixes or suffixes.

29. The laryngeals א, ה, ח, ע, ר, causing many seeming irregularities in the forms of words, deserve special attention.   [vowel.

30. Dåḡēš-fŏrtē[1] is in every case immediately preceded by a

31. The vowel of *open* syllables is long, of *closed*, short; of accented syllables it may be either long or short.

32. The letter of the article is ה; its vowel is regularly ◌ַ; it usually has D. f.[2] in the first letter of the word to which it is prefixed. But note הָ, in הָאָרֶץ.

4. GRAMMAR-LESSON.

Learn in the "Elements of Hebrew" the following sections:—

1. Under § 4. 1,   The laryngeals א, ה, ח, ע, and ר, cf. Obs. 29.
2. § 13. 1,   Dåḡēš-fŏrtē, cf. Obs. 30.
3. § 28. 1, 2,   Quantity of vowels in syllables, cf. Obs. 31.
4. § 47. 1,   The writing of the preposition בְּ (*in*).

5. WORD-LESSON.

(22) אוֹר *light*   (25) וַיּאֹמֶר *and-he-said*   (28) מְרַחֶפֶת *brooding*

(23) אִישׁ *man*   (26) וַיְהִי *and-(there)-was* (29) רָאָה *he-saw*

(24) מַיִם *waters* (27)   יְהִי *let-'there'-be* (30) רוּחַ *s,irit, wind*

---

[1] The *a* in this word is pronounced as *a* in *all*; the *e* like *ey* in *they*. The main accent is on the syllable ḡ ē š.

[2] D. f. = Dåḡēš-fŏrtē.

Notes.—(1) אוֹר means *light* or *light-of;* אִישׁ, *man* or *man-of;* רוּחַ, *spirit* or *spirit-of;* (2) The word for *waters* is מַיִם, but at the end of the verse, where the voice rests upon the word, it is written מָיִם.

6. EXERCISES.

1. To be translated into Hebrew:—(1) *Darkness* (was)[1] *upon+ the-waters, and-upon+(the)-faces-of the-earth;* (2) *In-beginning* (the) *spirit-of God* (was) *brooding upon the-waters;* (3) *God saw*)(*the-heavens, and-*)(*the-waters;* (4) (The)-*man-of God,* (the)-*light-of the-heavens;* (5) *And-he-said, he-said; he-was, she-was, let-*(there)-*be, and-*(there)-*was;* (6) *he-saw, he-created, he-was.*

2. To be translated into English:—(1) הַפָּנִים; (2) בְּאוֹר; (3) הָאָרֶץ; (4) הָאִישׁ, (5) הָאֱלֹהִים, (6) וַיֹּאמֶר, (7) וְרוּחַ, (8) מַיִם (9) הַמַּיִם, (10) הָאוֹר, (11) וְהָאוֹר.

3. To be written in English letters:—(1) רָאָה, (2) אִישׁ, (3) יְהִי, (4) מַיִם, (5) פַּת, (6) וְרוּחַ, (7) אוֹר, (8) וַיְהִי.

4. To be written in Hebrew letters:—(1) šîθ, (2) rû, (3) nê, (4) yïm, (5) 'îš, (6) mᵉrå, (7) mᵉrä, (8) šäl, (9) mär, (10) häm.

7. TOPICS FOR STUDY.

(1) Prep. בְּ, (2) Laryngeals. (3) Quantity of vowels in syllables. (4) Dåḡēš-förtē. (5) Sign of the feminine. (6) Sign of the participle. (7) Writing of the article. (8) Sign of the imperfect. (9) Root. (10) וְ and וַ. (11) Sharpened syllable.

LESSON IV.—GENESIS 1. 4.

1. NOTES.

22. וַיַּרְא—wăy-yăr' (two syllables)—*and-*(he)-*saw,* cf. 18. *c,* 21. *a:*

a. The conjunction וַ, forming, with י, a sharpened syllable, § 26. Note 1.

b. The letter י indicates the imperfect, יִרְא, cf. 18. *b.*

---

[1] Words in parentheses are not to be rendered in Hebrew.

c. Ŝᵉwâ under ר silent, § 11.; א here without force, § 43. 1. R. 1.

23. אֶת־הָאוֹר—'ēθ+hā-'ôr (three syllables)—)(+*the-light:*

a. In v. 1 אֵת is an *accented* closed syl.; here *un*-accented, because joined by Măḳḳēf to following word, § 17. 1. 2.; hence short ĕ appears in the unaccented syllable, § 29. 4. *a.*

b. Article her⁹ is הָ, as in הָאָרֶץ; but cf. -הַ in הַשָּׁמַיִם, הַמַּיִם.

c. 1st syl. unaccented closed; 2d, unac. open; 3d, accented closed, § 28. 1, 2.

d. The *o* is ô, not ō, same sound, but different value, § 7. 4.

24. כִּי־טוֹב—kî+ṭôv (two syllables) —*that*+*good:*

a. Three consonants: כ (k), cf. ך (χ); ט (ṭ), cf. ת; ב (v).

b. Two unchangeable vowels: ־י (î), וֹ (ô), § 30. 2. *b.*, 6. *c.*

c. On the use of letters to indicate vowel-sounds, § 6. 2, 3.

25. וַיַּבְדֵּל—wăy-yăv-dēl—*and-*(he)*-caused-a-division*, § 28. 1,2:

a. ד (d) a new letter; without the dot (ד), it is đ (= *th* in *this*).

b. 1st and 2d syl.'s unaccented closed (*short* vowel); 3d, accented closed (*long* vowel).

c. Ŝᵉwâ under ב is silent.

26. בֵּין—bēn—*between*, §§ 3. 2; 5. 3; 6. 3; 12. 1:

a. The letter *n* at the *end* of a word is written ן, not נ.

b. Both ê (י) and ē (_) are pronounced as *ey* in *they*.

c. The vowel here is unchangeable (ê), not changeable (ē).

d. There is a dot in ב, as there was in ב of בְּרֵאשִׁית

27. וּבֵין—û-vēn—*and-between*, §§ 12. 1; 49. 2:

a. Before the labial ב, the word for *and* is written וּ

b. Note that *between* is bēn, *and-between* is û-vēn.

28. הַחֹשֶׁךְ—hă(ḥ)-ḥō'-šĕχ—*the-darkness;* (cf. 12. *a, b, c*):

a. The article in this case is הַ; not הֶ·, nor הָ.

b. The accent falls on the vowel ō, the final ĕ being only a secondary vowel; cf. 5.*d*, 7.*c*, 12.*d.*

c. Note that הַ *appears* to be an unaccented open syllable with a short vowel. However, in the case of a strong laryngeal like ḥ a doubling is implied after the article. Cf. the same usage in 16.

2. THE OCCURRENCE OF SPIRANTS IN GENESIS I. 1—4.

בְּרֵאשִׁית	בּ (*b*, not *v*) follows nothing; ת (θ) follows î.
בָּרָא	בּ (*b*, not *v*) follows ת of the preceding word.
אֵת	ת (θ, not *t*) follows the vowel-sound ē.
הָיְתָה	ת (θ, not *t*) follows the vowel-sound ְ.
תֹהוּ וָבֹהוּ	ת (θ) follows â of preceding word; בֹ (*v*) follows â.
עַל־פְּנֵי	פּ (*p*) follows the consonant ל.
תְהוֹם	ת (θ) follows the vowel-sound ê of preceding word.
מְרַחֶפֶת	פ (*f* not *p*) follows ĕ; ת (θ) follows ĕ.
כִּי־טוֹב	כּ (*k*, not χ) follows ־; בֹ (*v*) follows ô.
וַיַּבְדֵּל	בְ (*v*) follows ă; דּ (*d*, not d) follows the consonant בְ
בֵּין	בּ (*b*) follows the preceding consonant ם.
וּבֵין חֹשֶׁךְ	בֵ (*v*) follows the vowel וּ; ךְ (χ) fol. ĕ.

3. OBSERVATIONS.

33. Six letters, called *spirants*, have two sounds: בּ *b*, בּ *v*, גּ¹ *g*, גּ ǧ (as in German *Tage*), דּ *d*, דּ ᵈ, כּ *k*, כּ χ, פּ *p*, פּ *f*, תּ *t*, ת θ.

34. Their smooth or hard sound, *b, g, d, k, p, t,* was indicated by a point called Dâḡēš-lēnē.

35. These letters receive this point whenever they do not immediately follow a vowel-sound, i. e., a vowel or vocal Š³wâ.

36. This lesson has two new letters: ט (ṭ), pronounced practically like ת; and דּ (*d*).

4. GRAMMAR-LESSON.

Learn in the "Elements of Hebrew," the following sections:
1. § 12. 1, and Note,   Spirants and Dâḡēš-lēnē.

---

¹ This letter is introduced here, in order to complete the list.

2. § 17. 1, 2,   Măḳḳēf and short vowel.

3. § 45. 1,   The usual form of the Article.

4. Under § 4. 1,   The letters ב, ו, מ, פ,

5. WORD-LESSON.

(31) בֵּין *between*   (34) וַיַּרְא *and-he-saw* (37) לָמַד *he-learned*

(32) ו *and*   (35) כִּי *that*   (38) נָתַן *he-gave*

(33) וַיַּבְדֵּל *and-he-caused-* (36) טוֹב *good*   (39) שֵׁם *name*
         a-division

Note.—The root of וַיַּבְדֵּל is בָּדַל *be-separate;* the root of וַיַּרְא

is רָאָה *see;* שֵׁם *= either name, or name-of.*

6. EXERCISES.

1. To be translated into Hebrew:—(1) *And-saw God)(the-heavens and-)(the-earth and-)(the-waters;* (2) *The-light the-good* (=
the good light); (3) *Good light* (in Heb., light good) *was upon the-
earth;* (4) *In-beginning* (was) *darkness; God created light; and-he-
caused-a-division between light and-between darkness;* (5) *God gave
)(+the-light;* (6) *He-gave the-light the-good* (= the good light);
(7) *Name, the-name,* (the) *name-of God;* (8) *Between the-heavens
and-between the-earth;* (9) *He-learned that the-light* (was) *good*
(Heb. order, *He learned the light that good*).

2. To be translated into English: — (1) הָאוֹר הַטּוֹב; (2) הַשֵּׁם
בְּשֵׁם הָאֱלֹהִים; (5) הָאֱלֹהִים הַטּוֹב; (4) הַחֹשֶׁךְ וְהָאוֹר; (3) הַטּוֹב
נָתַן אֱלֹהִים אֶת־הַמַּיִם; (7) וַיַּרְא אֱלֹהִים אֶת־הָאָרֶץ (6).

3. To be written in English letters:—(1) לָמַד, (2) שֵׁם, (3) נָתַן,
וּבֵין, (8) בֵּין, (7) וַיַּבְדֵּל, (6) בְּשֵׁם, (5) הַטּוֹב (5).

4. To be written in Hebrew letters:—(1) bên, (2) dēl, (3) bēn,
(4) dēl, (5) ṭôv, (6) ḥō, (7) θō'hû, (8) 'ôr, (9) bō'hû, (10) vên, (11)
dēl, (12) χî.

7. *TOPICS FOR STUDY.*

(1) Three ways of writing *and*. (2) Three ways of writing *the*. (3) Măḳḳēf. (4) Laryngeals. (5) Labials. (6) Dâğēš-lēnē. (7) Spirants (8) Sign of feminine, of participle. (9) Open, closed, and sharpened syllables. (10) Difference between ō and ô, ē and ê. (11) -וּ. (12) Plural ending.

LESSON V.—GENESIS I. 5.

1. *NOTES.*

29. וַיִּקְרָא—wăy-yiḳ-râ'—*And*-(he)-*called*, § **26.** 1. 2, N. 1.:

a. On ·וַ, see 18. *c;* on י see 18. *b;* wăy, a sharpened syl.

b. ק (ḳ), a new consonant pronounced practically like כּ (k), § **2.** 4.

c. The ְ under ק is silent, § **11.** 1.

d. יִקְרָא *he-will-call;* קָרָא *he-called,* cf. בָּרָא *he-created.*

30. לָאוֹר—lâ-'ôr—*to-the-light,* § **28.** 1, 2:

a. לְ the preposition *to,* with ָ, the vowel of article, § **47.** 4.

b. וֹ is ô, not ō.

c. Light = אוֹר ; *the-light* = הָאוֹר ; *to-the-light* = (not לְהָאוֹר) לָאוֹר, ה of the article being dropped out, § **45.** R. 3.

31. יוֹם—yôm—*day;* ô not ō.

32. וְלַחֹשֶׁךְ—wᵉlă(ḥ)-ḥṓ-šĕχ—*and-to-the-darkness:*

a. Four words: (1) וְ *and,* (2) לְ *to,* (3) הַ *the,* (4) חֹשֶׁךְ *darkness.*

b. הַ of article elided and its vowel (ă) given to לַ, § **45.** R. 3.

c. First syl. (wᵉlă(ḥ)) is unaccented and apparently open, but with a *short* vowel, contrary to § **28.** 1. The fact is D. f. is understood in ח, which, being a *laryngeal,* cannot receive it, § **14.** 3. N. 1.

33. קָרָא—ḳâ-râ'—*he-called,* § **55.** 1. 2:

a. This is the simple stem or root of the verb.

b. א, as always at the end of a word, is quiescent, § **43.** 1, a.

c. This word would regularly be accented on the ultima. It is

קְרָא here because of the acc. syl. לְ immediately following.

34. לַיְלָה—lắ'-y⁽ᵉ⁾lắ(h)—*night*, § **24.** 2, and N. 1:

a. ה is not a consonant, but used merely to represent the prec. ־ָ, § **6.** 1.

b. � and its šᵉwâ belong to the second syl.; the ־ָ is *initial*, § **10.** 1

c. Both ־ָ 's are *tone*-long (å), not naturally long (â).

35. וַיְהִי־עֶרֶב—wăy-hî 'é-rĕv—*and*-(there)-*was*+*evening:*

a. The first syl. (wăy) is unaccented and ends with a diphthong; there should be a D. f. in ﹐, but it has been lost, § **26.** 2. and N. 2; § **28.** 4; § **14.** 2.

b. The vertical line with ־ָ is called Méθĕǧ; it is a secondary accent written upon the second syl. before the principal accent, § **18.** 1.

c. The ־ֶ under עْ though short is accented, and the final ĕ is secondary.

36. וַיְהִי־בֹקֶר—wăy-hî+vṓ-ķĕr—*and*-(there)-*was*+*morning:*

a. On the syl. wăy and on Méθĕǧ see 35. a, b.

b. On the connective Măķķēf represented by +, § **17.** 1.

c. The ־ֹ is ō (tone-long), not ô (naturally long), § **31.** 3. b.

d. The final ĕ is secondary.

37. אֶחָד—'é(h)-ḥåḍ—*one:*

a. The ־ֶ is short ĕ, d. f. being understood in ח; cf. 32 c.

b. The ד is đ, like *th* in *the*, not d, which would be דּ.

2. *TABLE OF WORDS CONTAINING LONG VOWELS.*

1. Words with tone-long å: יִקְרָא, קָרָא, לַיְלָה, בָּרָא, קְרָא, etc.

2. Words with tone-long ē: יַבְדֵּל, אֵת.

3. Words with naturally long ê: פְּנֵי, בֵּין.

4. Words with tone-long ō: תֹּהוּ, חֹשֶׁךְ, בֹּקֶר, בֹּהוּ.

5. Words with naturally long ô: אוֹר, טוֹב, יוֹם.

R. The *o* of וַיֹּאמֶר and of אֱלֹהִים is ô, not ō, although not written וֹ.

3. OBSERVATIONS.

37. Tone-long vowels are vowels which are long because of their proximity to the tone; i. e., being originally short, they have become long through the influence of the accent.

38. Naturally long vowels are vowels which are long, generally, because of the contraction of two distinct elements, e. g., $\ddot{a}+w$ = ô, or $\ddot{a}+y$ = ê.

39. Tone-long vowels are, generally, indicated only by the vowel-sign.

40. Naturally long vowels are generally, but not always, indicated by a vowel-sign and also by a vowel-letter, e. g., ō is ‑ , but ô is וֹ; ē is ‑‑ , but ê is י‑‑.

41. Tone-long vowels, if the tone changes, are liable to change; but naturally long vowels are unchangeable.

42. The short accented ĕ, which always comes from ă, is especially worthy of note.

4. GRAMMAR-LESSON.

1. § 8.   The names of the vowels.

2. §§ 45. R. 3; 47. 4.   The article after a preposition.

3. § 55. 1, 2,   The root of a verb.

4. § 58. 1.   The simple verb-stem; its name.

5. § 30. (opening words), also Notes 1 and 2 under § 30. 7, } The naturally long-vowels,—(1) their origin, (2) their writing, (3) their character.

6. § 31. (opening words), also Note 1 under 3. } The tone-long vowels, (1) their origin, (2) their number, (3) their writing, (4) their character.

5. WORD-LESSON.

(40) אֶחָד *one*   (43) וַיִּקְרָא *and-he-called*   (46) עֶרֶב *evening*

(41) בֹּקֶר *morning*   (44) יָשַׁב *he-sat, dwelt*   (47) קוֹל *voice*

(42) יוֹם *day*   (45) לַיְלָה *night*   (48) קָרָא *he-called*

Note.—The word for *night* is לַיְלָה, but in the middle of the verse it is written and pronounced לָיְלָה.

6. EXERCISES.

1. To be translated into Hebrew:—(1) *To-(the)-beginning-of the-day God called morning; to-(the)-beginning-of the-night God called evening;* (2) *In-day one God created)(the-light;* (3) *God created)(the-light and-he-called to-the-light day;* (4) *The good day* (Heb., *the-day the-good*); (5) *(The)-name-of the-light* (is) *day, and-(the)-name-of the-darkness* (is) *night;* (6) *Heavens, the-heavens, to-the-heavens, in-the-heavens;* (7) *Earth, the-earth, in-the-earth, to-the-earth, and-to-the-earth;* (8) *(The)-voice-of God;* (9) *Day and-night;* (10) *The-waters, in-the-waters.*

2. To be translated into English:— (1) בְּקוֹל; (2) לְאוֹר; (3) בֵּין הַיּוֹם; (4) לְאִישׁ; (5) בָּאָרֶץ; (6) לַשָּׁמַיִם; (7) בַּיּוֹם; (8) וּלְאוֹר; (9) וּבֵין הַלַּיְלָה; יָשַׁב אֱלֹהִים בַּשָּׁמַיִם.

3. To be written in English letters:—(1) קוֹל, (2) יָשַׁב, (3) יוֹם, (4) אֶחָד, (5) עֶרֶב, (6) אוֹר, (7) בֵּין, (8) קָרָא.

4. To be written in Hebrew letters:—(1) lăm, (2) lâm, (3) lĕm, (4) lôm, (5) lōm, (6) lēm, (7) lêm, (8) yĭķ, (9) bēn, (10) rĕv, (11) yᵉlâ.

7. TOPICS FOR STUDY.

(1) Root. (2) Simple verb-stem. (3) Names of vowel-signs. (4) Article after a preposition. (5) Naturally long vowels. (6) Tone-long vowels. (7) Laryngeals and labials. (8) Dăḡĕš-lēnē.

LESSON VI.—GENESIS I. 6.

1. NOTES.

38. וַיֹּאמֶר—wăy-yṓ'-mĕr—*and-*(he)-*said* (see N. 18):

a. Syllables: (1) sharpened, (2) open, (3) closed.

b. Vowels: (1) Păθăḥ, (2) Ḥŏlĕm, (3) S'gŏl.

c. א, though a letter, has here no consonantal force; hence it has no š'wâ under it; it is quiescent, § 11. R.

39. אֱלֹהִים—'ĕlŏ-hîm—*God* (see N. 3):

a. Only two syllables: (1) open, (2) closed.

b. Vowels: (1) Ḥŏlĕm; (2) Ḥîrĕ̄ḳ; Ḥăṭēf-S'gŏl (ֱ), though a vowel-sound, is not a full vowel.

c. While ְ is *simple* Š'wâ, ֱ is a *compound* Š'wâ, § 9. 1, 2.

d. Š'wâs do not form syllables, § 27. 1.

40. רָקִיעַ—rå-ḳî(ă)'—*expanse;* cf. רוּחַ *spirit* (15):

a. Syl's: (1) open, (2) closed; vowels: (1) Ḳåmĕṣ, (2) Ḥîrĕ̄ḳ.

b. The ַ under ע is *not treated as a vowel;* it is called Păθăḥ-*furtive,* because in pronunciation it *steals* in before its conso-nant, cf. רוּחַ = rû(ă)ḥ, not rû-ḥă. Though pronounced, it is mere-ly a transition-sound from the labial *û* to the laryngeal consonant ', and is inserted for euphony, §§ 27. 1; 42. 2. *d.*

41. בְּתוֹךְ—b'θ̄ôx—*in-midst-of,* §§ 12. 1; 11. 2. *a*:

a. בּ has Dăḡēš-lēnē but ךְ has none.

b. The full vowel וֹ (= ô), is unchangeable.

c. This word means *in-midst-of,* not *in-midst.*

42. הַמָּיִם—hăm-mă'-yîm—*the-waters,*§§ 13. 1; 26. 1. 2. N. 1. 45. 1:

a. The ַ being unaccented and in a closed syl. must be ĭ, not î, § 28. 2.

b. Here ָ (1) indicates that the second vowel is accented, and also (2) marks the end of the clause, § 24. 2.

43. וִיהִי—wî-hî—*and-let-*(it)-*be:*

a. Let-(it)-be = יְהִי; and = וְ; but we have וַיְהִי in place of
וַיְהִי, since (1) when two Sᵉwâs would stand together at the
beginning of a word, the first is represented by ⁻; and (2) ⁻
(i) under וְ fol. by יִ (iy) = î, § 49. 4. N. 1; cf. the very different
וַיְהִי = and-(there)-was (21).

b. On the origin of ⁻ see § 36. 8. a.

44. מַבְדִּיל—măv-dîl—causing-a-division or dividing:

a. A participle (shown by מְ) from same root as וַיַּבְדֵּל (25).

b. Vowels: (1) Păɵăḥ, (2) Ḥîrĕḳ; but ⁻ is silent.

c. בּ (preceded by ⁻) without, דּ (preced. by בּ) with Dăğĕš
lēnē.

45. מַיִם לָמָיִם—mă'-yĭm lă-mă'-yĭm—waters to-waters:

a. Vowel under מַ in first word, ă; in second, â; because the
second word is the last in the verse, and so the voice rests upon
it and strengthens the vowel. Such a word is said to be in pause,
§ 38. 2.

b. The prepositions sometimes take a tone-long â, instead of ⁻,
when they are directly before the accented syllable, § 47. 5.

c. לָמָיִם = to-waters; not to-the-waters, which would be לַמָּיִם;
the stroke over מָ emphasizes the absence of Dăğĕš-fōrtē, § 16. 2.

2. WORDS WITHOUT POINTS OR VOWEL-SIGNS. GEN. I. 1—6

קרא,	פני	כי ,ל	יאמר	ה	ב	אור
ראשית	לילה	ויבדל	היתה	בהו	אחד
רקיע	מבדיל ,יום	יהי	ו	בין	אלהים
שמים	מים	יקרא	חשך	בקר	ארץ
תהו	ערב, על	וירא	טוב	ברא	את

3. OBSERVATIONS.

43. This verse has twenty-two syllables,[1] of which twelve are
closed, ten open; of the closed, two are sharpened.

44. This verse has twenty-six vowel-sounds: twenty-two full

---

[1] Let the student count the syllables and thus verify this statement.

vowels, three Šᵉwâs (two simple, one compound), one Păθăḥ-furtive.

45. This verse has *forty-four* letters, of which *nine* are silent; of these nine, seven are ׳, one ן and one א,

46. This verse has two silent Šᵉwâs.

47. The accent ⌐ ('Aθnâḥ) is written only in the *middle* of a verse.

48. The accent ⌐ (Sĭllûḳ) is written only at the *end* of a verse.

4. GRAMMAR-LESSON.

1. § 6. 1, 2, 3, and Notes 1—4,   The Vowel-letters.
2. § 14. 3, and Notes 1, 2,   Omission of D. f. from laryngeals.
3. § 9. 1, 2,   Simple and Compound Šᵉwâ.
4. § 11. 1, 2. *a*, and Remark,   Silent Šᵉwâ.

5. WORD-LESSON.

(49) מַבְדִּיל *dividing*   (50) מַיִם *waters*   (51) רָקִיעַ *expanse*

6. EXERCISES.

1. To be translated into Hebrew:—(1) *Between the-waters and-between the-waters;* (2) *Between the-waters to-the-waters;* (3) *Between waters to-waters;* (4) *Waters, waters* (in pause), *to-the-waters* (in pause), *to-waters* (in pause); (5) *Let-*(there)*-be, and-let-*(there)*-be, and-*(there)*-was;* (6) *Expanse and-spirit;* (7) *Expanse, the-expanse, to-the-expanse.*

2. To be translated into English:— (1) חֹשֶׁךְ; (2) אוֹר בַּיוֹם; (3) בַּלַּיְלָה; (4) טוֹב הָאוֹר; (5) הַמַּיִם עַל פְּנֵי הָאָרֶץ; (6) רָקִיעַ בְּרָקִיעַ, לְמַיִם, לְמָיִם, רָקִיעַ וִיהִי מַבְדִּיל.

3. To be written in English letters:—(1) חֹשֶׁךְ, (2) עֶרֶב, (3) יַבְדֵּל, (4) רָקִיעַ, (5) מַבְדִּיל, (6) בְּתוֹךְ.

4. To be written in Hebrew letters:—(1) 'ăl, (2) mă'-yĭm, (3) wî-hî, (4) dăl, (5) dēl, (6) dĕl, (7) ḥăđ, (8) dîl.

7. *TOPICS FOR STUDY.*

(1) Vowel-sounds rep. by **ִ**. (2) Vowel-sounds rep. by **ֻ**. (3) D.
f. rejected from laryngeals. (4) D. f. implied. (5) Compound Šᵉwâ.
(6) Silent Šᵉwâ. (7) Simple verb-stem. (8) Laryngeals and labials.
(9) Dåḡēš-lēnē, (10) Sharpened syllables. (12) Naturally long and
tone-long vowels. (13) Mǎḳḳêf. (14) Quantity of vowels in syllables.

LESSON VII.—GENESIS I. 7, 8.

1. *NOTES.*

46. וַיַּעַשׂ—wǎy-yǎ-'ǎś—*and-*(he)-*made:*

a. שׂ (ś) is to be distinguished from שׁ (š), § 2. 6.

b. The וַ is the same as in וַיֹּאמֶר (18), וַיִּקְרָא (21), וַיַּרְא (22).

c. The root is עָשָׂה *he-made;* the imperfect is יַעֲשֶׂה, a shorter
form is used with **וַ**.

d. The last ǎ is a helping-vowel.

47. הָרָקִיעַ—hå-rå-ḳî(ǎ)'—*the-expanse:*

a. The ⸗ is Pǎθǎḥ-furtive, cf. רוּחַ (rû(ǎ)ḥ); see 40. *b.*

b. The article is **הַ**, hence *the-expanse* should be הָרְקִיעַ; but ר
rejects D. f., and the preceding (short) ⸗ now standing in an
open syllable becomes ⸗, §§ **14.** 3; **36.** 1 *b;* **28.** 1.

c. The secondary accent is written on the second syllable before the
tone, § **18.** 1.

d. The accent ⸪ above ק and ע marks the end of a section; it is
used only when the verse has *three sections,* § **24.** 3.

48. אֲשֶׁר—'ᵃšĕr (one syllable)—*which,* §§ **9.** 2; **27.** 1:

a. The ⸗ is the compound Šᵉwâ of the A-class (cf. ⸗, of the I-class);
it is pronounced like ǎ, but with much less voice. It is not a full
vowel, and does not form a syllable.

b. The Relative particle does not vary for gender or number, § **53.**
1. *a.*

49. מִתַּחַת—mǐt-tȧ-ḥȧθ—*from-under* (for מִן תַּחַת), § **48.** 1:

a. The final letter (*n*) of מִן is assimilated, § 39. 1.

b. A letter thus assimilated is represented by D. f., § 39. N.

c. The point in תּ is D. f., because it follows a vowel, § 13. 1.

d. In this case the point is *also* Dȧǧēš-lēnē, since the sound doubled is *t*, not θ, § 13. 2. N. 1.

50. לָרְקִיעַ—lȧ-rȧ-ḳî(ȧ)ʿ—*to-the-expanse*, § 45. R. 3:

a. רְקִיעַ *expanse;* הָרְקִיעַ *the-expanse;* לָרְקִיעַ *to-the-expanse;* וְלָרְקִיעַ *and-to-the-expanse.*

51. מֵעַל—mē-ʿȧl—*from-upon:*

a. מִן (*from*) assimilates its final consonant, see 49. a; but

b. עַ refuses D. f., and ־ֽ is lowered to ־ֵ, § 48. 2.

52. וַיְהִי־כֵן—wȧy-hî+χēn—*and-*(it)*-was+so:*

a. ־ְ with ־ֵ is Méθěǧ, second syllable before tone, § 18. 1.

b. ־ְ with ־ֵ Sĭllûḳ, marking end of verse, § 24. 1. N.

53. שָׁמָיִם—šȧ-mȧ́-yǐm—*heavens*, cf. שָׁמַיִם of v. 1:

a. There is ־ָ under מ, instead of ־ַ, because *in pause,* § 38. 2; the Aθnȧ̂ḥ (־ֱ) is, next to Sĭllûḳ (ׁ), the strongest accent.

54. שֵׁנִי—šē-nî—*second:* tone-long, ē, not ĕ.

2. FORMS FOR SPECIAL STUDY.

(2)¹ רוּחַ	(5) לָאוֹר	(7) מִן	(3) אוֹר	(7) הָרְקִיעַ
(6) רְקִיעַ	(5) לַחֹשֶׁךְ	(7) מִתַּחַת	(4) טוֹב	(7) לָרְקִיעַ
(8) לָרְקִיעַ	(8) לִרְקִיעַ	(7) מֵעַל	(5) יוֹם	(7) וַיְהִי־כֵן

3. OBSERVATIONS.

49. Pȧθǡḥ-furtive, a mere transition-sound, does not form a syl.

¹ These numerals refer to the verse containing the word cited.

50. The ה of the article is elided after the preposition לְ (also בְּ).

51. The prep. *from* is *min*, but the *n* is often assimilated and represented by D. f.; if the following letter refuses D. f., the I is lowered to ē.

52. The naturally long ô, generally וֹ, in Hebrew does not change.

53. Where a verse has two sections, the end of the *first* is marked by ◌֑ ; the end of the *second* by◌֗. If the verse has *three* sections, the end of the *third* is marked by Sᵉḡōltâ (◌֓). In the use of the accents, we commence at the *end* of the verse, not at the beginning.

4. GRAMMAR-LESSON.

1. § **45**. 2, 3, The article before strong and weak laryngeals.

2. § **106**. 1, 2. c, 3—5, Affixes for gender and number.

3. § **107**. (opening), 1, 2, The absolute and construct states.

4. § **24**. 1—3, The three most important accents.

5. WORD-LESSON.

(52) אֲשֶׁר	who, which	(55) כֵּן	so	(58) שָׁלַח	he-sent
(53) וַיַּעַשׂ	and-he-made	(56) מִן	from	(59) שֵׁנִי	second
(54) יָם	sea	(57) עָשָׂה	he-made	(60) תַּחַת	under

6. EXERCISES.

(1) To be translated into Hebrew:—*In-the-waters which God made;* (2) *God* (is) *in-the-heavens and-upon the-earth;* (3) *The-waters* (are) *in-the-sea;* (4) *The-earth* (is) *beneath* (in Heb., *from-under to*) *the-sea;* (5) (A) *second day*[1]; (6) *The-day the-second*[1] (=the second day); (7) *God sent*)(*the light and-*)(*the darkness;* (8) *From+the-heavens to-the-earth;* (9) *Between the-sea and-between the-earth;* (10) *And-*(it)*-was+so.*

---

[1] The adjective, when attributive, follows its noun; and, if the noun is definite, the adjective receives the article.

2. To be translated into English:—(1) מֵעַל לָאָרֶץ (2) הָרֵאשִׁית;
(3) מִן־הָאָרֶץ (4) וּבַיִם; (5) הָאוֹר הַשֵּׁנִי; (6) הַמַּיִם אֲשֶׁר בַּיָּם;
(9) שָׁלַח אֶת־הַמַּיִם עַל־הָאָרֶץ (8) בַּבֹּקֶר וּבָעֶרֶב (7) לַשָּׁמַיִם;
עָשָׂה אֶת־הָרָקִיעַ .

3. To be written in English letters:—(1) שָׁלַח, (2) כֵּן, (3) כֵּן,
(4) יָם, (5) עָשָׂה (6) בֵּין, (7), פְּנֵי (8) שֵׁנִי (9) מֵעַל .

4. To be written in Hebrew letters:—(1) kēn, (2) bēn, (3) 'ôr,
(4) bó-hû, (5) măḥ, (6) 'ăl, (7) 'ăl, (8) 'ăs, (9) mē, (10) bēn.

7. TOPICS FOR STUDY.

(1) The three important accents. (2) The article before laryngeals. (3) The preposition (לְ and בְּ) before the article. (4) The
preposition *from*. (5) Assimilation. (6) The position of the attributive adjective. (7) The vowels ē and ê. (8) The vowels ō and ô.
(9) Secondary accent. (10) Păθăḥ-furtive. (11) Labials. (12) D. f.
in a spirant. (13) Laryngeals and D. f. (14) Sĭllûḳ and Mééθĕǧ.
(15) Măḳḳēf.

LESSON VIII.—GENESIS I. 9.

1. *NOTES.*

55. יִקָּווּ—yĭḳ-ḳå-wû—*Let*-(or, *shall*)-*be-collected:*
a. The י indicates the *imperfect;* וּ is the *plural*-ending of verbs.
b. The D. f. in ק is for an assimilated נ. which is the characteristic
of a *passive* verb-stem; the å under ק is pretonic.

56. הַמַּיִם—hăm-må-yĭm—*the-waters*, see 17:
a. מ has ־ַ, not ־ָ as in v. 2, since it is not *in pause.*
b. The article, written regularly with ă and D. f., § 45. 1.

57. אֶל־—'ēl+—*unto*, with which compare לְ *to.*

58. מָקוֹם—må-ḳôm—*place:*
a. Tone-long å, but naturally long ô; the former changeable, the
latter unchangeable.

b. The root is קוּם ; מ is a prefix often used in noun-formation.

59. וְתֵרָאֶה —w‘θē-rä-'é(h)—*and-*(she)-*shall-be-seen:*

a. Five letters, of which the root can have but *three,* § 55. 1; וְ=
and; תְ (= *shc*) is a prefix cf the *imperfect,* like י, which = *he.*

b. הֵרָאֶה should be תֵרָאֶה (with the same D. f. and å which are
in יָקוּם (55) above), for it is *passive;* but ר refuses D. f., and I
under תְ becomes ē, as in מֵעַל (51), § 48. 2.

c. Cf. closely the following forms:—

3 masc. sg.	יָקְוֶה	יֵרָאֶה	*he-will-be* etc.
3 fem. sg.	תָקְוֶה	תֵרָאֶה	*she-will-be* etc.
3 masc. pl.	יָקְוּ	יֵרָאוּ	*they-will-be* etc.

d. This is the first case of הֶ _ = é (h).

60. הַיַבָּשָׁה —hăy-yăb-bå-šå(h)—*the-dry* (land):

a. Four syllables,—two sharpened, two open, § 26. 1. N. 1.

b. Point in בּ is D. f. yet also Dåḡēš-lēnē, § 13. 2, and N. 1.

c. The final הַ stands for the preceding å, just as י stands for î, or
וּ for ô; cf. אֱלֹהִים and יוֹם.

2. HEBREW-ENGLISH WORD-REVIEW.*†

¹אוֹר	¹¹בֹּקֶר	²¹יְהִי	³²מַיִם	⁴²רָקִיעַ
²אֶחָד	¹²בָּרָא	²²יוֹם	³³מִן ,מִי, מֶ	⁴³שָׁמַיִם
³אֵל	¹³הַ, הֵ	²³יַעַשׂ	³⁴מָקוֹם	⁴⁴שֵׁנִי
⁴אֱלֹהִים	⁴¹הָיְתָה	²⁴יָקְוּ	³⁵מְרַחֶפֶת	⁴⁵תֹּהוּ
⁵אֶרֶץ	⁵¹וְ ,וָ ,וּ	²⁵יָקְרָא	³⁶עַל	⁴⁶תְהוֹם

* Every word is accented on the last vowel, unless the sign ָ indicates
that it is accented elsewhere.

† Omitting the prepositions and the relative particle (eleven words in all),
those that remain in this list, together with their related grammatical forms,
occur in the Bible about 27000 times. This would make about one hundred
and thirty pages, or about one tenth of the entire Old Testament.

אֲשֶׁר⁶ | חֹשֶׁךְ¹⁶ | יִרְא²⁶ | עֶרֶב³⁷ | תּוֹךְ⁴⁷

אֵת ,־אֶת⁷ | טוֹב¹⁷ | כִּי²⁷, לְ²⁸, | פְּנֵי³⁸ | תַּחַת⁴⁸

בְ⁸ | יֹּאמֶר¹⁸ | כֵּן²⁹ | קְרָא³⁹ | תֵּרָאֶה⁴⁹

בֹּהוּ⁹ | יַּבְדֵּל¹⁹ | לַיְלָה³⁰ | רֵאשִׁית⁴⁰

כֵּן¹⁰ | יַּבְשָׁה²⁰ | מַבְדִּיל³¹ | יְרוּחַ⁴¹

3. ENGLISH-HEBREW WORD-REVIEW.

46abyss	12created, he	38faces-of	30night	13the
15and	16darkness	33from	2one	28to
21let be	22day	4God	34place	48under
40beginning	45desolation	17good	18say, he will	3unto
10between	19divide, he will	43heavens	44second	36upon
35brooding	31dividing	8in	26see, he will	6which
25call, he will	20dry (land)	1light	49seen, let be	14was, she
39called, he	5earth	47midst-of	29so	9waste
24collected, let	37evening	11morning	41spirit-of	32waters
be	42expanse	23make, he will	27that	7(sign of object)

4. WORD-LESSON.

(61) אֶל־ unto

(64) מָקוֹם place

(62) יַבְּשָׁה dry (land)

(65) תֵּרָאֶה she-shall-be-seen

(63) יִקָּוּוּ they-shall-be-collected

5. GRAMMAR-LESSON

1. § **18**. 1,   Mě̄θĕğ, on second syllable before tone.
2. § **27**. 1, 2, 3,   Syllabification.
Review.—§§ **5**; **6**; **9**; **11**. 2. *a* and Rem.; **12**. 1; **13**. 1; **14**. 1, 2, 3;

17. 1, 2; **24.** 1—3; **26.** 1, 2; **28.** 1 2; **30.** (opening words), 7, N. 1,

2; **31.** (opening words), 3, N. 1; **45.** 1, 2, 3. and Rem. 3; **47.** 1, 4,

5; **49.** 1, 2; **55.** 1. 2; **58.** 1, 2. and N. 1; **106.** 1, 2. c, 3—5; **107.** 1, 2.

Note.—The stem seen in מָשַׁל, קְרָא, בְּרָא, etc., is the simple
active verb-stem, called Ḳăl, § **58.** 1; the stem seen in יִקְּוּ
and וַתֵּרָאֶה is the simple passive-stem, called Nif-'ăl § **58.** 2.

6. EXERCISES.

1. To be translated into Hebrew:—(1) In-the-place which (is)
between heavens and-between earth; (2) God will-be-seen upon+
the-earth; (3) The-waters will-be-seen in-the-sea; (4) The-earth (f.)
will-be-seen beneath (= from-under to) the-heavens; (5) The-waters
shall-be-collected unto+place one; (6) In-the-waters; (7) God created
)(the-dry (land).

2. To be translated into English:—(1) יִקָּווּ הַמַּיִם עַל־הָאָרֶץ;
יִרָאֶה הָאִישׁ (6); וּמָקוֹם (5); וּבַמָּקוֹם (4); וּלְאוֹר (3); וְלַמָּקוֹם (2)
וּמֵעַל, מֵעַל, עַל (8); יֵרָאוּ הַשָּׁמַיִם (7).

3. To be written in English letters:—(1) עֶרֶב, (2) אֶרֶץ, (3)
יָקֻוֶּה (6); וּבַמָּקוֹם (5) אֶחָד, (4) תֵּרָאֶה.

7. TOPICS FOR STUDY

(1) The sign of masc. sing. future, of fem. sing. future, of masc.
pl. fut. (2) The characteristic of the passive-stem. (3) A use of
Mêθěǧ. (4) Final ה. (5) Use of מ in formation of nouns. (6)
Various forms of ו conjunctive. (7) The words for sea and day.
(8) The position of the adjective when attributive. (9) The plural
affixes of nouns. (10) The feminine affixes.

LESSON IX.—GENESIS I. 10-11.

1. *NOTE-REVIEW.*

(1) וַיֹּאמֶר (18); (2) אֱלֹהִים (3); (3) הָאָרֶץ (7); (4) אֲשֶׁר (48);
(5) וַיְהִי־כֵן (52); (6) וַיְהִי־עֶרֶב (35); (7) וַיְהִי־בֹקֶר (36); (8) יוֹם (31).

2. *NOTES.*

61. לַיַּבָּשָׁה—lăy-yăb-bâ-šă(h)—*to-the-dry* (land), § **45.** R. 3.

62. אֶרֶץ—'ĕ-rĕṣ—*earth*,—with article הָאָרֶץ, § **45.** R. 2.
a. another case of a helping-vowel; like עֶרֶב (35).

63. וּלְמִקְוֵה—û-l'mîḳ-wê(h)—*and-to-collection-of:*
a. And is here written וּ, § **49.** 2; *to* is written, as usually, לְ.
b. The root is קָוָה, whence the passive future 3rd plural יִקָּווּ (55).
c. The מ is the prefix used in noun-formation, cf. מָקוֹם (58. *b*).
d. This noun (= *collection-of*) is in the construct state, § **107.** 2.

64. יַמִּים—yăm-mîm—*seas:*
a. The sing. is יָם from which the plural differs in that a D. f. appears in מ, and ă appears instead of â.
b. יָמִים (= yâm-mîm) would be an impossible form, § **28.** 2, 3; just as, on the other hand, מָקֹם (= mă-ḳôm) would be impossible, § **28.** 1.

65. תַּדְשֵׁא—tăd-šē'—(she)-*shall-cause-to-spring-forth:*
a. תּ, as in תֵּרָאֶה (59), = *she*, being the feminine prefix.
b. The ⸗ under דּ is silent, § **11.** 1.
c. דּ, שׁ, and א are the three root-letters; דְּשָׁא, cf. קָרָא, בָּרָא.
d. This stem is neither the simple nor the passive verb-stem, but a *causative* stem. It generally has ⸗ under the preformative, i. e., under the letter which is prefixed to the root to designate person or gender; cf. יַבְדֵּל (25), which has ⸗ under י, and means *he-causes-a-division.*

66. דֶּשֶׁא—dĕ́-šĕ'—*grass*, cf. the preceding root דֶּשֶׁא (65. c):

a. ד (preceded by ֵ) = d; but ד (preceded by —) = d̄.

b. This word, like אֶרֶץ, עֶרֶב, and others, has a secondary, or helping vowel.

67. עֵשֶׂב—'ĕ́-śĕv—*herb*: ב = v; שׂ = ś, not š (sh).

a. The secondary ĕ being only a helping vowel is not accented.

68. מַזְרִיעַ—măz-rî(ă)'—*causing-to-seed*, root זָרַע:

a. A new letter ז z; Pāᵭāḥ-furtive under עַ.

b. A participle, as shown by מַ, cf. מַבְדִּיל, (44) מְרַחֶפֶת (16)

c. A causative form, as shown by — under the preformative.

69. זֶרַע—zĕ́-răʻ—*seed*,—from the root זָרַע:

a. This word, like אֶרֶץ, עֶרֶב, דֶּשֶׁא and עֵשֶׂב has an unaccented helping vowel.

70. עֵץ—'ēṣ—*tree-of*; פְּרִי—pᵉrî—*fruit*.

71. עֹשֶׂה פְּרִי—'ō-śé(h) pᵉrî—*making fruit:*

a. The ô, here written over the right arm of שׂ (ś), is naturally long.

b. The ה —, like that in תִּרְאֶה, is ê.

c. The point in פ is D. f., being preceded by a full vowel (ê); it therefore joins the two words together and is called D. f. conjunctive, § 15. 3.

d. עֹשֶׂה accented on penult because closely followed by a monosyllable, § 21. 1.

e. עֹשֶׂה is a participle from עָשָׂה *he-made.*

72. לְמִינוֹ—lᵉmî-nô—*to-kind-his:*

a. The prep. לְ, the noun מִין, and the suffix וֹ (= *his*).

73. זַרְעוֹ־בוֹ—zăr-'ô+vô—*seed-his+in-him:*

a. זֶרַע *seed*, but זַרְעוֹ *his-seed*, the — being silent.

b. וֹ is a pronominal suffix meaning *his* or *him.*

c. בוֹ is made up of בְּ the prep. *in.* and וֹ the suffix *him.*

d. It is בוֹ (vô) not בֹּ. because of the preceding וֹ.

e. בּוֹ .... אֲשֶׁר = *which....in-him;* this is the idiom for *in which.*

3. FORMS FOR SPECIAL STUDY.

תָּרְשֵׂא, in wh. ת=*she*	and—under ת indic. a *causative* idea
מַבְדִּיל, " מ indic. a part.	and—under מ " " "
יַבְדִּל, " י=*he*	and—under י " " "
מַזְרִיעַ, " מ indic. a part.	and—under מ " " "

4. OBSERVATIONS.

54. There are in Hebrew (1) a *simple* verb-stem, (2) a *passive* verb-stem, and also (3) a *causative* verb-stem.

55. The characteristic of the passive stem is the letter נ, or a D. f. in the first radical representing נ assimilated.

56. The causative stem may be known by the — which always occurs under its preformative (י, ת or מ).

57. The name of the simple stem is Ḳăl, of the passive stem, Nif'ăl, of the causative stem, Hif'îl.

58. The letter י prefixed to verbal forms means *he*, the letter ת means *she*, while מ so prefixed indicates a participle.

5. GRAMMAR-LESSON.

1. § 1.   The names of the Hebrew letters.
2. § 13. 2. and N. 1,   Dăḡēš-fŏrtē in spirants.
3. § 57. 1—3,   Inflection.

6. WORD-LESSON.

(66) יַמִּים *seas*   (69) דֶּשֶׁא *grass*   (72) עֵץ *tree*

(67) מִקְוֶה *collection*   (70) זֶרַע *seed*   (73) תָּרְשֵׂא (see N. 65)

68, מִקְוֵה *collection-of* (71) מִין *kind, species*

7. EXERCISES.

1. To be translated into Hebrew:—(1) *To-the-tree making fruit*
(there is) *seed* (according)-*to-its-kind;* (2) *The-seed which+in-it*
(= in which) (is) *fruit;* (3) *The-day which+in-it* (is) *light;* (4)
The-earth shall-cause-to-spring-forth)(*the-grass and-*)(*the seed;* (5)
The-fruit (is) *in-the-seed, and-the-seed* (is) *in-the-earth.*

2. To be translated into English: — (1) הַיָּם אֲשֶׁר מַיִם בּוֹ;
(2) עֵץ הַפְּרִי (4) וַיְהִי־דֶשֶׁא; (3) הַלַּיְלָה אֲשֶׁר חֹשֶׁךְ בּוֹ (2)
(5) זַרְעוּ בָאָרֶץ.

3. To be written in English letters:—(1) תִּדְשָׁא, (2) דֶּשֶׁא, (3)
עֹשֶׂה (6) עֵץ, (5) בֵּין, (4) פְּרִי.

4. To be written in Hebrew letters:—(1) zĕ-rä', (2)   dĕ-šĕ', (3)
rû(ă)ḥ, (4) χēn, (5) 'ô-śê(h), (6) tôṣē', (7) vô, (8) wăy-hî.

8. TOPICS FOR STUDY.

(1) The characteristic of the Nif'al stem. (2) The characteristic
of the Hif'il stem. (3) The origin and character of tone-long and
naturally long vowels. (4) The sign of the participle. (5) The 3 sg.
masc. pron. suffix. (6) The character of ַ in עֹשֶׂה. (7) The D. f.
Conjunctive. (8) What inflection includes. (9) The names of the
Hebrew letters.

LESSON X.—GENESIS I. 12, 13.

1. NOTE-REVIEW.

(1) וַיֹּאמֶר (18); (2) וְרוּחַ (15); (3) אֶת־ (23); (4) יָמִים (64;
(5) תִּדְשָׁא (65).

2. NOTES.

74. וַתּוֹצֵא—wăt-tô-ṣē'—*and-*(she)-*caused-to-go-forth:*
a. Wāw Conversive ַו, and the feminine prefix תּ (= *she*).

b. The ׳ is a contraction of ‏וֹ‎_ (*aw*); hence ‏תּוֹצֵא‎ is for ‏תַּוְצֵא‎ ,
which, like ‏תַּרְשֵׁא‎ , has ‏ⵦ‎ under the pref. and is *causative.*

c. The root is ‏יָצָא‎ , which is for ‏וָצָא‎ , *he-went-forth.*

75. ‏לְמִינֵהוּ‎ --lᵉmî-nê-hû—*to-kind-his:*

a. An uncontracted form, with same meaning as ‏לְמִינוֹ‎ .

b. ‏הוּ‎ is the full form of suffix meaning *his* or *him;* ‏ⵦ‎ may, for
convenience, be called a connecting vowel.

76. ‏שְׁלִישִׁי‎ —šᵉlî-šî—*third;* cf. ‏שֵׁנִי‎ *second.*

3. FORMS FOR SPECIAL STUDY.

‏בָּקָר‎	‏הַמַּיִם‎	‏וַתֵּרָאֶה‎	‏מַזְרִיעַ‎
‏בָּהוּ‎	‏כַּבְדִּיל‎	‏וַתּוֹצֵא‎	‏לְמִינֵהוּ‎
‏מְרַחֶפֶת‎	‏הַמָּקוֹם‎	‏עֵשֶׂב‎	‏זַרְעוּ‎

4. OBSERVATIONS.

59. The full form cf the pronom. suffix 3rd p. sg. masc. is ‏הוּ‎ , the
short form is ‏וֹ‎ .

60. There are many nouns that take a supplementary helping-vowel, usually *ĕ,* under certain circumstances *ă,* which is never
accented.

5. GRAMMAR-LESSON.

1. § **47.** 1, 2, 4, 5.   The Inseparable Prepositions.
2. § **49.** 1, 2.   The Wâw Conjunctive.
3. § **45.**   The Article.

6. WORD-LESSON

(74) ‏תּוֹצֵא‎ (see N. **74**)   (77) ‏עֵשֶׂב‎ *herb*   (80) ‏שְׁלִישִׁי‎ *third*

(75) ‏מַזְרִיעַ‎ *yielding seed*   (78) ‏עָשָׂה‎ *making*

(76) ‏יָצָא‎ *he went-forth*   (79) ‏פְּרִי‎ *fruit*

7. EXERCISES.

1. To be translated into Hebrew:—(1) *The-day the-third* (= the

third day). (2) *The-earth shall-cause-to-go-forth*)(*the-herb and-*)(*the-tree.* (3) *Let-*(there)*-be* (a) *place between the seas and-the-land.* (4) *And-she-caused-to-go-forth*)(*the-spirit upon+the-waters.* (5) *And-· created God*)(*-the-light and-*)(*the-darkness in-day one.* (6) *Day and-seas and-waters.*

2. (1) וַיַּבְדֵּל בֵּין הַיָּם לָאָרֶץ, (2) הַיּוֹם אֲשֶׁר אוֹרוּ־בּוֹ טוֹב

(3) וַיִּבְרָא אֶת הָרָקִיעַ בַּיּוֹם (4) וַתּוֹצֵא הָאָרֶץ אֶת־הַדֶּשֶׁא

,הַשֵּׁנִי (5) וַיַּעַשׂ אֱלֹהִים אֶת הַיַּבָּשָׁה וְאֵת מִקְוֵה הַמַּיִם.

3. To be written in English letters: — (1) וְלַחְשֵׁךְ, (2) לָרָקִיעַ,

(3) מִתַּחַת, (4) מַזְרִיעַ, (5) זְרְעוֹ־בוֹ, (6) וַיְּרָא.

4. To be written in Hebrew letters:—(1) yĭḳ-ḳâ-wû, (2) bᵉθδχ, (3) 'ĕl+mâ-ḳôm, (4) lᵉmî-nô, (5) 'ēṣ, (6) 'ᵃšĕr, (7) zăr-'ô+vô, (8) šᵉlîšî.

8. *TOPICS FOR STUDY.*

(1) The helping vowel. (2) The syllable. (3) Păθăḥ furtive. (4) The forms of the conjunction *and.* (5) The origin of î under wʿ in וַיְהִי (6) The use of the imperfect with wâw conversive. (7) The sign of the definite object, its forms and usage. (8) The influence of laryngeals upon neighbouring vowels.

LESSON XI.—GENESIS I. 14, 15.

1. NOTE-REVIEW.

(1) יְהִי (19); (2) הַשָּׁמַיִם (5); (3) בֵּין (26); (4) יוֹם (31);

(5) לַיְלָה (34); (6) וַיְהִי־כֵן (52) .

2. NOTES.

77. מְאֹרֹת—mᵉ'ô-rôθ—*luminaries:*

a. Sing., מָאוֹר (like מָקוֹם *place*); but when the plur. ending ôθ is added the tone moves one syllable, and the original ā is reduced to ־ְ, § 109. 1. a.

b. Both ô's are naturally long, though written defectively, § **6.** 4 N. 2.

c. אוֹר = *light,* but מָאוֹר = *luminary;* on this use of מ, see 63.*c.*

78. בִּרְקִיעַ—bǐr-ḳî(ă)'—*in-expanse-of:*

a. Abs. רָקִיעַ (40); const. רְקִיעַ, the original ă being reduced to ־ְ, §109. 3. *a.*

b. Before רְ the prep. בְּ takes ־ִ instead of ־ְ, § **47.** 2.

c. The syl. בִּרְ (bǐr) is closed, § **26.** N. 2.

d. The šᵉwâ under רְ is silent, § **10.** 2.

79. לְהַבְדִּיל—lᵉhăv-dîl—*to-cause-a-division:*

a. An infinitive; the prefix הַ shows it to be *causative* (Hǐf'ǐl).

b. D. l. in דּ because it does not immediately follow a vowel-sound.

80. וְהָיוּ—wᵉhâ-yû—*and-they-shall-be:*

a. הָיָה = *he-was;* הָיְתָה = *she-was;* הָיוּ = *they-were.*

b. But וְ connects this with what precedes, and likewise carries on to the perfect the time-sense of the preceding context; cf. with this the form of the conjunction (וַ) which gives the *imperfect* the time-sense of the preceding context, see 18.

81. לְאֹתֹת—lᵉʾ-ô-ôôṯ—*for-signs:*

a. Sing. אֹת or אוֹת; plur. אֹתֹת, by the addition of ôθ, § **106.** 3.

b. Both vowels are naturally long (ô), written defectively.

82. וּלְמוֹעֲדִים—û-lᵉmô-ʿᵃdîm—*and-for-seasons:*

a. The conjunction, before a consonant with šᵉwâ, is written וּ § **49.** 2.

b. The וּ is ô, not ǒ; Méθěǧ is written before comp. šᵉwâ, § **18.** 3.

c. עֲ, being a laryngeal, takes a *compound* šᵉwâ, § **42.** 3.

d. The noun is in the plur. masc., as shown by îm.

83. וְלְיָמִים—û-lᵉyǎ-mîm—*and-for-days:*

a. Another case of וּ, instead of וְ, before a consonant with šᵉwâ, see 82. *a.*

b. This is an *irregular plural form from* יוֹם *day.*

84. וְשָׁנִים—wᵉšǎ-nîm—*and-years:*

a. A masc. pl. ending with a noun (שָׁנָה) which has feminine sg.
ending, § 106. 4. N.

85. לִמְאוֹרֹת—līm-'ô-rôθ—for-luminaries:

a. What was said in 78. b, c, concerning bĭr, applies to līm.

b. Here the first ô is written fully, the second defectively, § 6. 4. N. 2.

86. לְהָאִיר—lᵉhă-'îr—to-cause-to-shine; cf. אוֹר light:

a. Another causative infinitive (cf. הַבְדִּיל), but with ־ָ under ה
instead of ־ַ, because it is in an open syllable, § 28. 1.

3. FORMS FOR SPECIAL STUDY.

עֶרֶב	מְאֹרֹת	יְהִי	וְשָׁנִים
אֶרֶץ	אֹתֹת	מְאֹרֹת	וּבֵין
דֶּשֶׁא	יָמִים	בִּרְקִיעַ	וְלִמְוֹעֲדִים
זֶרַע	שָׁנִים	לִמְאוֹרֹת	וּלְיָמִים

4. OBSERVATIONS

61. The fem. plur. ending is ôθ, the masc., îm.

62. For the initial and so-called medial šᵉwâ, see § 10. 1, 2.

63. And is usually written וְ, but before labials and before consonants with šᵉwâ it is written וּ.

5. GRAMMAR-LESSON.

1. § 47. 1, 2, 4, 5,   The Inseparable Prepositions.
2. § 49. 1, 2,   The Wâw Conjunctive.
3. § 10. 1,2,   Initial and (so-called) Medial Šᵉwâ.
4. § 7. 1— 4,   Classification of Vowel-sounds.

6. WORD-LESSON.

(81) אוֹת sign   (83) מָאוֹר luminary   (85) שֶׁמֶשׁ sun

(82) יָרֵחַ moon   (84) מוֹעֵד season   (86) שָׁנָה year

7. EXERCISES.

1. To be translated into Hebrew:—(1) *The-sign, the-moon, the sun, the-year, the-season;* (2) *The-sun will-be-seen in-the-heavens;* (3) *Signs and-luminaries and-seasons and-years;* (4) *The-sun shall-be* (יִהְיֶה) *in-expanse-of the-heavens;* (5) *For-seasons and-for-luminaries;* (6) *To-cause-a-division between the-day and-between the-night;* (7) *Seas and-waters;* (8) *Days and-seas;* (9) *The-luminary, the-luminaries.*

2. To be translated into English:— (1) הַמְּאֹרֹת מֵעַל לָאָרֶץ;

(4) וַיַּבְדֵּל בֵּין הַשָּׁמַיִם וּבֵין הָאָרֶץ; (3) הַמָּאוֹר הַשֵּׁנִי (2)

(6) בְּרָקִיעַ, בְּרָקִיעַ, בְּרָקִיעַ; (5) בָּרָא אֱלֹהִים אֶת־הַשֶּׁמֶשׁ

הָרָקִיעַ אֲשֶׁר הַשֶּׁמֶשׁ בּוֹ (7); לַמְּאוֹרֹת, לְמָאוֹר.

3. To be written in English letters:— (1) יָרֵחַ, (2) מוֹעֵד, (3) יַבְדֵּל. (6) מוֹעֲדִים, (5) שָׁנָה, (4) שֶׁמֶשׁ.

4. To be written in Hebrew letters:—(1) hā-'îr, (2) 'ô-θôθ, (3) yôm, (4) yâ-mîm, (5) bĭr-ḳî(ă)'.

8. TOPICS FOR STUDY.

(1) Change of ⊤ to ⊤. (2) Prepositions בְּ and לְ with î. (3) Wâw Conversive with the past tense. (4.) Various forms of the verb הָיָה *he-was.* (5) ן and וְ. (6) ־ים and וֹת. (7) Difference between הַבְדִּיל and הָאִיר. (8) Nouns with helping vowels. (9) Initial and so-called Medial Š°wâ. (10) Classification of vowel-sounds according to formation, quantity, nature, value.

LESSON XII.—GENESIS I. 16, 17.

1. NOTE-REVIEW.

(78); בְּרָקִיעַ (4); (58) מָקוֹם (3); (56) הַמַּיִם (2); (77); מָאֹרֹת (1)

(29). וַיִּקְרָא (8); (22); וַיַּרְא (7); (28); הַחֹשֶׁךְ (6); (86); לְהָאִיר (5)

2. NOTES.

87. וַיַּעַשׂ—wăy-yǎ-'ăś—*and-*(he)-*made,* see 46:

a. Like יְהִי, a short form of the *imperfect,* root עָשָׂה.

b. Third syllable, has an unaccented helping or secondary vowel.

88. שְׁנֵי—šᵉnê—*two-of; cf.* פְּנֵי *faces-of:*

a. The construct state of the numeral שְׁנַיִם, of which ‏ַיִם is the *dual* ending, §§ 106. 5; 107. 6.

b. The word has but one syllable, ‏ְ not being a full vowel.

89. הַגְּדֹלִים—hăg-gᵉdô-lîm—*the-great* (ones):

a. The article written regularly with ‏ַ and D. f., § 45. 1.

b. An adjective in the plur. (note the ending ‏ִים) from גָּדוֹל.

c. The ‏ֹ is ô, though in the plural form written defectively.

d. The ‏ָ and ‏ְ under גּ in the sing. and plur. respectively, both arise from an original ă. In the singular this ă is in an open syl. immediately before the tone and therefore is rounded to â; in the plural the tone has moved away upon the addition of îm, and so original ă is reduced to šᵉwâ; cf. sg. m. גָּדוֹל, but sg. f. גְּדוֹלָה, pl. m. גְּדוֹלִים, pl. f. גְּדוֹלוֹת, in which, by the addition of an affix, the tone is changed. This change of a full vowel to šᵉwâ is called reduction, § 36. 2. *b.*

90. הַמָּאוֹר הַגָּדֹל—hăm-mâ-'ôr hăg-gâ-dôl—*the-luminary the-great* (one):

a. Both words have a tone-long â, and a naturally long ô, although in the adjective the ô is written defectively.

b. Both words have the article in its usual form.

91. לְמֶמְשֶׁלֶת—lᵉmĕm-šĕ-lĕθ—*for-dominion-of:*

a. Two unaccented closed syllables, one accented open.

b. The final ĕ is a helping vowel.

c. לְ is the prep.; מ, the formative prefix, cf. 58. *b;* ת, the fem. ending; the root being מָשַׁל.

92. הַקָּטֹן—hăk-ḳâ-ṭōn—*the-small;* with tone-long ō.

93. הַכּוֹכָבִים—hăk-kô-χâ-vîm—*the stars:*

a. The ָ under כּ is Méθěǧ, § **18.** 1; under כ it is Sillûḳ.

b. Cf. כּוֹכָב *star,* כּוֹכָבִים *stars,* הַכּוֹכָבִים *the-stars.*

94. וַיִּתֵּן—wăy-yĭt-tēn—*and-(he)-gave:*

a. יִתֵּן *he-will-give* is the Ḳăl Imperfect from נָתַן *he-gave.* With Wăw Conversive (cf. 18) it has the force of a Perfect (past).

b. The D. f. in תּ is for the first radical נ, which has been assimilated; cf. מִתַּחַת for מִן תַּחַת, see 49, § **39.** 1.

95. אֹתָם—'ô-θăm—)(-*them:* the pronominal suffix ם‍ָ with אֹת, another way of writing the sign of def. obj., § **51.** 2.

3. FORMS FOR SPECIAL STUDY.

הַמְּאֹרֹת הַגְּדֹלִים	*the-luminaries the-great* = the great luminaries.
הַמָּאוֹר הַגָּדֹל	*the-luminary the-great* = the great luminary.
הַמָּאוֹר הַקָּטֹן	*the-luminary the-small* = the small luminary.

4. OBSERVATIONS.

64. In the words cited above, the noun stands first, the *adjective*, second.

65. The noun is masculine,[1] the adjective is masculine.

66. When the noun is sing., the adjective is sing.; when the noun is plur., the adjective is plur.

67. The noun has the article, and so has the adjective.

68. The following is, therefore, the rule governing the position and agreement of an attributive adjective: *The adjective, when attributive, follows its noun, and agrees with it in gender, number and definiteness.*

---

[1] The noun מָאוֹר is *masculine,* although in the plural it has a feminine form.

5. GRAMMAR-LESSON.

1. § **57.** Notes 1, 2,	Tenses and Moods.
2. § **58.** 1.	The Simple Verb-stem, Ḳäl.
3. § **14.** 1—3,	Omission of Dåğēš-fŏrtē.
4. § **11.** 2. a, b,	Š͏ʻwå under final consonants.

6. WORD-LESSON.

(87) אוֹר *to shine*   (89) כּוֹכָב *star*   (92) רְבִיעִי *fourth*

(88) גָּרוֹל *great*   (90) מֶמְשָׁלָה *ruling*   (93) שְׁנַיִם *two*

(91) קָטֹן *small*

7. EXERCISES.

1. To be translated into Hebrew:—(1) *The great day;* (2) *In the great day;* (3) *And in the great day;* (4) *The great stars;* (5) *The small star;* (6) *The good God;* (7) *He-gave, he-ruled;* (8) *God gave)(the-luminaries for-(the)-ruling-of the-day and-for-(the)-ruling-of the-night;* (9) *The great luminary (is) the-sun; the small luminary, the-moon;* (10) *The-sun and-the-moon (are) in-(the)-expanse-of the-heavens;* (11) *God will-give)(the-day.*

2. To be translated into English:—'1) עָשָׂה אֶת־הַמָּאוֹר הַגָּרֹל; (2) הַשָּׁנָה הַשְּׁלִישִׁית; (3) מוֹעֵד אֶחָד; (4) הַכּוֹכָב הַטּוֹב; (5) הַמָּאוֹר הַקָּטֹן הַשֵּׁנִי; (7) הַמָּאוֹר הַשֵּׁנִי; (6) יְהִי כוֹכָבִים בַּלַּיְלָה; (8) הָעֵץ אֲשֶׁר־; (10) עֵץ הַפְּרִי; (9) וַיַּבְדֵּל בֵּין מְאֹרֹת לִמְאֹרֹת בּוֹ זָרַע.

3. To be written in English letters : — (1) יִתֵּן, (2) יַעַשׂ, (3) מְאֹרֹת, (8) לִמְשֹׁל, (7) בְּרָקִיעַ, (6) אַתֶּם, (5) כּוֹכָב, (4) מֶמְשָׁלֶת, (9) הַיּוֹם.

4. To be written in Hebrew letters:—yōm, (2) yôm, (3) šēχ, (4) lēχ, (5) ʼätt, (6) ṭălt, (7) yēšt, (8) hå-ʼôr.

8. TOPICS FOR STUDY.

(1) Affixes of the feminine. (2) Affixes of the masculine plural and dual, in absolute and construct. (3) Change of ⟋ to ⟍. (4)

The construction of the attributive adjective. (5) Mĕθĕḡ and Sĭllûḳ. (6) Assimilation of נ. (7) The infinitive of the root מָשַׁל. (8) The conjunction before a labial. (9) The ordinals meaning *second, third, fourth.* (10) Tenses and moods in Hebrew. (11) The form of the simple verb-stem (Ḳal). (12) Omission of Dåḡēš-fŏrtē. (13) Šᵉwâ under final consonants.

LESSON XIII.—GENESIS I. 18—20.

1. *NOTE-REVIEW.*

(1) הַמַּיִם (17); (2) הָאָרֶץ (7); (3) רְקִיעַ (40); (4) הַגְּדֹלִים (89);

(5) אֲשֶׁר (48); (6) לְמִינֵהוּ (75); (7) וַיַּרְא (22).

2. *NOTES.*

96. וְלִמְשֹׁל—wᵉlĭm-šōl—*and-to-rule:*

a. Conjunction וְ; prep. לְ with ־ָ, § 47. 2; the ־ָ under מ silent.

b. An infinitive from the root מָשַׁל, cf. **91**; tone-long ō.

97. בַּיּוֹם וּבַלַּיְלָה—bǎy-yôm û-vǎl-lǎy-lå̄(h)—*in-the-day and-in-the-night,* §§ 45. 4. R. 3; 47. 4; 49. 2.

98. וּלְהַבְדִּיל—û-lᵃhăv-dîl—*and-to-cause-a-division.*

a. וְ, § 49. 2; לְ, § 32. 3. *c;* הַבְדִּיל, see **79**.

b. The root is בָּדַל (pronounced bå-ḏăl).

99. רְבִיעִי—rᵉvî-ʻî—*fourth;* cf. שְׁלִישִׁי *third.*

100. יִשְׁרְצוּ—yĭš-rᵉṣû—(they) *shall-swarm:*

a. Ḳăl Imperfect 3 pers. plur. masc. from שָׁרַץ *he-swarmed;* יִשְׁרֹץ *he-will-swarm;* יִשְׁרְצוּ *they-will-swarm.*

b. Two Šᵉwâs—first, silent; second, vocal, § 11. 3. N. 1, 2.

c. The Imperfect tense represents an action as unfinished, incomplete, whether in past, present or future time.

101. שֶׁרֶץ—šĕʼ-rĕṣ—*swarm,* or, collectively, *swarms:*

a. Like זֶרַע ,דְּשֶׁא ,אֶרֶץ ,עֶרֶב and עֵשֶׂב; these nouns have but one essential vowel, viz., the first, since the second is inserted merely for euphony. They are called *Seğolates*.

b. The essential vowel in all these cases, except עֵשֶׂב, was origina·ly ă, which has been deflected to ĕ, § 89. 1. The essential vowel of עֵשֶׂב was originally ĭ.

102. נֶפֶשׁ —nĕ'-fĕš—*soul-of:* Another Seğolate, of which the primary form was נַפְשׁ; cf. the primary form of זֶרַע, viz., זַרְע, which appears before the suffix in זַרְעוֹ, see 73.

103. חַיָּה—ḥăy-yâ(h)—*life:* Feminine, as shown by הָ—.

104. וְעוֹף—wᵉ'ôf—*and-fowl:*

a. The Wâw Conjunctive pointed regularly with šᵉwâ.

b. A case of naturally long ô; the *final* form of ף (Pē).

105. יְעוֹפֵף—yᵉ'ô-fēf—(he) *shall-fly:*

a. An Imperfect from the root עוּף *to-fly*.

b. Unchangeable ô; both ף's are spirants.

3. FORMS FOR SPECIAL STUDY.

יִשְׁרַץ	לִמְשֹׁל	נֶפֶשׁ
יִשְׁרְצוּ	הִבְדִּיל	זֶרַע

4. OBSERVATIONS.

69. The Imperfect Ḳăl has a preformative in the 3d masc. the letter י, written with ĭ.

70. In forming the plural of the Ḳăl perf., the vowel of the second radical becomes vocal šᵉwâ.

5. GRAMMAR-LESSON.

1 § 50. 1,   The regular forms of the Personal Pronoun.

2. § 50. 2, 3.   Pausal forms and Remarks (*to be read only*).

6. WORD-LESSON.

(94) חַיָּה life   (96) עוּף to-fly   (98) שֶׁרֶץ swarm

(95) נֶפֶשׁ soul   (97) עוֹף fowl

7. EXERCISES.

1. To be translated into Hebrew:—(1) The-waters shall-swarm;
(2) God created)(the-earth, and-he-made)(the-heavens; (3) And-
saw God)(the-earth which he-had-created, and-(it)-was+good; (4)
I (am) God who created)(the-light; (5) Thou (art) in-the-heavens
and-I (am) upon+the-earth; (6) We (are) great; (7) Thou (m.)
(art) small; (8) Thou (f.) (art) good; (9) Ye (are) (the) light-of
the-earth.

2. To be translated into English : — (1) אָנֹכִי וְהוּא, (2) אַתְּ
בָּרָא (5) ,יִקְרְאוּ לַמַּיִם יַמִּים (4) ;גְּדֹלִים הַשָּׁמַיִם (3) ;גְּדֹלָה
הָעוֹף, ;אֱלֹהִים אֶת־הַנֶּפֶשׁ (6) .

3. To be written in English letters:—(1) שֶׁרֶץ, (2) וּלְמָשֹׁל, (3)
וּלְהַבְדִּיל, (6) נַפְשׁוֹ, (5) נֶפֶשׁ, (4) עוֹף.

4. To be written in Hebrew letters:—(1) ḳôl, (2) nĕ'-fĕš, (3)
mᵉ'ô-rôθ, (4) 'â-nô-χî, (5) 'ătt, (6) 'ăt-tĕm, (7) năḥ'-nû.

8. TOPICS FOR STUDY.

(1) Force of the Imperfect. (2) Seğolates. (3) The vowel ĕ, as
derived from ⁻. (4) The vowel ô. (5) The various ways of writing
the article. (6) The forms of the Personal Pronoun. (7) The simple
verb-stem. (8) The Passive. (9) The Causative.

LESSON XIV.—GENESIS I. 21—23.

1. NOTE-REVIEW.

(1) הַמַּיִם (42), (2) וַיֹּאמֶר (18`, (3) וַתּוֹצֵא 74 , (4) נֶפֶשׁ
חַיָּה (102. 103); (5) וַיַּעַשׂ (46) .

2. NOTES.

106. וַיִּבְרָא—wǎy-yǐv-rǎ'—*and-*(he)*-created:*

a. יִבְרָא *he-will-create,* but with ּ‎ו the force of the tense is changed.

b. Compare (1) קְרָא and וַיִּקְרָא with (2) בָּרָא and וַיִּבְרָא.

107. הַתַּנִּינִם—hǎt-tǎn-nî-nîm—*the-sea-monsters:*

a. Points in ת and נ are D. f., because preceded by vowels.

b. The ◌ִ under נ is î written defectively, § 6. 3. N. and 4. N. 2.

c. (1) Article ◌ַה, (2) noun תַּנִּין, (3) plural ending ◌ִים.

108. כָּל־נֶפֶשׁ—kŏl+nĕ'-fĕš—*every+soul-of:*

a. כָּל־ is an unaccented closed syllable, for the word before Mǎḳḳêf *always* loses its accent, § 17. 1, 2.

b. An *unaccented* closed syllable must have a short vowel, § 28. 2; but is ◌ָ a short vowel? *It is.* In this word we have for the first time ŏ, or Ḳâmĕṣ-ḥâṭûf, which is represented by the same sign[1] (◌ָ) as â, § 5. 5.

109. הַחַיָּה—hǎ(h)-ḥǎy-yǎ(h)—*the-life:* The article with its D. f. implied, § 45. 2; Mĕθĕǧ, second syllable before tone, § 18. 1.

110. הָרֹמֶשֶׂת—hâ-rô-mĕ'-śĕθ—*the-*(one)*-creeping:*

a. The article with D. f. rejected and ◌ַ rounded to ◌ָ, § 45. 3.

b. A participle (although without מ) fem. (ת) sg. from רָמַשׂ,

c. Observe that the ◌ֹ is ô, not ō, although defectively written.

111. שָׁרְצוּ—šâ-r‘ṣû—(they) *swarmed:*

a. He-swarmed שָׁרַץ, they-swarmed שָׁרְצוּ; cf. יִשְׁרַץ *he-will-swarm,* יִשְׁרְצוּ *they-will-swarm;* and so בָּרָא *he-created,* בָּרְאוּ *they-created;* קָרָא *he-called,* קָרְאוּ *they-called;* נָתַן *he-gave,* נָתְנוּ *they-gave.*

b. Ḳǎl Perf. 3 m. pl., as shown by the ending ּ‎ו.

---

[1] There is practically no difference in pronunciation between ◌ָ = â and ◌ָ = ŏ; but in this book they are transliterated differently in order to emphasize the difference in their origin.

112. לְמִינֵהֶם—lᵉ-mî-nê-hěm—*to-kinds-their:*

a. הֶם is pron. suf. 3 m. pl., as used with plur. nouns, § 51. 1. c.

b. ┬ (= ê) is a defective writing for ‏י‏ the plur. const. ending.

113. כָּנָף—kâ-nâf—*wing:*

a. The first ┬ is â, because *before* the tone and in an open syllable: the second is â because under the tone, § 31. 1. a. (1), c.

b. Const. sing. would be כְּנַף; *dual* would be כְּנָפַיִם.

114. וַיְבָרֶךְ—wăy-vâ'-rĕχ—*and-(he)-blessed:*

a. Root is בָּרַךְ, ‏י‏ being sign of Impf., and ‏ו‏ the conjunction.

b. D. f. of ‏ו‏ omitted from ‏י‏, which has only a šᵉwâ, § 14. 2.

c. The final ךְ has, as always, a šᵉwâ, § 11. 2. a.

d. In the syllable ‏וַי‏ ay forms a diphthong, hence the following ב is a spirant.

e. This stem is not at all like either (1) the simple verb-stem, as seen in יִקְרָא, or (2) the passive-stem, as seen in יָקוּן, or (3) the causative-stem, as seen in יַבְדִּיל, מַבְדִּיל. It is a *new* stem, viz., the *intensive*. The form would regularly be יְבָרֵךְ, but ר rejects the D. f., and the preceding ┬ becomes ┬, while, by a change of tone, ┬ yields to ┬; cf. אֶת, but אֶת- (23).

f. The characteristic of the intensive-stem is Dâgēš-fŏrtē in the second radical, not, as in יָקוּן (55), in the first.

115. לֵאמֹר—lê'-mōr—*to-say,* generally translated *saying:*

a. Inf. const. of אָמַר *say* is אֱמֹר; cf. מְשֹׁל (96) from מָשַׁל.

b. Before 'א, the prep. ל takes ┬, giving לֵאמֹר, § 47. 3.

c. א being weak, finally quiesces, carrying ┬ along with it, and in compensation ┬ becomes ê.

116. פְּרוּ—pᵉrû—*be-ye-fruitful:* A Ḳâl Imperative plural.

117. וּרְבוּ—û-rᵉvû—*and-multiply-ye:* Ḳâl Imperative plur. with Wâw Conjunctive, here ‏ו‏ before a consonant with šᵉwâ, § 49. 2.

118. וּמִלְאוּ—û-mĭl-'û—*and-fill-ye:*

a. Wâw Conjunctive before a labial is written וּ, § 49. 2.

b. Šᵉwâ is *silent*, §§ 10. 2. b; 26. 4. N. 2; 28. 4.

c. Ḳål Imperative plural of מְלָא, וּ indicating the plural.

119. בַּיָּמִים—băy-yăm-mîm—*in-the-seas:*

a. יָם *sea*, יַמִּים *seas*, הַיַּמִּים *the-seas*, בַּיַּמִּים *in-the-seas.*

b. Cf. יוֹם *day*, יָמִים *days*, הַיָּמִים *the-days*, בַּיָּמִים *in-the-days.*

120. וְהָעוֹף—wᵉhā-'ôf—*and-the-fowl*, §§ 49. 1; 45. 3.

121. יֶרֶב—yĭ'-rĕv—*let-*(him)-*multiply:*

a. Ḳål Impf., short form, from same root as רָבֻ (117).

b. י is the pref. of the Impf.; ר and ב, radicals; third radical lacking.

c. ◌ֶ is a helping vowel.

122. חֲמִישִׁי—ḥami-šî—*fifth*, § 9. 2.

3. FORMS FOR SPECIAL STUDY.

יְקָרֶא – קָרָא	מְרַחֶפֶת	הַמַּיִם
יִבְרָא – בָּרָא	מְמַשֶּׁלֶת	הַחַיָּה
יִשְׁרְצוּ – שָׁרְצוּ	רֹמֶשֶׂת	הָרֹמֶשֶׂת

4. OBSERVATIONS.

71. Upon the addition of וּ in the Impf. as well as in the Perf. the vowel of the second radical becomes vocal Šᵉwâ.

72. The feminine ending ת is often preceded by an unaccented ◌ֶ, inserted for euphony.

73. The article is ◌ַ הַ; while הַ (also הַ) takes the D. f. by implication, ר (also ע and א) entirely rejects it.

74. The quiescense of a consonant is usually compensated for by the strengthening of the preceding vowel.

5. GRAMMAR-LESSON.

1. § **106.** 2. *b,* The fem. ending ת attached to a stem by means of ־ֶ‚

2. § **106.** 2. *c,* The fem. ending ת changed to ה‎ָ‎‚

3. § **42.** 1. 3¹ The peculiarities of laryngeals.

6. WORD-LESSON.

(99)   כָּל־   *all, every*   (102)   תַּנִּין   *sea-monster*

(100)   כָּנָף   *wing*   (103)   בֵּרַךְ   *he-blessed*

(101)   רָמַשׂ   *he-crept*   (104)   מָלֵא   *he-filled*

7. EXERCISES.

1. To be translated into Hebrew:—(1) *God said, "Let-there-be (an)-expanse" and-he-created*)(+ *the-heavens.* (2) *And-he-made*)(+*the-great stars* (lit. *the-stars the-great*). (3) *Fill-ye the-waters and-multiply-ye in-the-seas.* (4) *And-blessed God every winged fowl* (lit. *every+fowl-of wing*). (5) *Let-multiply the-fowl upon+the-earth.* (6) *God blessed*)(*every* + *living-thing that creeps* (lit.)(*every soul-of the-life the-creeping*); (7) *The-waters swarmed according-to-their-kinds.*

2. To be translated into English : — (1) וַיִּבְרָא אֱלֹהִים אֶת־

(2) הַתַּנִּינִם לְמִינֵהֶם‚   (3) וַיִּשְׁרְצוּ הַמַּיִם בַּיּוֹם הַחֲמִישִׁי

(4) בֵּרַךְ אֹתָם אֱלֹהִים‚   (5) יִרֶב הָעוֹף עַל־הָאָרֶץ לֵאמֹר

נָתַן אֹתָם אֱלֹהִים בַּיַּמִּים וְעַל־הָאָרֶץ.

3. To be written in English letters : — אֹתָם, יְבָרֶךְ, שָׁרְצוּ,

הַגְּדֹלִים, הַתַּנִּנִים, וּרְבוּ, חֲמִישִׁי.

4. To be written in Hebrew letters:—(1) kōl, (2) kŏl+, (3) yĭ'-rĕv, (4) šĕ'-rĕṣ, (5) hă(h)-hăy-yâ(h), (6) năf-šô, (7) š°nê.

¹ Learn only the general statement, not the sub-sections marked *a, b, c,* etc.

8. *TOPICS FOR STUDY.*

(1) The plural (masc.) of verbal forms. (2) The feminine ending ‎ה. (3) The dual ending. (4) The intensive stem. (5) The peculiar-ities of laryngeals. (6) Compensatory strengthening of vowels.

LESSON XV.—GENESIS I. 24—26.

1. *NOTE-REVIEW.*

(1) ‎כָּל־ (108); (2) ‎וְלִמְשֹׁל (96); (3) ‎וּבַלַּיְלָה (97); (4) ‎לְהָאִיר
86; (5) ‎אֶת־הָאוֹר (23; (6) ‎וַיְהִי (43).

2. *NOTES.*

123. ‎תּוֹצֵא—tô-ṣē'—*Let-*(her)*-cause-to-go-forth:*

a. ‎וֹ (ô) is contracted from ‎וְ_; ‎תּוֹצֵא is like ‎תַּדְשֵׁא (65).

b. Hif'îl Impf. 3 fem. sg. from the root ‎יָצָא *he-went-forth.*

124. ‎לְמִינָה—l°mî-nâh—*to-kind-her:*

a. ‎ל *to,* ‎מִין *kind,* ‎ה_ *her;* cf. ‎לְמִינֵהוּ, לְמִינוֹ.

b. The point in ‎ה is neither D. f. nor D. l.; it is inserted to show that ‎ה has a consonantal force and is *not* silent, for ‎ה at the end of a word is always silent unless it has this point, called Măppîḳ, § **16.** 1.

125. ‎בְּהֵמָה—b°hē-mâ(h)—*cattle:*

a. ‎ה, having no Măppîḳ, is silent; the noun is fem., § **106.** 2. *c.*

126. ‎וָרֶמֶשׂ—wâ-rĕ'-mĕś—*and-creeper:*

a. Wâw Conj. before the tone-syl. receives ‎ָ, § **49.** 4; cf. ‎וָבֹהוּ (11).

b. ‎רֶמֶשׂ is a Seğolate noun from the same root as ‎רֹמֶשֶׂת (110).

c. The secondary, helping vowel is not accented.

127. ‎וְחַיְתוֹ־אֶרֶץ—w°ḥăy-θô+'ĕ'-rĕṣ—*and-beast-of +earth:*

a. ‎חַיָּה (absolute) = *life* or *beast;* ‎חַיַּת is construct, § **107.** 2, 4.

b. ‎וֹ is an old ending, now obsolete, § **105.** 1. Rem.

c. חִיתוֹ is for חַיְתוֹ, but ־ under וּ has become silent ־ָ, D. f. in וּ being dropped, and וּ forms a diphthong; hence ת is spirant.

128. חַיְת—ḥäy-yäθ—*beast-of:* with the same meaning as the preceding *archaic* form חִיתוֹ; here D. f. remains.

129. הָאֲדָמָה—hă-'ăḍă-mă(h)—*the-ground:*

a. The article before a weak laryngeal has ־ָ, § 45. 3.

b. The vowel before a compound Šᵉwâ always has Méθĕğ, § 18. 3.

c. א, a laryngeal, takes compound rather than simple Šᵉwâ, § 9. 2.

d. ה, having no Măppîḳ (§ 16. 1), is silent; the word is feminine, § 106. 2. c.

130. נַעֲשֶׂה—nă'-ᵃśé(h)—*we-will-make,* or, *let-us-make:*

a. Of these four consonants only *three* can be radicals; the root is עָשָׂה.

b. The נ, from pronoun אֲנוּ *we,* indicates 1 p. pl., *we,* just as וּ indicates 3 m. sg., *he,* and ת, 3 fem. sg., *she.*

c. The laryngeal ע takes *compound* Šᵉwâ, § 9. 2.

d. Méθĕğ, as always, before a compound Šᵉwâ, § 18. 3.

c. The vowel ה_ is *é,* cf. same vowel in וְתֵרָאֶה (59) and עָשֶׂה (71).

f. To the first syl. ᵃ is an overhanging sound helping in the transition from the laryngeal to the following sibilant.

131. אָדָם—'ă-ḍăm—*man:* both vowels changeable.

132. בְּצַלְמֵנוּ—bᵉṣäl-mē'-nû—*in-image-our:*

a. Prep. בְּ; noun צֶלֶם; connecting-vowel ־ֵ; suffix נוּ.

b. The accent ־ֶ is disjunctive, separating the word from what follows.

133. כִּדְמוּתֵנוּ—kîḍ-mû-θē'-nû—*according-to-likeness-our:*

a. כְּ has D. l. because of preceding disjunctive accent, § 12. 3.

b. The Šᵉwâ becomes silent, as in לִמְשֹׁל (96), after the inseparable preposition.

c. The noun is דְּמוּת, the suf. and connecting-vowel being נוּ.

---

134. וְיִרְדּוּ—wᵉyîr-dû—*and-they-shall-have-dominion:*

a. וְ = *and;* ⸾ indicates Impf. ‪ן‬, plural; radicals, ר and ד.

135. בִּדְנַת—vĭd-ğăθ—*in-fish-of:*

a. The stroke over בּ is Râfê, § **16.** 2.

b. Prep., before a consonant with šᵉwâ, takes ⸗, § **47.** 2.

c. On ğ, see §§ **10.** 2, *d.* and **28.** 4.

d. Noun in abs., דָּגָה; in const., דְּנַת, § **106.** 2. *a.* (2).

136. הָרֶמֶשׁ הָרֹמֵשׂ—hâ-rĕ'-mĕś hâ-rô-mĕś—*the-creeper the-creep-*
ing: the noun and the participle, both with article.

---

3. *FORMS FOR SPECIAL STUDY.*

לֶאֱמֹר *for* לַאמֹר	חָיָה	פְּרוּ	וְבֹהוּ
הַוֹּצֵא *for* תּוֹצֵא	חַיַּת	רְבוּ	וְרֶמֶשׂ
לְמִינָה *for* לְמִינָה	חַיְתוֹ	מָלְאוּ	לָמִּים

---

4. *OBSERVATIONS.*

75. Contractions are common; thus ‪ו‬_ (ăw) becomes ô; הָ_
(å-hå) becomes הָ_ (âh). The result is always a naturally long
vowel.

76. The original fem. ending, was ת_, which is retained in the
construct, but in the absolute the ת is lost and the preceding ⸗ becomes ⸗.

77. The Imperative has only a second person.

78. Before a tone-syllable Wâw Conjunctive and the inseparable
prepositions *may* take a tone-long ⸗.

5. *GRAMMAR-LESSON.*

1. § **51.** 1. *a—c,*   Pronominal Suffixes,—separate forms.

2. § **51.** 2,   Pronominal Suffixes with אֵת.

6. WORD-LESSON.

(105) אֲדָמָה   *ground*   (108) רָבָה   *he-multiplied*

(106) בְּהֵמָה   *cattle*   (109) רֶמֶשׂ   *creeper*

(107)   פָּרָה   *he-was-fruitful*

7. EXERCISES.

1. To be translated into Hebrew:—(1) *God created*)(*-them;* (2) *He-said to-the-sea-monsters, Fill-ye*)(+*the-seas;* (3) *The-fowl multiplied upon*+*the-earth;* (4) *The-day the-fifth;* (5) (*The*) *beast-of the-earth was* (*fem.*) *upon*+*the-ground;* (6) *To-kind-his, and-to-kind-her, and-to-kinds-their;* (7) *His-day, my-day, her-day;* (8) *God made*)(+ *the-creeper upon*+*the-ground;* (9) *The-cattle the-good* (f.); (10) *The good beast;* (11) *And-saw God all*+*that he-had-created, and-*(it)-*was* +*good;* (12) *The-waters* (are) *in-the-seas and-upon*+*the-earth.*

2. To be translated into English:—(1) וְהָעוֹף יָעוֹף; (2) וַתּוֹצֵא

וַתּוֹצֵא הָאָרֶץ אֶת־הַבְּהֵמָה וְאֶת־ (3) ,הָאָרֶץ דֶּשֶׁא וְעֵשֶׂב וָעֵץ

.וַיְבָרֶךְ אֶת־כָּל־רֶמֶשׂ הָאֲדָמָה (4) ;הָרֶמֶשׂ וְאֶת חַיַּת הָאָרֶץ

3. To be written in English letters: — (1) מָלֵא, (2) רָבָה, (3)

תּוֹצֵא, (7) לֵאמֹר, (6) לְמִינָה, (5) בְּהֵמָה, (4) בָּרַךְ.

4. To be written in Hebrew letters:—(1) kōl, (2) kŏl+, (3) bên, (4) bēn, (5) bēn+, (6) rĕ′-mĕś, (7) hăy-θô, (8) băy-yăm-mîm, (9) ′ăšĕr, (10) rēX, (11) vâ′-rĕX.

8. TOPICS FOR STUDY.

(1) The Intensive-stem. (2) Omission of D. f. (3) Inf. const. of אָמַר with prep. לְ. (4) Difference between the words for *sea, seas* and *day, days.* (5) The ordinals 2d to 5th. (6) Pron. suf. of 3d per. fem. (7) Măppîḳ. (8) Relation between the fem. affixes ָה and ָת. (9) Pronominal suffixes,—separate forms. (10) Pronominal suffixes with אֵת.

LESSON XVI.—GENESIS I. 27—29.

1. *NOTE-REVIEW.*

(1) וְעוֹף (104); (2) בְּהֵמָה (125); (3) וָרֶמֶשׂ (126); (4) וַיִּבְרָא
(106); (5) אֹתָם (95); (6) וַיְבָרֶךְ (114); (7) פְּרוּ (116); (8) וּרְבוּ
(117); (9) וּמִלְאוּ (118); (10) חַיָּה (103); (11) הָרֹמֶשֶׂת (110).

2. *NOTES.*

137. בְּצַלְמוֹ—bᵉṣäl-mô—*in-image-his:*

a. בְּ *in;* צַלְמ, *see* 132. *a;* וֹ *his,* as in לְמִינוֹ (72), זַרְעוֹ (73).

b. The accent over מ is disjunctive, cf. ־ֵ (132. *b*).

138. בְּצֶלֶם—bᵉṣĕ'-lĕm—*in-image-of:*

a. בְ has D. 1. because of preceding disjunctive accent, § **12. 3.**

b. This is the usual form of the noun, but צַלְמ (137. *a*) is the *primary* form, to which suffixes are attached. Cf. זֶרַע, but זַרְעוֹ
(73); and so אֶרֶץ, but אַרְצוֹ, עֶרֶב, but עַרְבוֹ, נֶפֶשׁ, but נַפְשׁוֹ
etc., § **109. 4.** *a, b.*

139. אֹתוֹ—'ô-θô—)(*-him,* § **51.** 2.

140. זָכָר וּנְקֵבָה—zä-χär û-nᵉḳē-vå(h)—*male and-female:*

a. זָכָר is a noun like אָדָם, with two tone-long vowels which were
originally short, § **90. 1.** *a.*

b. Wåw Conj., before a consonant with šᵉwå, is וּ § **49.** 2.

c. The ending ־ָה is the feminine affix, § **106. 2.** *c.*

141. לָהֶם—lå-hĕm—*to-them,* §§ **47.** 5; **51.** 3. *b.* and N.

142. וְכִבְשֻׁהָ—wᵉχĭv-šû'-hå—*and-subdue-ye-her:*

a. וְ *and;* כְּבֹשׁ for כִּבְשׁוּ [cf. מִלְאוּ (118)] *subdue-ye* ־ָה *her;*
the root being כָּבַשׁ.

b. ־ֻ is usually ŭ, but here a defective writing for וּ (û), the sign of
the plural; ŭ is sounded as *u* in *put,* but û as *oo* in *tool.*

143. וּרְדוּ—û-rᵉδû—*and-have-ye-dominion:*

a. On וֹ see § **49.** 2; the accent ֻ over רֹ is disjunctive.

144. בִּדְגַת—bĭd-ğăθ—*in-fish-of;* cf. בְּדְנַת (135):

a. בְּ has D. l., because of preceding disjunctive accent, § **12.** 2, 3.

145. הִנֵּה—hĭn-nē(h)—*behold!* an interjectional adverb.

146. נָתַתִּי—nă-θăt'-tî—*I-have-given:*

a. D. f. in תָּ is for נ assimilated, נָתַתִּי = נָתַנְתִּי; root נָתַן.

b. The ending תִּי =*I;* cf. אָמַר *he-said,* אָמַרְתִּי *I-said;* יָדַע *he-knew,* יָדַעְתִּי *I-knew;* מָשַׁל *he-ruled,* מָשַׁלְתִּי *I-ruled.*

147. לָכֶם—lă-xĕm—*to-you* (m.):

a. Prep. has ָ, cf. לָמַיִם (45), לָהֶם (141).

b. כֶם is the pronominal suffix for the 2d. pl. masc.

148. זֹרֵעַ זֶרַע—zô-rē(ă)' ză'-ră'—*seeding seed:*

a. זֹרֵעַ is the active participle of the Ḳăl stem—note the ô.

b. On ָ under עַ read § **42.** 2. *d.*

c. זֶרַע is for זֶרְע (69), on account of the accent (ָ), § **38.** 2.

149. יִהְיֶה—yĭh-yê(h)—*he-*(i. e., *it*)*-shall-be:*

a. Observe the Mḗθĕğ with ָ and that the š•wâ is silent, § **18.** 5.

b. Root, הָיָה; י indicates Impf. cf. shortened form יְהִי (19).

150. לְאָכְלָה—l•'ŏx-lă(h)—*for-food:*

a. The ָ under אָ, in an unaccented closed syl. is ŏ, not ă.

b. The root is plainly אָכַל *he-ate;* הָ_ indicates fem.

3. FORMS FOR SPECIAL STUDY.

בְּצַלְמוֹ בְּצֶלֶם	צֶלֶם	צַלְמֵנוּ	אֹתָם	כִּבְשָׁהָ
וּרְדוּ בִּדְנַת	צַלְמוֹ	אֹתוֹ	לָהֶם	כִּבְשָׁהָ

4. OBSERVATIONS.

79. When a disjunctive accent stands between a spirant and the

preceding vowel, the spirant does not *immediately* follow the vowel, and hence takes Dåḡēš-lēnē.

80. Seḡolates before suffixes take what is called their primary form, i. e., the original form of the noun, which had but one vowel, that vowel standing under the first radical.

81. The suffix meaning *him* is וֹ, *them* הֶם or ם.

82. The personal *pre*-fix 1 p. pl. meaning *we* is the letter נ; the pronominal *suf*-fix *our* is נוּ; *her* is הָ.

83. Syllables ending with laryngeals and having a short vowel followed by a compound šᵉwâ are loosely closed; the šᵉwâ eases the transition between the laryngeal and the following consonant.

5. *GRAMMAR-LESSON.*

1. § **52.** 1. *a, b, c,* and 2,   The Demonstrative Pronouns.
2. § **53.** 1. *a. b,*   The Relative Particle.
3. § **54.** 1, 2. *a—d,*   The Interrogative Pronouns.

6. *WORD-LESSON.*

(110) אָדָם *man*   (113) זָכָר *male*   (116) צֶלֶם *image*

(111) דָּגָה *fish*   (114) כָּבַשׁ *he-subdued* (117) רָדָה *he-subdued*

(112) דְּמוּת *likeness* (115) נְקֵבָה *female*   (*had-dominion*)

7. *PRINCIPLES OF SYNTAX.—THE ARTICLE.*

הַמָּאוֹר הַגָּדֹל = *the-luminary the-great* = the great luminary.

הַמָּאוֹר הַקָּטֹן = *the-luminary the-small* = the small luminary.

Principle 1.—The adjective, when attributive, follows its noun, and, if the noun is definite, receives the article.

הַיּוֹם הַזֶּה = *the-day the-this*   = this day.

הָאָרֶץ הַזֹּאת = *the-earth the-this* (f.) = this earth.

הַשָּׁמַיִם הָאֵלֶּה = *the-heavens the-these* = these heavens.

Principle 2.—The demonstrative pronoun, when attributive, follows its noun, *both noun and demonstrative receiving the article.*

8. EXERCISES.

1. To be translated into Hebrew:[1]—(1) *The great place;* (2) *The great heavens;* (3) *The good seed;* (4) *The good luminaries;* (5) *This male and this female;* (6) *These luminaries which* (are) *in the heavens;* (7) *This good place;*[2] (8) *These great luminaries;* (9) *This spirit* (f.), (10) *Who created man in his image?* (11) *Who made this light?* (12) *To whom* (are) *these heavens and this earth?* (13) *What did God create in beginning?*

2. To be translated into English : — (1) הָאֲדָמָה הַזֹּאת; (2) מַה־ (5) ;הַיּוֹם הַגָּדֹל (4) ;הַפְּרִי הַטּוֹב הַזֶּה (3) ;הַשָּׁנִים הָאֵלֶּה לְמִי הַשֶּׁמֶשׁ (7) ;מַה־קָּרָא לַיַּבָּשָׁה (6) ;נָתַן אֱלֹהִים לָהֶם אֱלֹהִים אֲשֶׁר הָאָרֶץ לוֹ (8) ;וְהַיָּרֵחַ.

3. To be written in English letters:—(1) זֶה, (2) זֹאת, (3) אֵלֶּה, (4) אֲשֶׁר, (5) מִי, (6) מָה, (7) זָכָר, (8) נְקֵבָה.

4. To be written in Hebrew letters:—(1) d‘mûθ, (2) ǧăθ, (3) dă-ǧă(h), (4) lă-hĕm, (5) ’ô-θô.

9. TOPICS FOR STUDY.

(1) Laryngeals with compound S‘wâ. (2) The vowel הַ_. (3) Accents ־ֵ, ־ִ, ־ֻ. (4) Loosely closed syllables. (5) Medial S‘wâ. (6) D. l. after a disjunctive accent. (7) Râfê. (8) Primary form of Segolates. (9) אֵת, אֶת־, אֹת. (10) The vowel ־ֵ. (11) Demonstratives. (12) Relative. (13) Interrogatives. (14) Rule for attributive adjectives. (15) Rule for attributive demonstrative.

---

[1] In this and in following exercises, words making in Hebrew *one* word will not be joined together by hyphens.

[2] The order will be: (1) noun, (2) adjective, (3) demonstrative, the article being written with each word.

LESSON XVII—GENESIS I. 30, 31.

1. NOTE-REVIEW.

(1) עֵשֶׂב (67); (2) זֶרַע (69); (3) אֲשֶׁר־בּוֹ (73. e); (4) חַיַּת (128);

(5) נֶפֶשׁ חַיָּה (102,103); (6) וַיַּרְא (22); (7) וַיְהִי־בֹקֶר (36).

2. NOTES.

151. רוֹמֵשׂ—rô-mēś—*creeper* (literally, *creeping*):

a. Naturally long ô, tone-long ē; Ḳāl act. part., cf. זֹרֵעַ (148).

b. This ô (in Ḳāl act. part.) is seldom written fully, as here.

152. אֶת־כָּל־יֶרֶק—'ĕθ+kŏl+yĕ'-rĕḳ—)(+*every*+*greenness-of:*

a. On the short vowels ֶ and ֵ see § 17. 2.

b. יֶרֶק, like אֶרֶץ and many others, is an *a*-class Seġolate.

153. עָשָׂה—'ā-śā(h)—*he-made:*

a. Ḳāl Perf. 3 m. sg.,—the *root-form* from which came וַיַּעַשׂ (46), and עָשָׂה (71).

154. מְאֹד—m*'ŏđ—*exceedingly:* an adverb.

155. הַשִּׁשִּׁי—hăš-šĭš-šî—*the-sixth.*

3. FORMS FOR SPECIAL STUDY.

אֶת־כָּל־עֵשֶׂב	וּלְכָל־חַיַּת	נָתַתִּי (I)
אֶת־כָּל־יֶרֶק	וּלְכָל־עוֹף	לָכֶם (you)
אֶת־כָּל־אֲשֶׁר	וּלְכֹל רוֹמֵשׂ	בּוֹ (him)

4. OBSERVATIONS.

84. Note, in cases cited above, how ֶ and ֵ give place to ֵ and ֶ (ŏ), when, as when the word is joined by Măḳḳēf to the following word, the tone has passed away from them.

85. The conjunction וְ is written וּ before a consonant with Š°wâ.

86. תִּי = I; כֶם = you; וְ for הוּ = him.

5. GRAMMAR-LESSON.

1. § **2.** 4, 5, 7,	Pronunciation of ק, ט, צ.
2. § **3.** 2, 3,	Letters with double forms, and with similar forms.
3. § **4.** 1, 2.	Classification of Letters.
4. § **12.** 2, 3,	Spirants with Šᵉwâ preceding, with disjunctive accent preceding.
5. § **15.** 1, 3,	Dâḡēš-fŏrtĕ compensative and conjunctive.
6. § **16.** 1, 2,	Măppîḳ and Râfê.
7. § **26.** 2, N. 1.	Sharpened syllables.

6. WORD-LESSON.

(118) אָכְלָה food   (120) נָתַן he-gave   (122) מְאֹד exceedingly

(119) הִנֵּה behold (121) יֶרֶק greenness   (123) שִׁשִּׁי sixth

7. PRINCIPLES OF SYNTAX.—THE ARTICLE.

עַל־פְּנֵי הַמָּיִם = upon+faces-of the-waters = upon the face[s] of the waters.

רוּחַ אֱלֹהִים = spirit-of God = the spirit of God.

לְמִקְוֵה הַמַּיִם = to-collection-of the-waters = to the collection of waters.

כָּל־נֶפֶשׁ הַחַיָּה = all+soul(s)-of the-life = all the souls of life.

בִּדְנַת הַיָּם = in-fish-of the-sea = in the fish of the sea.

Principle 3.—The article cannot be prefixed to a noun in the construct state; if the article is needed, it is given to the noun following.

Principle 4.—If the second of the nouns in the construct relation is definite, because it is a proper noun, or because it has the article, the first noun is also to be regarded as *definite*.

8. EXERCISES.

1. To be translated into Hebrew:—(1) *I know that thou* (m.) (art) *good;* (2) *I gave to the cattle and to the beast(s) of the earth grass and herb(s) for food;* (3) *The tree yielded* (Heb., *made*) *good fruit;* (4) *God gave to the fowl of the heavens the seed of the earth for food;* (5) (There) *was fruit in all the earth;* (6) *All that God made was exceedingly good.*

2. To be translated into English:—(1) בְּיוֹם אֶחָד עָשָׂה אֱלֹהִים

אֶת־הָאוֹר (2) ;בְּיוֹם הַשֵּׁנִי עָשָׂה אֶת־הָרָקִיעַ (3) בְּיוֹם הַשְּׁלִישִׁי

בְּיוֹם הָרְבִיעִי נָתַן בְּרָקִיעַ (4) ;הָיְתָה הַיַּבָּשָׁה וַתּוֹצֵא עֵשֶׂב וָעֵץ

בְּיוֹם הַחֲמִישִׁי בָּרָא אֱלֹהִים אֶת־עוֹף (5) ;הַשָּׁמַיִם אֶת־הַמְּאֹרֹת

בְּיוֹם הַשִּׁשִּׁי עָשָׂה אֶת־הַבְּהֵמָה (6) ;הַשָּׁמַיִם וְאֶת דְּגַת הַיָּם

,וַיִּבְרָא אֶת־הָאָדָם בְּצֶלֶם אֱלֹהִים

3. To be written in English letters:—(1) אָכְלָה, (2) יָרָק, (3) זֶרַע,

בֵּין (7), כֵּן (6) בָּקָר, (5) יוֹם, (4)

4. To be written in Hebrew letters:—(1) hû, (2) xĕm, (3) hâ,
(4) hᵃmî, (5) xâ, (6) nû, (7) 'ēllê.

LESSON XVIII.—REVIEW.

[*To the student*:—This lesson is a review of all that have preceded it.
Nothing is so necessary, in the acquisition of a language, as constant and
thorough review. One should carry forward with him at least nine-tenths of
what he has learned. The first chapter of Genesis contains one hundred and
two different words, and about four hundred and fifty different forms. The
most common, and most important principles of the language have been considered. Many additional principles might have been brought forward in
connection with this chapter, but it has been deemed wise to hold them in
reserve. It is understood that in no case will the student proceed to take
up Lesson XIX., until this Lesson with all which it includes has been learned.
Let every word, every verse, every principle be mastered absolutely.]

1. WORD-REVIEW.

[In this list of words, the superior figures indicate the verse in which the
word, or its derivative, is found. In the case of nouns, the singular absolute
is given, in the case of verbs, the root. The student is expected to compare
with each word as here given, the various forms of that word which occur in
the chapter, e. g., with הָיָה, he will compare הָיְתָה *she was,* יְהִי *let-*(there)-
be, וַיְהִי *and-let-*(there)-*be,* וַיְהִי *and-*(there)-*was,* וְהָיוּ *and-they-shall-be,* יִהְיֶה
it-shall-be.]

1. VERBS.

רָדָה²⁶	קָוָה⁹	נָתַן¹⁷	יָצָא¹²	בָּרַךְ²²	*אוֹר¹⁵
רָחַף²	קָרָא⁵	*עוּף²⁰	כָּבַשׁ²⁸	יָדְשָׁא¹¹	אָמַר³
רָמַשׂ²¹	רָאָה⁴	עָשָׂה⁷	מָלֵא²²	הָיָה²	בָּדַל⁴
שָׁרַץ²¹	רָבָה²²	פָּרָה²²	מָשַׁל¹⁸	זָרַע¹¹	בָּרָא¹

* The Infinitive form, see § 55, 3.

2. NOUNS, PARTICLES, ETC.

רָקִיעַ⁶	עוֹף²⁰	לְ⁵	חֲמִישִׁי²³	בֶּהֱמָה²⁴	אָדָם²⁶
שְׁלִישִׁי¹³	עַל²	לַיְלָה⁵	חֹשֶׁךְ²	בֵּין⁴	אֲדָמָה²⁵
שָׁמַיִם¹	עֵץ¹¹	מְאֹד³¹	טוֹב⁴	בֹּקֶר⁵	אוֹר³
שָׁנָה¹⁴	עֶרֶב⁵	מָאוֹר¹⁴	יַבָּשָׁה⁹	גָּדוֹל¹⁶	אוֹת¹⁴
שֵׁנִי⁸	עֵשֶׂב¹¹	מוֹעֵד¹⁴	יוֹם⁵	דָּגָה²⁶	אֶחָד⁵
שְׁנַיִם¹⁶	פָּנִים²	מַיִם²	יָם¹⁰	דְּמוּת²⁶	אָכְלָה²⁹
שֶׁרֶץ²⁰	פְּרִי¹¹	מִין¹¹	יֶרֶק³⁰	דֶּשֶׁא¹¹	אֵל⁹
שִׁשִּׁי³¹	צֶלֶם²⁶	מֶמְשָׁלָה¹⁶	כׇּ²⁶	·ה'¹	אֱלֹהִים¹
תֹּהוּ²	קָטֹן¹⁶	מִן⁷	כּוֹכָב¹⁶	הִנֵּה²⁹	אֶרֶץ¹
תְּהוֹם²	רֵאשִׁית¹	מִקְוֶה¹⁰	כִּי⁴	וְ¹	אֲשֶׁר⁷
תָּוֶךְ⁶	רְבִיעִי¹⁹	מָקוֹם⁹	כֹּל²¹	זָכָר²⁷	אֵת¹
תַּחַת⁷	רוּחַ²	נֶפֶשׁ²⁰	כֵּן⁷	יֶרַע¹¹	בְּ¹
תַּנִּין²¹	רֶמֶשׂ²⁴	נְקֵבָה²⁷	כָּנָף²¹	חַיָּה²⁰	בֹּהוּ²

2. VERSE-REVIEW.

1. Pronounce the pointed text of ea h verse until it can be read aloud rapidly and without hesitation (see p. 181).

2. Write out on paper the unpointed text, one verse at a time, and then, without the aid of either pointed text or translation, insert the necessary points and vowel-signs. Compare the result with the pointed text, and note the mistakes; repeat the exercise till each verse can be pointed without mistake (see p. 203).

3. Write the Hebrew of the chapter, verse by verse, with only the English translation before the eye. Here also correct the result each time by the pointed text (see p. 192).

4. Write the Hebrew of the chapter, verse by verse, from the transliteration, noting with care, in the case of each word, the exact English equivalent for each sign or character in the Hebrew (p. 213).

3. *GRAMMAR-REVIEW.*

1. The alphabet, § **1**. 1-3.
2. Pron. of א, ע, ח, ק, § **2**. 1-4.
3. Pron. of ט, שׁ, צ, ו, § **2**. 5-8.
4. Extended, final, and similar letters, § **3**. 1-3.
5. Classification of letters, § **4**. 1, 2.
6. Pronunciation of ◌ָ § **5**. 1.
7. Pron. of ◌ָ, § **5**. 6. *a*.
8. Vowel-letters, א, ו, יְ, § **6**. 1, 2, 3, and Notes 1-4.
9. Classificat'n of vowel-sounds, § **7**. 1-4.
10. Names of vowels, § **8**.
11. Simple Šᵉwâ, § **9**. 1.
12. Compound Šᵉwâ, § **9**. 2.
13. Initial Šᵉwâ, § **10**. 1, 2.
14. Silent Šᵉwâ, § **11**.
15. Dåḡēš-lēnē, § **12**. 1, and N. 1.
16. D. l. after a Šᵉwâ, § **12**. 2.
17. D. l. after a disj. acc., § **12**. 3.
18. Dåḡēš-förtē, § **13**. 1, 2, and Note 1.
19. Omission of D. f., § **14**. 1-3. Notes 1, 2.
20. D. f. compensative and conjunctive, § **15**. 1, 3.
21. Măppîḳ and Râfê, § **16**. 1, 2.
22. Use of Măḳḳēf, § **17**. 1-2.
23. Mếθḗḡ, § **18**. 1.
24. More common accents, § **24**. 1-3.
25. Kinds of syllables, § **26**. 1, 2. N. 1. 2.
26. Syllabification, § **27**. 1-3.

27. Quantity of vowels in syllables, § **28**. 1-4.
28. Naturally long vowels, § **30**. (opening words) and Notes 1, 2, under § **30**. 7.
29. Tone-long vowels, § **31**. (opening words) and Notes 1, 2, under **31**. 3.
30. Peculiarities of laryngeals § **42**. 1-3.
31. The article, § **45**. 1, 2, 3, & R. 3.
32. Inseparable prepositions, §**47**. 1-5.
33. Wåw conjunctive, § **49**. 1-4.
34. Personal pron., § **50**. 1-3.
35. Pronominal suffixes, § **51**. 1. *a-c*, 2.
36. Demonstrative pronoun, § **52**. 1. *a-c*, 2.
37. Relative particle, § **53**. 1. *a, b*.
38. Interrogative pronouns, § **54**. 1, 2. *a-d*.
39. Roots, § **55**. 1, 2.
40. Inflection, § **57**. 1-3.
41. Tenses and Moods, § **57**. 3. Notes 1, 2.
42. Simple verb-stem, § **58**. 1, 2. *a-c*.
43. Gender of nouns, § **106**. 1, 2, *a, b*.
44. Number of nouns, § **106**. 3-5.
45. States of nouns, § **107**. 1, 2.

4. *EXERCISE.**

To be translated into Hebrew:—

1. *The name of the light is day, and the name of the darkness is night.*
2. *Waters, to waters, the waters, to the waters.*
3. *The earth will be seen beneath the heavens.*
4. *The day, in which is light.*
5. *The fruit, in which is seed.*
6. *The fruit is in the seed, and the seed is in the earth.*
7. *The sun will be seen in the heavens.*
8. *To cause-a-division between the day and the night.*
9. *And in the great day. The great stars.*
10. *The great luminary is the sun; the small luminary is the moon.*
11. *The sun and the moon are in the expanse of the heavens.*
12. *Thou art in the heavens, and I am upon the earth.*
13. *And God saw all which he had created, and it was good.*
14. *God created the earth, and he created the heavens.*
15. *The waters are in the seas and upon the earth.*
16. *His day, her day, my day.*
17. *The beast of the earth was upon the ground.*
18. *This good place.*
19. *These great luminaries.*
20. *God gave to the fowl of the heavens the seed of the earth for food.*

LESSON XIX.—GENESIS II. 1-3.

1. *NOTE-REVIEW.*

(1) הַשָּׁמַיִם (5); (2) וְהָאָרֶץ (8); (3) עָשָׂה (153); (4) אֹתָם
(95); (5) כִּי (24); (6) בוֹ (73); (7) אֲשֶׁר (48).

---

* These sentences are selected from preceding exercises.

2. NOTES.

156. וַיְכֻלּוּ—and-(they)-were-finished; cf.[1] וַיְבָרֶךְ (114), יָקֻוּ 55):

a. D. f. omitted from י, § 14. 2; וּ indicates the plural number.

b. The ﬩, in verbal forms, always marks the *passive;* under the first radical it indicates the Pŭ'āl (intensive passive) stem, § 58. 4. a. c.

c. Root is כָּלָה, meaning in Pī'ēl, *finish*, in Pŭ'āl, *be-finished.*

157. וְכָל־צְבָאָם—and-all+host-their; cf. אֶת־גְּדֹלִים (89. d):

a. וְ acc. to § 49. 1; ◌ָ is ŏ, because in a closed syllable which has lost its tone, § 29. 5.

b. צָבָא host, *but* צְבָאָם host-their; the original ◌ָ which became ◌ָ in an open syl. before the tone, is reduced to ◌ְ when the tone moves farther away, § 36. 2. b.

c. ◌ָם is the pron. suf. of the 3 masc. plur., § 51. 1.

158. וַיְכַל—and-(he)-finished; cf. וַיְכַלּוּ, וַיְבָרֶךְ:

a. Shorter form for וַיְכַלֶּה, the Pī'ēl of כָּלָה (156. c).

b. Two D. f.'s omitted: one from י because without a full vowel, one from ל because final, § 14. 1, 2.

159. בַּיֹּם הַשְּׁבִיעִי—in-the-day the-seventh:

a. The accent ◌ֽ over הַשְּׁבִיעִי marks the end of a *secondary section*. It is called Zâḳēf ḳâṭōn, i. e., little Zâḳēf, § 24. 4.

160. מְלַאכְתּוֹ—work-his; cf. רֵאשִׁית, זַרְעוֹ:

a. Abs. sg. מְלָאכָה; א has lost its consonantal force.

b. The original ◌ָ of ל is retained unchanged because it is in a closed unaccented syl., § 29. 1. a.; in the abs. form ◌ָ is rounded to ◌ָ, being in an open, pretone syl.

c. The abs. has ◌ָה, but the form with suf. has ◌ְת, § 106. 2. a.

161. וַיִּשְׁבֹּת—and-he-rested; cf. וַיִּקְרָא, וַיִּבְרָא:

---

[1] Every old word, suggested for comparison with the new word under consideration, has at least *one* important point in common with that new word.

a. This is the regular form of the Ḳăl Impf., the ֶ in יִקְרָא and
יִבְרָא leing due to the presence of the weak letter א.

b. The ◌ in this word is ō (tone-long), not ô.

c. The root is plainly שָׁבַת *he-rested*, see below, 163.

162. וַיְקַדֵּשׁ—*and-he-sanctified;* cf. וַיֹּכַל, וַיְבָרֶךְ:

a. D. f. omitted from י, as in וַיְהִי, וַיְבָרֶךְ, וַיְכֻלּוּ, וַיֹּכַל.

b. The root is קָדֵשׁ, meaning, as a verbal form, *he-was-holy.*

c. The first radical has ◌, the second radical, D. f.; these indicate
a Pĭ'ēl form; read §§ 58. 3.; 65. 2. *a. b.*

d. Compare each vowel-sound in יְקַדֵּשׁ and יְבָרֶךְ, and note that the
latter has ◌ instead of ◌, because ר refuses D. f., and ◌ instead
of ◌, because the accent is on the penult.

e. The root means *be-holy;* the Pĭ'ēl, here intensive or causative,
means *make-holy, sanctify,* § 58. 3. *c.*

163. שָׁבַת—*he-rested;* cf. עָשָׂה, קָרָא, בָּרָא:

a. Ḳăl Perf. 3 masc. sing. of the strong verb שָׁבַת.

164. לַעֲשׂוֹת—*to-make,* i. e., *in-making.*

a. The prep. לְ with ◌, because of following laryngeal, § 47. 3.

b. עֲשׂוֹת is a Ḳăl Inf. const. of עָשָׂה.

c. Further information concerning this form will be given later.

3. FORMS FOR SPECIAL STUDY.

יִשְׁבֹּת	מְאֹר but מְאֹרֹת	יְבָרֶךְ but יְבָרֵךְ	
יָקֵוּ	גָּדֵל but גְּדֹלִים	מְלָאכָה but מְלַאכְתּוֹ	
יְקַדֵּשׁ	אָדָם but אֲדָמָה	כָּל־ but כֹּל	
יְכֻלּוּ	צָבָא but צְבָאָם	אֶת־ but אֵת	
יַבְדֵּל	כָּנָף but כְּנָפַיִם	זַרְעוֹ but זֶרַע	

4. *OBSERVATIONS*

87. Short vowels are retained in *closed* unaccented syllables.

88. In *open* unaccented syllables, short vowels give away to š°wâ. This change is called *reduction*.

89. The Ḳăl Impf. has no special characteristic; unles$ one of the radicals is a weak letter, it generally has ō for the vowel of its second radical.

90. The Nif'ăl Impf. has D. f. in and ⟂ under the first radical, while the other *passive* stem (Pŭ'ăl) has ⟂ under the first radical and D. f. in the second.

91. The Pǐ'ēl Impf. has (besides D. f. in the second radical) ⟂ under the first radical; the Hǐf'îl Impf. has ⟂ under the preformative.

5. *GRAMMAR-LESSON.*

1. § **58.** 1.	Simple verb-stem, Ḳăl.
2. § **60.** (& p. 195)	Tabular view, Inflection of the Ḳăl Perfect.
3. § **60.** 1—3.	Remarks on inflection.
4. § **36.** 2. *a.*	Reduction of an ultimate vowel in verbal inflection.
5. § **36.** 2. N. 2.	[This covers the reduction to ⟂ in the forms

‎וְקָטַלְתָּ ,קְטַלְתָּ ,קְטַלְתֶּם.

6. *WORD-LESSON.*

1. Learn from the Hebrew word-lists under List I., verbs occurring 500 to 5,000 times, those words numbered 1-10.

2. Make a list of the new words in Gen. II. 1-3.

7. *EXERCISES.*

1. To be translated into Hebrew:—(1) *I said, we said, she said, thou* (f.) *didst say, they said, ye* (m.) *said;* (2) *She ruled, they*

ruled, ye (f.) *ruled, I ruled, we ruled, thou* (m.) *ruledst;* (3) *They gave, we gave, I gave, she gave, thou* (m.) *gavest, he gave;* (4) *I knew, she knew, we knew, they knew, thou* (m.) *didst know.*

2. To be translated into Hebrew:—(1) *The heavens will be fin-ished;* (2) *The waters will be collected;* (3) *God will sanctify the seventh day;* (4) *God rested in the seventh day;* (5) *He created the heavens and all their host;* (6) *He made the great luminaries;* (7) *He will rest in this day;* (8) *We rested, she rested, ye* (m.) *rested, they rested.*

3. To be translated into English:—(1) מִי שָׁבַת מִכָּל־מְלַאכְתּוֹ;

(4) זֶה ;שָׁבַתִּי בַּיּוֹם הַשִּׁשִּׁי (3); מִי יִשְׁבַּת בַּיּוֹם הַשְּׁבִיעִי (2)

הַיּוֹם הַשְּׁבִיעִי אֲשֶׁר־בּוֹ שָׁבַת אֱלֹהִים.

4. To be written in English letters:—*The first three verses of Genesis II., from the pointed text.*

5. To be written with points and vowel-signs:—*The first three verses of Genesis II., from the unpointed text.*

8. *TOPICS FOR STUDY.*

(1) Omission of D. f. (2) Characteristics of Pŭ'äl stem. (3) Reduction of a penultimate vowel, of an ultimate vowel. (4) The Ḳäl Imperfect. (5) The Pī'ēl Imperfect. (6) Retention of short vowels. (7) Difference between the vowels of שָׁבַת and בָּרָא, וַיְקַדֵּשׁ and וַיְבָרֶךְ,(8) Original form of the simple verb-stem. (9) Form in use. (10) Its inflection. (11) Forms of the Ḳäl Perf. containing S⁶wâ. (12) The various personal termination and their origin.

LESSON XX.—GENESIS II., 4-6.

1. *NOTE-REVIEW.*

(1) אֶרֶץ (62); (2) יִהְיֶה (149); (3) הָאֲדָמָה (129); (4) פְּנֵי (13).

2. NOTES.

165. אֵלֶּה—*these;* cf. זֶה (m.), זֹאת (f.).

166. תּוֹלְדוֹת—*generations-of;* cf. מְאֹרֹת, מוֹעֲדִים :

a. Plur. fem., never found in sing.; two syllables.

b. Absence of D. l. in ד because preceding Šᵉwâ is vocal, § 12. 2.

c. Three spirants; both o's are ô, not o.

167. בְּהִבָּֽרְאָם—*in-being-created-their;* cf. יְקַוּוּ, צְבָאָם :

a. בְּ pointed with Šᵉwâ; ‎ָם same as in צְבָאָם (157).

b. It is קָטַל, but קְטָלָה; so הִבָּרֵא, but הִבָּֽרְאָם, i. e., the ultimate vowel is reduced when ‎ָם is added, § 36. 2. a.

c. הִבָּרֵא has D. f. *in* and ‎ִ *under* the *first* radical, the characteristics of the Nif'âl or passive stem, § 72. R. 2.

d. This is an Inf. const. governed by the prep. בְּ ,

e. The small ה written above the line is a traditional writing handed down by the Massoretic Editors (§ 19.).

168. עֲשׂוֹת—*to-make,* or *making-of:* see 164.

169. יְהֹוָה —Written *Jehovah* in the Revised English Bible. But this pronunciation is due to an error dating as far back as the 14th. century A. D. The present vocalization of the Hebrew name is due to the later Jewish reverence for the ancient name of their God, which made them fear to pronounce it. The original pronunciation seems to have been יַהְוֶה. For this, the later Jews regularly substituted אֲדֹנָי, *Lord.* In order to remind themselves of this change, they regularly point יהוה not with its own vowels, but with those of אֲדֹנָי, (*Lord*) as here, thus indicating that אֲדֹנָי should be pronounced, and not יַהְוֶה.

170. שִׂיחַ—*shrub-of:* one syllable, § 27. 1; cf. רוּחַ ,

171. הַשָּׂדֶה—*the-field;* cf. יִהְיֶה, עָשָׂה :

a. The accent ‎⌐ over הַשָּׂדֶה, like ‎⌐ over הַשְּׁבִיעִי (159. a), marks a secondary section. It is called Rᵉvî(ă)', § 24. 5. b.

172. טֶרֶם—tĕ'-rĕm—*not-yet:* an adverb.

173. יִצְמַח—(he) *will-sprout-forth;* cf. יִשְׁבֹּת:
a. Ḳäl Impf. 3 m. sg. of צָמַח *he-sprouted-forth.*
b. The ◌ַ under מ is pausal for ◌ְ, § 38. 2.
c. This verb has ◌ַ (in pause ◌ָ) rather than ◌ְ, as seen in יִשְׁבֹּת, because of the laryngeal ח, § 42. 2. b.

174. לֹא—lō'—*not;* cf. זֹאת, יֹאמַר.

175. הִמְטִיר—(he) *had-caused-to-rain;* cf. מַבְדִּיל, הַבְדִּיל:
a. Here are three radicals, making מָטַר *he-rained.*
b. The prefix הִ (originally הַ) indicates the Hif'îl Perfect, § 58. 5. a. b; and § 59. 3.
c. Cf. the vowel of the preformative in the forms תַּרְשֵׁא, יַבְדֵּל, מַזְרִיעַ, מַבְדִּיל, הַבְדִּיל, with that in הִמְטִיר, § 72. R. 6.

176. אַיִן—a noun meaning *nothing,* but always used as a predicate, *there is not, there was not;* hence the phrase means *and man was not,* or *and there was no man.*

177. לַעֲבֹד—*to-serve;* cf. לִמְשֹׁל, לַעֲשׂוֹת:
a. The עֲבֹד is Ḳäl Inf. const. of עָבַד *he-served;* but ע has ◌ֲ, where מ of מְשֹׁל, a similar form, has ◌ְ, because it is a laryngeal, § 42. 3. a.
b. The prep. ל takes ◌ַ, as in לַעֲשׂוֹת, according to § 47. 3.

178. וָאֵד—wᵉ'- êd—*and-(a)-mist.*

179. יַעֲלֶה—(he) *will-go-up,* or (he) *used-to-go-up;* cf. יִהְיֶה:
a. י is the pref. of the Impf.; the root is עָלָה *he-went-up.*
b. The vowel under י in יִשְׁבֹּת and יִצְמַח is ◌ִ, but in this word it is ◌ַ, because of the following ע, § 42. 2. a.
c. Just as an original ◌ַ is retained under the preformative of all Hif'îl forms except the Perfect, where it has been *attenuated* (§ 36. 3) to ◌ִ (cf. הִמְטִיר), so an original ◌ַ has been retained

under the performative of the Ḳăl Impf. *before laryngeals*, where otherwise it is attenuated to ⊤.

d. In יִשְׁבַּת the first rad. has ⊤, but in יַעֲלֶה it has ⊤, § 42. 3. *b.*

e. The Imperfect here expresses customary action in past time.

180. מִן—*from:* so written only before the article; cf. ← מֶ, מָ, § 48. 1, 2.

181. וְהִשְׁקָה—*and-used-to-cause-to-drink;* cf. הִמְטִיר:

a. Another Hif'îl Perf., as indicated by הִ; root שָׁקָה.

b. The וְ here is Wâw Conv., and gives to the verb the force possessed by יַעֲלֶה, which preceded it, § 70. 1. *b,* 2. *b.*

3. FORMS FOR SPECIAL STUDY.

עֵשׂוֹת	הִמְטִיר	יִקְרָא	רוּחַ
לַעֲבֹד	הִשְׁקָה	יִשְׁבּוֹת	רָקִיעַ
יַעֲלֶה	יַבְדֵּל	יִצְמַח	מַזְרִיעַ
יִצְמַח	תַּדְשֵׁא	יַעֲלֶה	שִׂיחַ

4. OBSERVATIONS.

92. A laryngeal will take (1) *under* it a compound instead of a simple šᵉwâ; and (2) *before* it the vowel ⊤ rather than ⊤ or ⊤.

93. The Hif'îl stem has, under the preformative, the vowel ⊤ except in the Perfect, where it has been *attenuated* to ⊤ (cf. Latin *facilis,* but *difficilis*).

94. The vowel of the preformative in the Ḳăl Imperfect was originally ⊤, but this has been retained only before laryngeals, being elsewhere attenuated to ⊤.

95. The Ḳăl Imperfect may have for its stem-vowel either ō, or ă. In the cases cited above, note how ⊤ before א and in pause has been rounded to ⊤, while before ה it has become ĕ.

96. Păθăḥ-furtive creeps in under the final laryngeals ח, ה, ע, when they are preceded by any long vowel except ־ָ.

5. GRAMMAR-LESSON.

1. § **58**. 3. *a, b, c.*	Origin and use of the Pī'ēl stem.
2. § **58**. 4, *a, b, c.* '	Origin and use of the Pŭ'ăl stem.
3. § **58**. 7 *a, b, c.*	Origin and use of the Hīθpă'ēl st.
4. § **62**. 1. *b,* 2. *a, b,* (& pp. 194, 195)	Inflection of these stems in Perf.
5. § **36**. 3. *a, b.*	Attenuation of ־ַ to ־ִ

6. WORD-LESSON.

1. In the Word-Lists, under List I., the verbs numbered 11—20.
2. Make a list of the new words in Genesis II. 4—6.

7. EXERCISES.

1. To be translated into Hebrew:—(1) *He sanctified* (קִדַּשׁ, Pī), *we sanctified, they sanctified, I sanctified, ye* (m.) *sanctified;* (2) *She spoke* (דִּבֶּר in Pī'ēl), *I spoke, we spoke, they spoke, thou* (f.) *didst speak, ye* (m.) *did speak;* (3) *He was sanctified* (Pŭ'ăl), *I was sanctified, we were sanctified, they were sanctified;* (4) *She purified herself* (קִדַּשׁ in Hīθpă'ēl), *we purified ourselves, they purified themselves, I purified myself.*

2. To be translated into Hebrew:—(1) *Yahweh God sanctified this day and this place;* (2) *This* (is) *the day which God sanctified;* (3) *These* (are) *the heavens and the earth which God created;* (4) *The shrub and the herb will be in the field;* (5) *There was no man upon the earth in those days;* (6) *God did not cause it to rain upon the dry* (land); (7) *The herb will sprout forth upon the field;* (8) *These generations;* (9) *This earth;* (10) *This day.*

3. To be translated into English:—(1) קִדַּשְׁתִּי אֶת־הַיּוֹם; (2)

הִמְשִׁיל אֱלֹהִים אֶת־הָאָדָם (3); נָתַתָּ לוֹ אֶת הָאָרֶץ הַזֹּאת
בָּרָא אֶת־הָאָדָם (4); בְּרֹנַת הַיָּם וּבְעוֹף הַשָּׁמַיִם וּבְכָל־הָאָרֶץ
לַעֲבֹד אֶת־הָאֲדָמָה.

4. To be written in English letters:—*Verses* 4—6 *of chapter II. from the pointed text.*

5. To be written with points and vowel-signs:—*Verses* 4—6 *of chapter II. from the unpointed text.*

8. TOPICS FOR STUDY.

(1) Forms of the Dem. pron. (2) Use of D. l. (3) Reduction of an ultimate vowel in verbal forms. (4) Characteristics of the Nif'al. (5) The word יְהֹוָה. (6) Pāθāḥ-*furtive.* (7) The difference in pointing between יְשֵׁבֶת and יִצְמַח, between יְשֵׁבֶת and יִקְרָא, between יְשֵׁבֶת and יַעֲלֶה. (8) Attenuation of ־ to ־. (9) Hif'îl Perfect. (10) אָיִן, לֹא and טֶרֶם. (11) Difference between עֲבֹד and מָשַׁל. (12) Force of the tense in יַעֲלֶה. (13) Peculiarities of laryngeals. (14) The origin, use, and inflection of the three intensive stems. (15) The form קְטָלָה. (16) The form קְטַלְתֶּם. (17) Rounding of vowels. (18) The Personal pronoun.

LESSON XXI.—GENESIS II. 7-9.

1. NOTE-REVIEW.

(1) יְהֹוָה (169); (2) מִן־ (180); (3) נֶפֶשׁ חַיָּה (102,103); (4) כָּל־
(108); (5) בְּתוֹךְ (41); (6) עֵץ (70); (7) טוֹב (24).

2. NOTES.

182. וַיִּיצֶר—*and-*(he)-*formed;* cf. וַיֹּאמֶר:

a. The first ‬ is the preformative, the second, the radical.

b. Ḳăl Impf. 3 m. sg. of the root יָצַר *he-formed.*

c. The ־ֶ under צ is ĕ; consideration of it may be postponed.

183. עָפָר—*dust:* with the article it would be הֶעָפָר, § **45. 4.**

184. וַיִּפַּח—*and-he-breathed;* cf. מִתַּחַת, יִצְמַח:

a. For יִנְפַּח, the נ being assimilated; root נָפַח.

b. On ־ַ instead of ־ִ before ח see § **42. 2.** *b.*

185. בְּאַפָּיו—bᵉʼăp-pâw—*in nostrils-his:*

a. אַף *nose;* אַפַּיִם *nostrils;* אַפָּיו *his-nostrils.*

b. Learn that ־ָיו, pronounced âw (the י having no force), is the form of 3 masc. sg. suf. when attached to plural or dual nouns.

c. The D. f. in פ stands for נ, the original form being אַנְף.

186. נִשְׁמַת—nĭš-măθ—*breath-of;* cf. דְּנַת, חַיַּת:

a. Abs. sg. is נְשָׁמָה. but in const. ה־ַ goes back to the orig.ת־ַ; the other changes will come up later.

187. חַיִּים—*lives;* cf. חַיָּה *life, beast.*

188. וַיִּטַּע—*and-(he)-planted;* cf. יִפַּח:

a. So far as concerns vowels and form, the same as וַיִּפַּח (184); from the root נָטַע *he-planted.*

189. גַּן—*garden;* cf. below in v. 9 הַגָּן *in pause.*

190. מִקֶּדֶם—mĭḳ-ḳĕ'-đĕm—*from-east;* cf.עֶרֶב:

a. The prep. מִן with נ assimilated, § **48. 1.**

b. An *a*-class Seǵolate, primary form קֶדֶם, § **89. 1.** *a.*

191. וַיָּשֶׂם—*and-he-put:* learn (1) this form, (2) its meaning, (3) its root שִׂים *to-put.*

192. שָׁם—*there:* an adverb.

193. יָצָר—*he-formed,* or *he-had-formed;* cf. וַיִּצֶר:

a. Pausal for יָצַר, the root form, see 182. *b.*

194. וַיַּצְמַח—*and-(he)-caused-to-sprout-forth;* cf. וַיַּבְדֵּל:

a. Cf. with Ḳăl יַצְמִח (173), which has ־ִ under י instead of ־ַ.

b. The ־ֵ under the preformative is the indication of the Hif'îl (except in Perf.).

c. יַבְדֵּל has ־ֵ under 2d rad., but יַצְמַח has ־ַ; why? § 42. 2. *b.*

d. Hîf. Impf. 3 m. sg. of the root צָמַח *he-sprouted.*

195. נֶחְמָד—nĕḥ-mâd—*desirable,* or *desired:*

a. The šᵉwâ, though under a laryngeal, is silent.

b. The root is חָמַד, נ indicating a Nif'ăl.

c. On the vowel ־ֶ see § 42. 2. c; on ־ָ, § 68. 2.

196. לְמַרְאֶה....לְמַאֲכָל—*for-sight....for-food:*

a. Two nouns formed by the prefix מ; cf. מִקְוֶה, מָקוֹם; § 96.

b. The roots are רָאָה *he-saw,* אָכַל *he-ate.*

197. הַחַיִּים—hă(ḥ)-ḥăy-yîm—*the-lives;* cf. הַחֹשֶׁךְ:

a. The D. f. of the article is implied in ה, §§ 42. 1. *b;* 45. 2.

b. Mĕθĕğ on the second syllable before the tone.

198. הַדַּעַת—*the-knowing* — a verbal noun from יָדַע *he-knew,* with the article pointed as usual; it has here a direct object.

b. A one-vowel noun originally; the final ă is a helping vowel.

199. וָרָע—wâ-râ'—*and-evil;* cf. וְבֹהוּ:

a. Wâw Conj., before a tone-syllable, takes sometimes ־ָ, § 49. 4.

b. רָע, instead of רַע, because in pause, § 38. 2.

3. FORMS FOR SPECIAL STUDY.

נֶפֶשׁ	אֶרֶץ	דֶּשֶׁא	עֵשֶׂב	בָּקָר
קֶדֶם	עֶרֶב	שֶׁרֶץ	עֵדֶן	חֹשֶׁךְ

4. OBSERVATIONS.

97. Nouns with two vowels, and having an accented ־ֶ as their first vowel, are *always* a-class Seğolates, the ĕ being a deflection of an original ă.

98. Nouns with two vowels, and having an accented ־ֵ as their

first vowel, are *always* *i*-class Seġolates, the ē coming from an original ī.

99. Nouns with two vowels and having an accented ‒ for their first vowel, are *always* *u*-class Seġolates, the ō coming from an original ŭ.

100. The final unaccented ‒ in all these nouns is merely an inserted helping-vowel (§ 37. 2).

5. GRAMMAR-LESSON.

1. § **58.** 5*a*. *b*. *c*,   Origin and use of the Hif'îl stem.
2. § **62.** 2. *c*,   Inflection of this stem (cf. p. 184.)
3. § **89.** 1,   Origin of Seġolates.
4. § **36.** 2*a*. *b*. N. 1,   Changes of ă, ĭ, ŭ, due to the tone.

6. WORD-LESSON.

1. In the Word-Lists, Lists I. and II., the verbs numbered 21—30.
2. Make out a list of the new words in Genesis II. 7—9.

7. EXERCISES.

1. To be translated into Hebrew:—(1) *He caused to rain, they caused to rain, I caused to rain, we caused to rain;* (2) *He caused to kill, she caused to kill, they caused to kill, ye* (m.) *caused to kill;* (3) *He divided* (Hîf. of בָּדַל), *she divided, they divided, I divided, we divided.*

2. To be translated into Hebrew:—(1) *And God breathed into his nostrils;* (2) *In the garden which God planted in Eden was fruit;* (3) *This fruit was good for food;* (4) *The good fruit;* (5) *The evil fruit;* (6) *The good tree and the evil tree;* (7) *And he caused to sprout forth grass and herb(s) and tree(s).*

3. To be translated into English : — (1) הִבְדִיל אֱלֹהִים בֵּין הָעֵץ אֲשֶׁר בְּתוֹךְ הַגָּן עֵץ הַחַיִּים (2) ;הַטּוֹב וּבֵין הָרָע

נָתַן אֱלֹהִים אֶת־הָאָדָם בַּגַּן אֲשֶׁר (4 ;נָטַע אֶת־הָעֵץ־הָגָּן (3)
‏,הִבְדִּילָה (5 ;נָטַע וַאֲשֶׁר־בּוֹ הַצֹּמִיחַ כָּל־עֵץ נֶחְמָד לְמַרְאֶה
‏הִבְדַּלְתֶם‏ ‏,הִבְדַּלְנוּ‏ ‏,הִבְדִּילוּ‏ •

4. To be written in English letters:—*Verses 7—9 of chapter II.,
from the pointed text.*

5. To be written with points and vowel-signs:—*Verses 7—9 of
chapter II., from the unpointed text.*

8. TOPICS FOR STUDY.

(1) Assimilation. (2) The vowels ◌ and ◌ in the stem of the
Ḳāl Imperfect. (3) Pronunciation and meaning of the affix יִן◌.
(4) The root *to-put*, the form *and-he-put*. (5) Difference between
יַבְדֵּל and יַצְמַח. (6) מ as a prefix in the formation of nouns. (7)
A-class Seğolates. (8) I-class Seğolates. (9) U-class Seğolates. (10)
Origin, use and inflection of the Hif'îl stem. (11) Effect of tone
upon vowels. (12) The helping-vowel ĕ.

LESSON XXII.—GENESIS II. 10-12.

1. NOTE-REVIEW.

(1) מְלַאכְתּוֹ (160); (2) וַיִּשְׁבֹּת (161); (3) תּוֹלְדוֹת (166); (4)
יַעֲלֶה (179). (5) ;(173) יַצְמַח.

2. NOTES.

200. כְּנָף, אָדָם—cf. ; *river*,-a) ′*and*—וְנָהָר.

a. This noun belongs to a large class, formed from the root by means
of two primary short vowels, both of which, the one *before*, and
the other *under*, the tone, have undergone change, § **90. 1.** *a.*

201. יָצָא—yô-ṣē′—*going-forth,=goes-forth;* cf. רֹמֵשׂ.

a. The active participle of Ḳāl, used, as often, for a present tense.

b. The first vowel is ô, not ō; the root, יָצָא *he-went-forth.*

202. מֵעֵדֶן—*from-Eden;* cf. מֵעַל, § 48. 2; עָיֵב, § 89. 1. *b:*

a. Note the Zâḳēf-ḳâṭōn (⸱); it marks the end of a secondary section and also the accent of מֵעֵדֶן, cf.. 159. *a.*

203. לְהַשְׁקוֹת—*to-cause-to-drink,* i. e., *to-water;* cf. עֲשׂוֹת, הַבְדִּיל:

a. Like הַבְדִּיל, this word has the pref. הַ; it is Hîf. Inf. const.

b. Like עֲשׂוֹת, it ends in וֹת.

c. Cf. also the Hîf. Perf. 3 m. sg. הִשְׁקָה (181).

204. וּמִשָּׁם—*and-from-there;* cf. מִתַּחַת, וּבֵין.

205. יִפָּרֵד—*it-will-be-divided,* or *it-divides-itself:*

a. D. f. *in* and å *under* פ indicate at once the Nîf'âl.

b. The root is פָּרַד; Nîf. Perf., נִפְרַד; cf. יָקוּו (55).

206. לְאַרְבָּעָה—*for-four;* cf. רְבִיעִי *fourth.*

207. רָאשִׁים—râ(')šîm—*heads:* an irregular plural from רֹאשׁ.

a. א here is silent, as always after a vowel.

208. שֵׁם—šēm—*name:* same as the proper name *Shem.*

209. הַסֹּבֵב—*the-*(one)-*surrounding;* cf. יָצָא, רֹמֵשׁ:

a. On ◌ see 171. *a.*

210. הַחֲוִילָה—hă(h)-hʰwî-lå(h)—*the-Havilah:*

a. The *article* here belongs really to אֶרֶץ, the phrase = *all the land of Havilah,* not *all land of the Havilah,* see Principle 3 (p. 69).

211. אֲשֶׁר־שָׁם—*which+there,=* *where;* cf. אֲשֶׁר־בּוֹ= *in which.*

212. זָהָב—*gold:* A noun like נָהָר, אָדָם, כָּנָף, § 90. 1. *a.*

213. וּזְהַב—û-zʰhåv—*and-gold-of:*

a. The Wåw, before a consonant with Šʰwâ is וּ, § 49. 2.

b. Comp'd Šʰwâ, under ז, preceding a laryngeal, § 32. 3. *c.*

c. Méθēǧ with וּ before compound Šʰwâ, § 18. 3.

d. זְהַב differs from זָהָב in that the form is treated as if the

accent had passed from it to the following word. This is virtu-
ally true, for the noun is in the construct state, § **107.** (opening
words); § **109.** 3. *a, b.* The ground-form of the noun is זָהָב.
In the absolute, both vowels are rounded to â, because of tonal
influence, one being under the tone and the other in an open
syl. before the tone. In the construct, the final ă remains unchanged, being in a closed, unaccented syl. but the preceding ă
is reduced to š⁴wâ, being in an open unaccented syl.

e. Cf. נָהָר abs., *but* נְהַר const.; כָּנָף abs., *but* כְּנַף const.

214. הַהוּא—hă(h)-hî' (*not* hă(h)-hîw')—the-that; cf. הַחשֶׁךְ:

a. הוּא is archaic for הִיא, § **50.** 3. *a;* here used as a Demonstrative, § **52.** 2.

b. The Demonstrative follows its noun, *and has the article.*

c. ה being a laryngeal implies the doubling; hence ă of the article
is only *apparently* in an open syl.

215. הַבְּדֹלַח—hăb-bᵉdō'-lăḥ—*the-bdellium.*

216. אֶבֶן הַשֹּׁהַם—'ĕ'-vĕn hăš-šō'-hăm—*stone-of the-onyx:*

a. Two Seğolates,—one *a*-class, one *u*-class.

b. Helping-vowel in first is ־, in second, after ה, ־, § **37.** 2. *a.*

3. *FORMS FOR SPECIAL STUDY.*

יֵצֵא	הָאָחֵר	חַיָה abs., but חַיַּת *const.*
סָבַב	וְזָהָב	נְשָׁמָה abs., but נִשְׁמַת *const.*

4. *OBSERVATIONS.*

101. The *o* of the Ķăl active Participle is ô, not ō.

102. Note, in the words cited above, Mêθĕğ written (1) on second syl. before the tone, (2) with a vowel before compound š⁴wâ.

103. The original fem. ending in Hebrew was ת־; but this
has been weakened to ה־, except where something closely follow-

ing protects it. On account of the following noun, it is preserved in the construct state.

5. *GRAMMAR-LESSON.*

1. § **72**. Table,	General view of the Verb-stems.
2. § **72**. R's 1—7,	Changes from original vowels.
3. § **58**. 2. *a, b, c.*	Origin and use of the Nĭfăl stem.
4. § **58**. 6. *a, b, c.*	Origin and use of the Hŏfăl stem.
5. § **62**. 1. *a, c.*	Inflection of the Nĭfăl and Hŏfăl perfects.

6. *WORD-LESSON.*

1. In the Word-Lists, under List II., verbs numbered 31—40.
2. Make out a list of the new words in Genesis II. 10—12.

7. *EXERCISES.*

1. To be translated into Hebrew:—(1) *Thou* (m.) *wast caused to divide, I was caused to kill, we were caused to kill;* (2) *He was killed, they were killed, she was killed;* (3) *Thou* (m.) *wast sanctified* (Nif.), *ye* (f.) *were sanctified, they were sanctified;* (4) *We were kept, thou* (f.) *wast kept, she was kept.*

2. To be translated into Hebrew:—(1) (The) *river of that land is* (a) *great river;* (2) (The) *name of that river is Pishon;* (3) *The river which goes forth from Eden will be divided;* (4) (The) *gold of* (the) *land of Havilah is good gold;* (5) *Thou shalt call the river which surrounds* (=the one surrounding) *that land Pishon.*

3. To be translated into English:—(1) אֶחָד קָטֹן כּוֹכָב ;(2)

נָהָר גָּדֹל ;(4) שֵׁם הַגָּן הוּא עֵדֶן ;(3) יָצַרְתָּ אֶת־הָאָדָם עָפָר

לֹא יָדַעְתִּי הַמָּקוֹם אֲשֶׁר ;(5) סָבַב אֶת־הָאָרֶץ אֲשֶׁר־שָׁם זָהָב

תִּשְׁבַּתִּי בַּיּוֹם הַשְּׁבִיעִי ;(6) שָׁם הוּא עֵדֶן.

4. To be written in English letters:—*Verses* 10—12 *of chapter II., from the pointed text.*

5. To be written with points and vowel-signs:—*Verses* 10—12 *of chapter II., from the unpointed text.*

6. To be written:—(1) The verbs שָׁמַד ,פָּרַד, and מָשַׁל in the perf. 3 m. sg. of the Nifăl; (2) the verbs שָׁמַר ,מָלַך, and לָמַד in the perf. 1st p. plur. of the Hŏfăl.

8. TOPICS FOR STUDY.

(1) Nouns formed by prefixing מ. (2) Nouns which had originally two short vowels. (3) A-class, I-class and U-class Seğolates. (4) The vowels of the Ķăl Part. act. (5) A comparison of הַשְׁקוֹת with הַבְדִיל and עֲשׂוֹת. (6) The word meaning *he-was-divided.* (7) The construct state of nouns like נָהָר, זָהָב, etc. (8) The construct state of Seğolates. (9) The two forms of the fem. ending הַ_, and תָ_. (10) Mĕθĕğ. (11) The original forms of the various Perfect stems.

LESSON XXIII.—GENESIS II. 13-14.

1. NOTE-REVIEW.

(1) מֵעֵדֶן (202); (2) לְמַאֲכָל (196); (3) יִצְמַח (173); (4) יַעֲלֶה (179); (5) וַיִּשְׁבֹּת (171); (6) יִפָּרֵד (205).

2. NOTES.

217. חִדָּקֶל—hĭd-dĕ'-ķĕl—*Tigris.* This name is written *I-dig-lat* in the Assyrian inscriptions.

218. הַהֹלֵך—hă(h)-hô-lēx—*the-*(one)-*going;* cf. הַסֹּבֵב:
a. D. f. of article is implied in ה, cf. הַהוּא (214), § **45.** 2.
b. Ķăl act. Part. (ô, not ō) of הָלַך *he-went.*

219. קִדְמַת—ķĭd-măθ—*eastward-of;* const. of קִדְמָה:
a. The original תָ_ is retained in the const state, § **106.** 2. a. (3)

b. A fem. form related to קֶדֶם (190).

220. הוּא פְּרָת—*is Euphrates.*

3. FORMS FOR SPECIAL STUDY.

שֵׁם - הַנָּהָר	קַדְמַת	הוּא הַסּוֹבֵב
וְשֵׁם הַנָּהָר	הָרְבִיעִי	הוּא הַהֹלֵךְ

104. Note in words cited above, Mĕθĕğ written (1) with a tonal vowel in a closed syl. before Makkēf, (2) with Ḳâmĕṣ before a vocal Šᵉwâ, (3) with a primary short vowel (ă) before a laryngeal with doubling implied.

105. Note that the participle often serves as the equivalent of a relative clause.

5. GRAMMAR-LESSON.

§ **63.** Tabular View.   Inflection of Ḳăl Imperfect (active).

§ **63.** R. 1.   Various prefixes and affixes used.

§ **63.** R. 2.   Original Stem of the Ḳăl Imperfect.

§ **63.** R. 3, 4.   The terminations ִי_, וּ and נָה_.

6. WORD-LESSON.

Make out a list of the new words in Genesis II, 13-14.

7. PRINCIPLES OF SYNTAX.—THE PERSONAL PRONOUN

הוּא הַסּוֹבֵב   He [or IT] (is) the (-one-) surrounding.

וּזְהַב הָאָרֶץ הַהוּא   And the gold of THAT land.

וְהַנָּהָר הָרְבִיעִי הוּא פְּרָת   And the fourth river IS Euphrates.

Principle 5.—The personal pronoun besides (1) its ordinary use as a *personal* pronoun, may have (2) the force of a remote demonstrative pronoun (*that*), and (3) the force of a *copula*, i. e., to mark the relation between the subject and the predicate.

8. EXERCISES.

1. To be translated into Hebrew: — (1) *He will rest, I shall rest, we shall rest, they will rest, thou* (f.) *shalt rest;* (2) *They* (m.) *will swarm, he will swarm, she will swarm, they* (f.) *will swarm, ye* (m.) *shall swarm;* (3) *He will call, she will call, I shall call, we shall call, thou* (m.) *shalt call;* (4) *He will plant, I shall plant, thou* (m.) *shalt plant, she will plant, they will plant;* (5) *He will give, she will give, I shall give, we shall give, thou* (m.) *wilt give.*

2. To be translated into Hebrew: — (1) *The river which surrounds* (the) *land-of Cush is Gihon;* (2) *The river which goes eastward-of Assyria is Euphrates;* (3) (The) *name-of the great river is Tigris;* (4) *She will rest in* (the) *land-of Havilah;* (5) *We shall give that land.*

3. To be translated into English: — (1) הָאָרֶץ הַהוּא קַדְמַת

(2) אַשּׁוּר; (2) כֻּל־אֶרֶץ כּוּשׁ; (3) הַנָּהָר הַהוּא הַסּוֹבֵב אֶת־כָּל־אֶרֶץ

(4) יִשְׁרְצוּ הַמַּיִם שֶׁרֶץ נֶפֶשׁ; (4) שָׁבַת אֱלֹהִים בַּיוֹם הַהוּא

(5) חַיָּה; (5) יִפָּרֵד הַנָּהָר הַגָּדוֹל וְהָיָה לְאַרְבָּעָה רָאשִׁים.

4. To be written in English letters: — *Genesis II* 13-14 *from the pointed text.*

5. To be written with points and vowel-signs: — *Genesis II,* 13-14, *from the unpointed Hebrew text.*

6. To be written: — The verbs שָׁבַת and מָשֵׁל in the Ḳāl Imperfect tense throughout.

9. TOPICS FOR STUDY.

(1) Inflection of the Ḳāl Imperfect (active). (2) Prefixes of the Imperfect. (3) Affixes of the Imperfect as compared with those of the Perfect. (4) The difference in the stem-vowels of יִשְׁבַת,

יִקְרָא, and יִטַע.

LESSON XXIV.—GENESIS II. 15-16.

1. *NOTE-REVIEW.*

(1) וַיִּפַּח (184); (2) לֵאמֹר (115); (3) מִקֶּדֶם (190); (4) הַדַּעַת

(198); (5) וְרָע (199).

2. *NOTES.*

221. וַיִּקַּח—*and*-(he)-*took;* cf. וַיִּפַּח, וַיִּטַּע:

a. For וַיִּלְקַח, but ל is assimilated (like נ), § 39. 3.

b. The laryngeal ח has ־ (ă) before it, rather than ō, § 42. 2. b.

222. וַיַּנִּחֵהוּ—wăy-yăn-nî-ḥē-hû—*and-he-caused-to-rest-him:*

a. The וַ is Wăw Conver.; ־הוּ is the pron. suf. of 3 m. sg.

b. The root is נוּחַ *to-rest;* the form is an *irreg.* Hîf'îl.

223. לְעָבְדָהּ וּלְשָׁמְרָהּ—l'ŏv-dâh ûl'šŏm-râh:

a. The translation of these words is: *to-serve-her and-to-keep-her.*

b. The insep. prepositions are as usual; וְ before ל becomes וּ, § 49. 2.

c. The final הּ is a consonant, as indicated by Măppîḳ, § 16. 1.

d. The ־ under עְ and שְׁ, if it were â, would have Mĕθĕğ, § 18. 2.

e. ־הָ is a contraction of ־הָ; cf. וּ for ־הוּ, § 108. 1. R. 1.

f. These forms are Ḳăl Inf's const. (cf. מְשֹׁל), and without suffixes
would read עֲבֹד and שְׁמֹר (§ 70. 2); but, before the suffix, a
different form is used.

g. The syllables ŏv- and sŏm being unaccented and having short
vowels must be closed. Š'wâ is therefore silent. The absence
of d. l. from ד is a survival from a period when there was a
short vowel under בְ (cf. §§ 10. 2. d; 28. 4.). This survival was
aided by the fact that the spirant letter בְ greatly facilitated the
spirant articulation of the following

224. וַיְצַו—*and*-(he)-*commanded;* cf. וַיְכַל from כָּלָה:

a. Long form וַיְצַוֶּה, Pî'ēl Impf. of צָוָה *he-commanded.*

b. D. f. omitted (1) from **י** and (2) from **נ**, § **14.** 1, 2.

c. The unfailing indication of the Pī'ēl is here, viz., ־ under 1st rad.

d. **צִוָּה**, in Pī'ēl, = *he-commanded;* so **כִּלָּה**, in Pī'ēl, = *he-finished.*

225. **אָכֹל**—'ă-xôl—*to-eat,* or *eating:*

a. Ḳăl Inf. *absolute* of **אָכַל** *he-ate;* second vowel *unchangeable.*

b. Cf. with this the form of the Inf. const. **אֲכֹל** (cf. **מְשֹׁל**) = 'ăxôl, the *o* being *changeable,* § **67.** 1. *b,* 2.

c. Cf. **מָשֹׁל** (ô) and **מְשֹׁל** (ō); **שָׁמֹר** (ô) and **שְׁמֹר** (ō).

226. **תֹּאכֵל**—tô'-xēl—*thou-shalt-eat:*

a. **ת** indicates the Impf. 2 m. sg. (*thou*), root **אָכַל**.

b. Cf. with this **וַיֹּאמֶר** *and-he-said,* from **אָמַר**.

3. FORMS FOR SPECIAL STUDY.

וַיִּקַּח	וַיְקַדֵּשׁ	וַיַּבְדֵּל	יָקוּ	אָכֹל
וַיִּטַּע	וַיְצַו	וַיְצְמַח	יְפָרֵד	שָׁמְרָה
וַיִּפַּח	וַיְבָרֶךְ	תַּדְשֵׁא	תֵּרָאֶה	עָבְדָה

4. OBSERVATIONS.

106. Verbs whose third radical is a laryngeal must have ־ for their stem-vowel in the Imperfect.

107. The Pī'ēl Impf. may always be distinguished by the ־ (or, if the second radical is a laryngeal, the ־ֽ) which is under the first radical.

108. The Hĭf'îl Impf. may be distinguished by the ־ which is under the personal preformative.

109. The Nĭf'ăl Impf. may be distinguished by the D. f. *in* and the ־ֽ *under* the first radical.

110. The *o* of the Inf. abs. is ô unchangeable; but the *o* of the Inf. const. is tonal ō, and varies with the position of the accent.

5. GRAMMAR-LESSON.

1. § **65. 2.** a, b,　　The stᴣm and inflection of the Pī'ēl Impf. (cf.
　　　　　　　　　　　 p. 185)

2. § **65. 3,** a, b,　　The stcm and inflection of the Hīθpă'ēl Impf.
　　　　　　　　　　　 (cf. p. 184)

3. § **65. 5.** a, b,　　The stem and inflection of the Hīf'îl Impf. (cf.
　　　　　　　　　　　 p. 184)

6. WORD-LESSON.

1. In the Word-Lists, under List II., verbs numbered 41—50.

2. Make out a list of the new words in Genesis II. 15—16.

7. EXERCISES.

1. To be translated into Hebrew:—(1) *He will keep, they will keep, we shall keep, thou* (f.) *shalt keep.* (2) *She will sanctify, I shall sanctify, ye will sanctify, they* (f.) *will sanctify, we shall sanctify;* (3) *She will sanctify herself, you will sanctify yourselves;* (4) *IIe will cause to divide,*[1] *they* (m.) *will cause to divide, we shall cause to divide, thou* (f.) *wilt cause to divide, ye* (f.) *shall cause to divide;* (5) *I shall rule, they* (f.) *will cause to rule.*

2. To be translated into Hebrew:—(1) *Thou mayest eat from all the fruit which God has given;* (2) *Thou shalt divide between the good and between the evil;* (3) *Thou mayest not eat from the tree which is in the midst of the garden.*

3. To be translated into English: — (1) אָכֹל תֹּאכֵל‎; (2) שְׁמוֹר‎

(3) תִּשְׁמֹר‎; (4) יְקַדֵּשׁ אֱלֹהִים אֶת־הַיּוֹם הַזֶּה‎; עָשָׂה אֱלֹהִים

(5) וַיְצַו אֱלֹהִים אֶת־הָאִישׁ לֵאמֹר לָאָדָם אֶת־הָאָרֶץ

תֹּאכֵל פְּרִי‎.

4. To be written in English letters:—*Verses* 15—16 *of chapter II., from the pointed text.*

---

[1] Use the root בָּדַל‎ in Hif'îl.

5. To be written with points and vowel-signs:—*Verses* 15—16 *of
chapter II., from the unpointed text.*

6. To be written:—(1) The verbs מָשַׁל, מָלַךְ and לָמַד throughout the Imperfect of the Pī'ēl, Hiθpǎ'ēl and Hīf'îl stems.

8. *TOPICS FOR STUDY.*

(1) Assimilation of לְ. (2) Dif. between the *o* of the Inf. abs.
and the *o* of the Inf. const. (3) The Inf. const. before suffixes. (4)
The words meaning *being-of, to-serve-her.* (5) Peculiarities of
laryngeals. (6) Tonal vowels. (7) Méθĕğ, Măppîḳ, Rằfệ and
Măḳḳēf.

LESSON XXV.—GENESIS II 17-18.

1. *NOTE-REVIEW.*

(1) וַיִּקַּח (221); (2) וַיְכַל (158); (3) יִפְרַד (205); (4) וַיְקַדֵּשׁ
(162); (5) תּוֹצֵא (123).

2. *NOTES.*

227. וּמֵעֵץ—*and-from-tree-of:* וּ, § **49.** 2; מֵ, § **48.** 2.
a. A new disjunctive accent, called rᵉvî(ă)ʻ; § **24.** 5. b.

228. תֹּאכַל—Another spelling of תֹּאכֵל (226).

229. מִמֶּנּוּ כִּי בְיוֹם—*from-him* (= *it*); *for, in-day-of:*

a. מִן takes a special form before suffixes, viz. מִמֶּן; with הוּ,
מִמֶּנּוּ = מִמֶּנְהוּ, in which the ה is assim. backwards and
represented by D. f. in נ, § **51.** 5. b, and ־ is deflected to ־֑.

b. D. l. in כ and in בְ because of prec. disj. accent, § **12.** 3.

230. אָכְלְךָ—ʻᵃ-ẋŏl-ẋ̇ằ—*thy-eating:*

a. The Inf. const. is אֲכֹל, but before ךָ, אָכְל (ŏ), § **71.** 3. *a.* (1).

b. Cf. (1) reg. form קְטֹל, (2) form before ךָ. קְטָל, (3) form before ה_ (see Note 223 *f*), קְטָל (ŏ).

231. מוֹת תָּמוּת—môθ tă-mûθ—*dying thou-shalt-die:*

a. The Ḳăl Inf. abs., and Impf. 2 m. sg. of מוּת *to-die.*

b. The explanation of these forms will be given later.

232. הֱיוֹת—hᵉyôθ—*being-of;* cf. עֲשׂוֹת *making-of:*

a. Ḳăl Inf. const. of הָיָה *he-was,* translated as a verbal noun.

b. Under the laryngeal ה appears a compound šᵉwâ.

233. לְבַדּוֹ—*to* or *in-separation-his:* לְ, prep.; בַּד, noun; וֹ, suffix.

234. אֶעֱשֶׂה־לּוֹ—'ĕ-ᵉśé(h)l+lô—*I-will-make+for-him:*

a. א indicates the *first* pers. sg.; root is עָשָׂה *he made.*

b. The D. f. in לְ is conjunctive (cf. עֲשֵׂה־פְּרִי), § 15. 3.

c. Cf. וַיַּעַשׂ (46), עָשָׂה (71), עֲשׂוֹת, all from עָשָׂה.

235. עֵזֶר—'é-zĕr—(a)*help* or *helper;* cf. אֶבֶן עֵזֶר *Ebenezer:*

a. Like עֶשֶׂב and עֶדֶן an *i*-class Seğolate, § 89. 1. b.

236. כְּנֶגְדּוֹ—*as-over-against-him:* כְּ, נֶגֶד, וֹ.

3. GRAMMAR-LESSON.

1. § **65. 1.** a, b.   The stem and inflection of the Nĭf'ăl Impf.

2. § **65. 4.**   The stems and inflections of the Pŭ'ăl and Hŏf'ăl
Impf.

4. WORD-LESSON.

1. Make out a list of the new words in Genesis II 17-18.

5. EXERCISES.

1. To be translated into Hebrew:—(1) *He will be divided,*[1] *they
will be divided, thou* (f.) *shalt be divid·d, we shall be divided;* (2)
Thou (f.) *shalt be sanctified, I shall be sanctified, ye shall be
sanctified, we shall be sanctified, she will be sanctified;* (3) *Thou*
(f.) *shalt be divided,*[2] *we shall be. divided, ye shall be divided;* (4)

---

[1] Use פָּרַד in the Nĭf'al.   [2] Use בָּדַל in Hŏf'ăl.

I shall be ruled, thou (m.) *shalt be ruled, we shall be ruled;* (5)
Thou (f.) *shalt rule thyself, we shall rule ourselves, he will rule
himself.*

2. To be translated into Hebrew:—(1) *In that day thou shalt
die;* (2) *In the day of thy eating from the tree of fruit. thou shalt
surely die;* (3) *And the man was not alone in the midst of the
garden;* (4) *And there was a helper over-against-him.*

3. To be translated into English:—(1) מוֹת תָּמוּת; (2) הִתְקַדֵּשׁ

וַיִּקַּח מִמֶּנּוּ (4) ;וַיַּעַשׂ אֱלֹהִים לָאָדָם עֵזֶר (3) ;בְּיוֹם הָרְבִיעִי

‏לֹא טוֹב הֱיוֹת הָאָדָם לְבַדּוֹ (5) ;פְּרִי לְמִינֵהוּ

4. To be written in English letters:—*Genesis II*, 17-18 *from the
pointed text.*

5. To be written with points and vowel-signs:—*Genesis II*, 17-18
from the unpointed text.

6. To be written:—The verbs מָשַׁל and קָדֵשׁ throughout the
Imperfect of the Pī'ēl, Hīθpä'ēl and Hif'îl stems.

8. *TOPICS FOR STUDY.*

(1) The characteristics distinguishing the various Imperfects.
(2) The stems of the various Imperfects. (3) The inflection of the
various Imperfects. (4) The use of the Infinitive Absolute. (5) The
use of the Infinitive Construct.

LESSON XXVI.—GENESIS II. 19-20.

1. *NOTE-REVIEW.*

(1) הָאֲדָמָה (129); (2) חַיַּת (128); (3) הַשָּׂדֶה (171); (4) וַיִּקְרָא
(29); (5) בְּהֵמָה (125); (6) כְּנֶגְדּוֹ עֵזֶר (235,236); (7) וַיִּקַּח (221).

2. NOTES.

237. וַיְצֶר‎—a defective writing of וַיִּיצֶר‎ (182).

238. וַיָּבֵא‎—and-he-caused-to-come; cf. וַיַּבְדֵּל‎:

a. Clearly a Hif'îl Impf. 3 m. sg. of the root בּוֹא‎ to-come-in.

b. Instead of ⸗, the preformative ◊ has ⸗ in an open syllable.

239. לִרְאוֹת‎—lîr-'ôθ—to-see; cf. לִמְשֹׁל, לַעֲשׂוֹת‎:

a. רְאוֹת‎ is the Inf. const. of the verb רָאָה‎ he-saw.

b. לְ‎, before a letter with šᵉwâ, takes ⸗, § 47. 2.

240. מַה־יִּקְרָא־לוֹ‎—mă(h)y+yîḳ-râ'+lô—what+he-will-call+to-it:

a. The Interrogative what? pointed like the article, § 54. 2. a.

b. לוֹ‎ = to-him, just as בּוֹ‎ = in-him.

241. הוּא‎—literally he, = is; cf. Principle 5 (3).

242. שְׁמוֹ .... שֵׁמוֹת‎—his-name....names:

a. Before the suffix וֹ the ⸗ of שֵׁם‎ becomes ⸗; but

b. The ⸗ is retained before the fem. plur. affix ôth.

c. Rᵉvî(ä)' (⸚) over שֵׁמוֹת‎, §24. 5. b; (cf. 227, and 229).

243. מָצָא‎—he-found; cf. בָּרָא, קָרָא‎:

a. ⸗, instead of ⸗ as in שָׁבַת‎, because א‎ is silent.

b. Lit., he-found; here impersonal, = there-was-found; cf. French on dit = it is said, and German man sagt.

3. FORMS FOR SPECIAL STUDY.

מִן־הָאֲדָמָה	הָאָדָם	הַשָּׁמַיִם (v. 20)	וַיִּתֵּן
מִתַּחַת	לֹא־מָצָא	וּלְאָדָם (v. 20)	וַיִּפַּח
מֵעַל	הַשָּׂדֶה	שֵׁמוֹת (v. 20)	וַיִּטַּע

4. OBSERVATIONS.

109. The preposition מִן‎ from is written separately chiefly before the article; elsewhere it is joined to the following word, the נ suf-

fering assimilation; but, if the following word begins with a laryngeal, the D. f. is rejected and the preceding ⁻⁻ becomes ⁻.

110. The syl. standing second before the tone receives Mêθĕğ,
if it is an *open* syllable.

111. Three accents of high rank are ⊥ Zâķēf ķâţōn, ⊥ Zâķēf
gâḏôl, ⊥ R•vî (ă)', § 24. 4, 5. *a, b.*

112. Verbs whose first radical is נ assimilate the נ whenever it
would stand at the close of a syllable. It is then represented by D.
f. in the second radical. Such forms are liable to be confused with
Pī‘ēl forms.

5. GRAMMAR-LESSON.

1. § 66. 1. *a—c,*   The *stem* of Imperatives.

2. § 66. 2. *a, b,* and N. 1,   The *inflection* of Imperatives.

6. WORD-LESSON.

1. In the Word-Lists, under List V., nouns numbered 1—15.

2. Make out a list of the new words in Genesis II., 19-20.

7. EXERCISES.

1. To be translated into Hebrew:—(1) *Rule thou* (m.), *keep ye*
(f.), *sanctify thou* (f.), *divide ye* (m.), *fill ye, subdue ye, be thou* (f.)
separated, sanctify yourselves, swarm ye.

2. To be translated into Hebrew:—(1) *What will God call the
great lúminary?* (2) *Who formed every fowl of the heaven?* (3)
Who gave (Heb., *called*) *names to the fowl of the heaven, and to the
beast of the earth?* (4) *Gold, the gold, to the gold, in the gold, and
in the gold;* (5) *He found the fruit in the garden.*

3. To be translated into English : — (1) שְׁמִי־מַה; (2) מַה־שְּׁמוֹ;

(3) יָצַרְתִּי; (4) מַה־יִּקְרָא הָאָדָם לְכָל־הַבְּהֵמָה; (5) לְמִי־זֹאת; (6) אֹתוֹ;

(7) יָצַרְתָּ אַתָּה; בַּבְּהֵמָה וּבְחַיַּת הָאָרֶץ וּבְדֹנַת הַיָּם;

• וּבְעוֹף הַשָּׁמַיִם לֹא נִמְצָא עֵזֶר לְאָדָם כְּנֶגְדּוֹ

4. To be written in English letters:—*Verses* 19-20 *of chapter II., from the pointed text.*

5. To be written with points and vowel-signs:—*Verses* 19-20 *of chapter II., from the unpointed text.*

6. To be written:—The verbs שָׁמַר, מָשַׁל and פָּקַד in the Imv. of all the stems.

8. TOPICS FOR STUDY.

(1) The Interrogative Pronouns. (2) Verbs with א as their third radical. (3) Verbs with נ as their first radical. (4) Nouns which had originally two short vowels. (5) Preposition מִן. (6) The accents Zâḳēf ḳâṭon, Zâḳēf gâḍôl, and R°vî(ä)'. (7) The stems and inflection of the various Imperatives.

LESSON XXVII.—GENESIS II. 21, 22.

1. *NOTE-REVIEW.*

(1) אָדָם (131); (2) זָהָב (212); (3) מֶ in מֵאִישׁ (202); (4) וְהָיוּ (80); (5) אֶחָד (37); (6) לֹא (174).

2. *NOTES.*

244. וַיַּפֵּל—wăy-yăp-pēl—*and*(he)-*caused-to-fall:*

a. This form is for וַיַּנְפֵּל, which is, like וַיַּכְדֵּל, in Hif'íl.

b. Root נָפַל, of which נ is assimilated and represented by D. f.

c. נָפַל, נָפַח, נָטַע, נָתַן all have נ for their first radical; the old Jewish paradigm-word was פָּעַל, the first radical of which is פ; hence, technically, these verbs are called פ"ן, i. e., Pē Nûn, § 77. 1.

245. תַּרְדֵּמָה—(a)-*deep-sleep:* on formation see § 98. and R.

246. וַיִּישָׁן—wăy-yî-šăn—*and-he-slept;* cf. וַיִּיצֶר:

a. The ־ָ is pausal for ־ַ, § 38. 2.

b. The radical י becomes silent after the preceding ־ִ.

247. אַחַת—'ă(ḥ)-ḥăθ—*one:* fem. of אֶחָד (37).

a. A d. f. is implied in ח, hence ă is really in a closed syllable.

248. מִצַּלְעֹתָיו—mĭṣ-ṣāl-'ô-θăw—*from-ribs-his:*

a. The מִן with נ assimilated, § **48. 1.**

b. צַלְעֹת is plur. const. of צֵלָע (v. 22), a feminine noun.

c. יו‍ַ is the same as in אַפָּיו, see Note 185. *b.*

249. וַיִּסְגֹּר—wăy-yĭs-gōr—*and-he-closed;* cf. וַיִּשְׁבֹּת.

a. Perfects: הִסְגִּיר, נִסְגַּר, סֻגַּר, סָגַר.

b. Imperfects: יַסְגִּיר, יִסָּגֵר, יִסֹּגֵר, יִסְגֹּר.

c. The o is ō, not ô; as it always is in Ḳăl Impf.

250. בָּשָׂר—*flesh;* cf. עָפָר, נָהָר, זָהָב, כָּנָף, אָדָם, § **90. 1.** *a.*

251. תַּחְתֶּנָּה—tăḥ-tĕ'n-nă(h)—*instead-of-her:*

a. Prep. תַּחַת, see 49; a connecting syllable, נ‍ַ; the fem. suf., ה.

b. ה is assim. backwards, so that תַּחְתֶּנָּה becomes תַּחְתֶּנּ; then the vowel-letter ה is added, § **6. 1. N. 1.**

252. וַיִּבֶן—wăy-yĭ'-vĕn—*and-(he)-built;* cf. יֶרֶב:

a. Long form יִבְנֶה (root בָּנָה), as יֶרֶב and יִרְבֶּה (root רָבָה).

b. The ending ה‍ַ is *always* lacking in verbal forms with Wăw Conversive; so וַיְהִי, not וַיִּהְיֶה, וַיַּעַשׂ, not וַיַּעֲשֶׂה.

c. יִבְן is difficult to pronounce, so ֶ is inserted under ב, § **82. 5. b. (3).**

d. From the root בָּנָה *build,* come בֵּן *son,* בַּת *daughter.*

253. הַצֵּלָע—*the-rib;* cf. the form before suf. צַלְעֹת (248).

254. לָקַח—*he-took;* cf. the Ḳăl Impf. יִקַּח (221).

255. לְאִשָּׁה—lᵉ-'ĭš-šă(h)—*for-woman;* cf. אִישׁ (v. 23).

256. וַיְבִאֶהָ—wăy-vî-'ĕ'-hă—*and-he-caused-to-come-her:*

a. Root בּוֹא; cf. וַיָּבֵא (238); D. f. omitted from י

b. The ה is 3 f. sg. suffix *her.*

c. The ֵ is î, though written defectively.

d. In יְבָא ă has become å before the tone; but in יְבָאָה, this original ă has become ־ָ, because of the removal of the tone, § **32**. 1. *c.*

e. The connecting element before the suffix is ĕ, a short vowel in an open syl., but under the tone; § **28**. 5. Cf. similar forms in 252, 172, 176 and הִשִׁיאַנִי (330) and אִישְׁתְּךָ (351).

3. FORMS FOR SPECIAL STUDY.

יְרֵב *for* יִרְבֶּה	מָאוֹר *but* מְאֹרֹת	עֵרֶב
יִבֶן *for* יִבְנֶה	בְּשָׁר *but* בְּשָׂרִי	זֶרַע
יַעַשׂ *for* יַעֲשֶׂה	יְבָאָה *but* יְבָא	תַּחַת

4. OBSERVATIONS.

113. The ending ־ֶה with which all Imperfects of verbs having ה for the third radical end, is lacking with Wåw Conversive.

114. Two consonants with Š^ewâ seldom stand at the end of a word; a helping vowel (־ֵ or ־ָ) is generally inserted for euphony.

115. A primary short vowel in an open syl. is dependent upon the position of the tone for its form; when pretonic, it modifies its quality (e. g. ă becomes å, ĭ becomes ē, and ŭ becomes ō), but when the tone moves away, it is reduced to Š^ewâ.

116. Some Seǧôlates have two S^eǧôls; others, those with a laryngeal for the third radical, have one S^eǧôl and one Păθăḥ; still others, those with a laryngeal for the second radical, have two Păθăḥs.

5. *PRONOUNS, PERSONAL TERMINATIONS, PRONOMINAL SUFFIXES.*

אֹתָנוּ שָׁמַר הוּא	He kept or has kept us.
אֹתָךְ שְׁמָרָה הִיא	She has kept thee (f.).
אֹתוֹ שְׁמַרְתָּ אַתָּה	Thou (m.) has kept him,
אֹתָהּ שָׁמַרְתְּ אַתְּ	Thou (f.) has kept her.
אֹתְךָ שְׁמַרְתִּי אָנֹכִי	I have kept thee (m.).
אֹתִי שָׁמְרוּ הֵם	They (m.) have kept me.
אֶתְכֶן שָׁמְרוּ הֵן	They (f.) have kept you (f.).
אֹתָם שְׁמַרְתֶּם אַתֶּם	Ye (m.) have kept them (m.).
אֹתָן שְׁמַרְתֶּן אַתֶּן	Ye (f.) have kept them (f.).
אֶתְכֶם שָׁמַרְנוּ אֲנַחְנוּ	We have kept you (m.).

[**Note.**—Let this exercise be thoroughly mastered; it will be found a most helpful acquisition.]

6. *GRAMMAR-LESSON.*

1. § 67. 1. *a, b,*   The Infinitive Absolute.
2. § 67. 2. *a, b,*   The Infinitive Construct.
3. § 30. 6. *a,*   The ô that comes by rounding from â.
4. § 30. 7. *c, d,*   The ô that comes by contraction of *au* or *aw*.

7. *EXERCISES.*

1. To be translated into Hebrew:—(1) *to rule* (abs.), *to cause to rule* (abs.), *to keep* (const.), *to sanctify* (const.), *to sanctify oneself;* (2) *to be kept* (abs.), *to be created* (const.), *to be called* (const.), *to cause a division* (const.), *to rule* (const.), *to be ruled* (abs.).

2. To be translated into Hebrew: (1) *This* (is) *the woman whom God created from the man;* (2) *I will close the flesh;* (3) *God caused*

a deep sleep to fall upon the man; (4) *Rib from his ribs and flesh from the man;* (5) *The waters shall be called seas.*

3. To be translated into English: — (1) אָדָם אֶחָד (2) הַיּוֹם; (5) לְקַחְתִּי מִן־הַמַּיִם (4) לָקַח הָאִישׁ מִן־יְהֹעָפָר (3) הָאַחֵר; הָאִישׁ הַטּוֹב הַזֶּה (7) הַנָּהָר יָצָא מֵעֵדֶן (6) לְאוֹר יִקְרָא יוֹם (8) הָאִשָּׁה הַטּוֹבָה הַזֹּאת,

4. To be written in English letters:—*Verses 21, 22 of chapter II., from the pointed text.*

5. To be written with points and vowel-signs:—*Verses 21, 22 of chapter II., from the unpointed text.*

6. To be written:—(1) The verb פָּקַד in the Infinitive Absol. and Infinitive Construct of all stems; (2) the verb מָשַׁל in the Imperative 2 m. pl. of all stems.

9. *TOPICS FOR STUDY.*

(1) Absence of הָ‎ . (2) Insertion of ◌ַ and ◌ָ. (3) The demonstrative pronoun. (4) The personal pronoun. (5) The pronominal suffixes with the sign of the definite object. (6) The personal terminations of the Perfect. (7) D. f. conjunc. (8) D. f. omitted. (9) Pu'äl stem. (10) Reduction. (11) The vowels of Seǧolates.

LESSON XXVIII.—GENESIS II. 23.

1. *NOTE—REVIEW.*

(1) וַיַּפֵּל (244); (2) וַיָּבֵא (256); (3) וַיְצַו (224); (4) וַיִּפַּח (184); (5) לִמְאֹרֹת (85).

---

[1] See § 45. 4.

2. NOTES.

257. זֹאת—zô(')θ—*this* (f.); cf. אֵלֶּה (165), § 52. 1. c

a. א is silent here after the vowel ô.

258. הַפֶּעַם—hăp-pä'-'ăm—*the-stroke,* = *now:*

a. An a-class Seğolate, original ă retained, § 89. 2. a.

b. ־ used as a helping-vowel instead of ־ַ, § 42. 2. a.

c. Article has here its original *demonstrative* force, *this,* i. e., *this* stroke or time, meaning *now.*

259. מֵעַצְמַי—mē-'ªşă-măy—*from-bones-my:*

a. מֵ for מִן; cf. מֵעַל and מֵאִישׁ (v. 23), § 48. 2.

b. עַצְמַי is the form taken by עֶצֶם in the *plural* with the suffix meaning *my;* §§ 108. 3. a. (1); 109. 4. c.

260. מִבְּשָׂרִי—*from-flesh-my;* cf. מְאֹרֹת, גְּדֹלִים:

a. Not בְּשָׂרִי, but בְּשָׂרִי; cf. 256. d, § 32. 1. c.

b. A *singular* noun with suffix of 1 person sg.

261. יִקָּרֵא—yĭķ-ķă-rē'—*he-*(i. e., *it)-shall-be-called:*

a. Nif. Impf. 3 m. sg. of the verb קָרָא *call.*

b. Note the D. f. *in,* and pretonic ־ַ *under* the first radical.

262. לְקֳחָה־זֹּאת—lŭķ-ºhă(h)z+zô(')θ—*was-taken+this:*

a. ־ָ indicates Pŭ'ăl; comp'd Sᵉwâ under ק, though not a laryngeal.

b. ה־ָ indicates Perf. 3 fem. sg., cf. הָיְתָה.

c. D. f. conjunctive in ז, § 15. 3; Méθĕğ before comp'd Sᵉwâ.

d. D. f. omitted from ק and the line *Râfê* placed over ק to call attention to the absence of d. f. §§ 14. 2; 32. 3. b.

e. Compound Sᵉwâ of the ŭ-class to agree with the preceding ŭ.

3. GRAMMAR-LESSON.

1. § 63. 1. a, c,   The Ķăl active and passive Participles.
2. § 63. 2, 3,   The Nif'ăl and remaining Participles
3. § 61. 1—3,   Inflection of Ķăl Perfect Statives.
4. § 64. 1—3 and Notes,   Inflection of Ķăl Imperfect Statives.

4. WORD-LESSON.

1. In the Word-Lists, under List V., nouns numbered 16—30.
2. Make out a list of the new words in Genesis II. 23.

4. EXERCISES.

1. To be translated into Hebrew:—(1) *Ruling, ruled, causing to rule, ruling oneself, being caused to rule;* (2) *Resting, causing to to rest, closing, closed, caused to close;* (3) *Eating, causing to rain, finding, serving, sanctifying* (Pī'ēl), *sanctified* (Pŭ'ăl), *keeping.*

2. To be translated into Hebrew:—(1) *This woman was taken from this man;* (2) *Thou* (m.) *art old, he is heavy, thou* (f.) *art small, he loves;* (3) *He will be heavy, she will be holy, we shall be old;* (4) *From my flesh, she will keep her, they will keep us;* (5) *We shall keep the garden in the midst of the rivers.*

3. To be translated into English: — (1) בָּרָא אֱלֹהִים אֶת־הָאִישׁ; (2) הַזֶּה וְאֶת־הָאִשָּׁה הַזֹּאת וַיִּקַּח הָאִישׁ שְׁנַיִם מִכָּל־; (3) הַבְּהֵמָה עַל־הָאָרֶץ; (4) לְקָחָה הָאִשָּׁה מִבְּשַׂר הָאָדָם; (5) יִכְבַּד, זָקֵן, קָדַשׁ, קָטֹן, נִכְבַּד וַיְקַדֵּשׁ אֹתוֹ בַּיּוֹם הַהוּא.

4. To be written in English letters:—*Genesis II, 23 from the pointed text.*

5. To be written with points and vowel-signs:—*Genesis II, 23 from the unpointed text.*

6. To be written:—(1) The verbs זָקֵן *old* and קָטֹן *small* throughout Ḳăl Perfect; (2) The verbs כָּבֵד *heavy* and גָּדַל *great* throughout the Ḳăl Imperfect.

5. TOPICS FOR STUDY.

(1) Ḳăl Participles; (2) Other Participles; (3) Stative Verbs; (4) Ḳăl Perfect (stative); (5) Ḳăl Imperfect (stative).

LESSON XXIX.—GENESIS II. 24, 25.

1. *NOTES.*

263. עַל־כֵּן—*upon+so,* = *therefore;* cf. ē of כֵּן and ê.of בֵּין.

264. יַעֲזָב־—yă'-ăzŏv+—*he-will-forsake+:*

a. For יַעֲזֹב, but before Măķķēf ŏ instead of ō; root עָזַב.

b. יַעֲזָב instead of יַעְזֹב (cf. יִקְטֹל), because the laryngeal prefers (1) ־ֲ to ־ְ, and (2) ־ַ to ־ִ, §§ **42.** 2. *a.* 3. *b.*

c. Ķăl Impf. 3 m. sg. of the laryngeal verb עָזַב; synopsis in Ķăl,

עָזַב, יַעֲזֹב, עָזוֹב, עָזֹב, עָזַב, עָזוֹב, עָזֹב, יַעֲזֹב, עָזַב.

265. אָבִיו—'ă-vîw—*father-his:*

a. אָב *father;* ־ִי appears in its construct form and before suffixes.

b. ו is all that is left of הוּ *his* or *him;* cf. ו in אָפִיו.

266. אִמּוֹ —'ĭm-mô—*mother-his:*

a. אֵם *mother;* ו, the suffix of the 3 masc. sg.

b. In אֵם d. f. is lacking from ם, because it is final, and under the tone an original ĭ becomes ē; but in אִמּוֹ d. f. is present and original ĭ is retained in an unaccented syllable before a doubled consonant.

267. וְדָבַק—*and-shall-cleave;* cf. וְהָיוּ :

a. Synopsis in Ķăl, דָּבוֹק, דָּבֹק, דָּבַק, יִדְבַּק, דְּבַק, דְּבוֹק, דָּבֹק, דָּבַק, דָּבוֹק.

b. ו with the Perf. is Wăw Conversive; cf. וַ with the Imperfect.

268. בְּאִשְׁתּוֹ—b•'ĭš-tô—*in-wife-his:*

a. An irregular form of אִשָּׁה, before the suffix.

269. וַיִּהְיוּ—wăy-yĭh-yû—*and-they-were;* cf. וְהָיוּ :

a. Š•wâ under ה is silent.

b. Méθĕğ with ־ִ, to facilitate the pronunciation of the fol. ה.

c. Ķăl Impf. 3 m. pl. of the verb הָיָה, with Wăw Conversive.

270. שְׁנֵיהֶם—(the) *two-of-them,* = *they-two;* cf. שְׁנֵי, לָהֶם :

a. שְׁנֵי is the construct state of the dual שְׁנַיִם *two.*

b. הֵם is the pronominal suffix of the 3 plur. masc.

271. עֲרוּמִּים—ʿrŭm-mîm—*naked:*

a. The Šʿwâ under ע, because of distance from the tone.

b. The ן must here be regarded as a short vowel (i. e., an incorrect *full* writing of ŭ), on account of the D. f. following.

272. יֵתְבֹשָׁשׁוּ—yîθ-bô-šä′-šû—*they-will-be-ashamed:*

a. A formation after the manner of the Hiθpä'ēl.

b. Imperfect 3 masc. plur. of the root בּוֹשׁ.

c. The ◌ָ in pause for ◌ַ.

3. FORMS FOR SPECIAL STUDY.

פָּנִים	שְׁנַיִם	אִם	אֶת	וַיְהִיוּ	יַעֲזֹב־
פְּנֵי	שְׁנֵי	אִמוֹ	אֶת־	וְהָיוּ	יַעֲלֶה

2. OBSERVATIONS.

117. The ◌ָ which is seen in יְקְטֹל was originally a Pǎθǎḥ; this original Pǎθǎḥ is retained before laryngcals.

118. Wâw Conversive with the Impf. is וַ◌; with the Perfect, it is וְ◌.

119. An original ī is deflected in a closed unaccented syl. to ◌ָ.

120. An original ī is retained unchanged in an unaccented sharpened syllable.

121. The plur. ending ◌ִים becomes in the construct ◌ֵי.

122. The dual ending ◌ַיִם also becomes in the construct ◌ֵי

3. PRONOUNS, PERSONAL PREFIXES AND TERMINATIONS, PRONOMINAL SUFFIXES.

לָנוּ	יִכְתֹּב	הוּא	He will write to us.
לָךְ	תִכְתֹּב	הִיא	She will write to thee (f.).
לוֹ	תִכְתֹּב	אַתָּה	Thou (m.) wilt write to him.
לָה	תִכְתְּבִי	אַתְּ	Thou (f.) wilt write to her.
לָךְ	אֶכְתֹּב	אָנֹכִי	I will write to thee (m.).
לִי	יִכְתְּבוּ	הֵם	They (m.) will write to me.
לָכֶן	תִכְתֹּבְנָה	הֵן	They (f.) will write to you (f.).
לָהֶם	תִכְתְּבוּ	אַתֶּם	Ye (m.) will write to them (m.).
לָהֶן	תִכְתֹּבְנָה	אַתֶּן	Ye (f.) will write to them (f.).
לָכֶם	נִכְתֹּב	אֲנַחְנוּ	We will write to you (m.).

5. GRAMMAR-LESSON.

1. § **72.**   General View of the Strong Verb.

2. § **72.** R's 1—7,   Characteristics of Stems.

Note 1.—The synopsis of a stem includes (1) the Perf. 3 m. sg., (2) the Impf. 3 m. sg., (3) the Imv. 2 m. sg., (4) the two Infinitives, (5) the Participle or Participles.

Note 2.—In this general review of the strong verb, master the synopsis of each stem, so that it can be pronounced without hesitation, and written with perfect accuracy.

Note 3.—In this work use the following verbs in addition to the paradigm word: (1) מָשַׁל *rule,* (2) כָּתַב *write,* (3) לָכַד *capture.*

6. WORD-LESSON.

1. In the Word-Lists, Lists V. and VI., nouns numbered 31—45.

2. Make out a list of the new words in Genesis II. 24, 25.

7. EXERCISES.

1. To be translated into Hebrew:—(1) *He will rule, he ruled himself, he will be caused to rule, be thou* (m.) *ruled;* (2) *He will be kept, keep thyself* (Nĭf.), *he caused to keep, to be caused to keep;* (3) *He was holy, he will be sanctified, sanctify thou* (Pĭ'ēl and Hĭf'ĭl), *it will be sanctified;* (4) *To be created, being created, causing to divide, to cause to call, ruled, being caused to keep.*

2. To be translated into Ḥebrew:—(1) *God will not forsake me;* (2) *My mother will write to me;* (3) *The man and the woman became* (Heb., *were for*) *one flesh;* (4) *The man was called Adam;* (5) *The woman forsook her mother, and clave to her husband.*

3. To be translated into English:—(1) שׁי נַפְ֫שִׁי; (2) לֹא

הָיוּ שְׁנֵיהֶם (3) תַּעֲזֹב אִשְׁתְּךָ; (4) לֹא תַעֲזֹב הָאִשָּׁה אֶת־אִישָׁהּ

.אָדָם אֵין בְּיוֹם עֲשׂוֹת אֱלֹהִים אֶ֫רֶץ וְשָׁמָ֫יִם; (5) טוֹבִים

4. To be written in English letters:—*Genesis II* 24, 25 *from the pointed text.*

5. To be written with points and vowel-signs:—*Genesis II* 24, 25 *from the unpointed text.*

6. Synopses to be written:—(1) *Of* בָּדַל *in* Nĭ. *and* Hĭ.; (2) *of* בָּקַשׁ *in* Pĭ *and* Pŭ.; (3) *of* בָּשַׁל *in* Ḳăl, Pĭ., Pŭ. *and* Hĭ.; (4) *of* זָכַר *in* Ḳăl, Nĭ. *and* Hĭ.; (5) *of* פָּקַד *in all seven stems;* (6) *of* כָּבֵר (which has ă in Ḳăl Impf. and Imv.) *in* Ḳăl, Nĭ., Pĭ., Pŭ., Hĭ., Hĭθp.

8. TOPICS FOR STUDY.

(1) Attenuation of ă to ĭ in the preformatives of the Ḳăl Impf. (2) The occurrence of an original ă before laryngeals in the preformatives of the Ḳăl Impf. (3) Wâw Conversive, with the Perf., with the Impf. (4) The words for *man, woman, his-wife, her-husband.* (5) Dual ending in absolute and construct. (6) Changes of the vowel ĭ. (7) Synopses in various stems. (8) Characteristics of various stems. (9) Classes of weak verbs.

LESSON XXX.—REVIEW.

1. *WORD-REVIEW.*

[In this list of words, the superior figures indicate the verse in which the word, or its derivative, is found. In the case of nouns, the singular absolute is given, in the case of verbs, the root. The student is expected to compare with each word as here given, the various forms of that word which occur in the chapter, e. g., with שָׁקָה　he will compare הִשְׁקָה　*he-caused-to-drink,* לְהַשְׁקוֹת　*to-cause-to-drink.*]

1. VERBS.

³קָדַשׁ	²⁴עָזַב	⁷נָפַח	¹⁷מוּת	¹⁷חָמַד	¹⁶אָכַל
⁸שׂוּם	⁶עָלָה	²¹נָפַל	⁵מָטַר	¹⁹יָדַע	¹⁹בּוֹא
²שָׁבַת	¹⁰פָּרַד	¹¹סָבַב	²⁰מָצָא	⁷יָצַר	²⁵בּוֹשׁ
¹⁵שָׁמַר	¹⁶צָוָה	²¹סָגַר	¹⁵נוּחַ	²¹יָשֵׁן	²²בָּנָה
⁶שָׁקָה	⁵צָמַח	⁵עָבַד	⁸נָטַע	¹כָּלָה	²⁴דָּבַק
				¹⁵לָקַח	¹⁴הָלַךְ

2. NOUNS, PARTICLES, ETC.

⁵שִׂיחַ	¹צָבָא	¹⁸נָגָר	⁷חַיִּים	²²אִשָּׁה	²⁴אָב
²שְׁבִיעִי	²¹צֶלַע	¹⁰נָהָר	⁵טֶרֶם	¹⁸בַּד	¹²אֶבֶן
¹²שֹׁהַם	⁸קֶדֶם	⁷נְשָׁמָה	⁷יהֹוָה	¹²בְּדֹלַח	⁶אֵד
⁸שָׁם	¹⁴קִדְמָה	¹⁸עֵזֶר	⁵לֹא	²¹בָּשָׂר	⁵אַיִן
¹¹שֵׁם	¹⁰רֹאשׁ	⁷עָפָר	⁹מַאֲכָל	⁸גַּן	²³אִישׁ
⁴תּוֹלֵדָה	⁹רַע	²³עֶצֶם	¹⁹מָה	¹¹הוּא	²⁴אִם
²¹תַּרְדֵּמָה	⁵שָׂדֶה	²⁵עֵרוֹם	²מְלָאכָה	⁴זֶה	⁷אַף
		²³פַּעַם	⁹מַרְאֶה	¹¹זָהָב	¹⁰אַרְבָּעָה

2. *VERSE-REVIEW.*

1. Pronounce the pointed text of each verse until it can be read aloud rapidly and without hesitation.

2. Write out on paper the unpointed text, one verse at a time, and then, without the aid of either pointed text or translation, insert the necessary points and vowel-signs. Compare the result with the pointed text, and note the mistakes; repeat the exercise till each verse can be pointed without mistake.

3. Write the Hebrew of the chapter, verse by verse, with only the English translation before the eye. Here also correct the result each time by the pointed text.

4. Write out the transliteration of each verse, referring in doubtful cases to the transliteration of particular words given in the Notes from time to time.

3. GRAMMAR-REVIEW.

1. Long ô = â, § 30. 6.

2. Long ô = aw, § 30. 7.

3. Changes of ă, ĭ, ŭ, § 31. 2. 3.

4. Reduction, § 36. 2. a, b, and N. 1—4.

5. Attenuation, § 36. 3. a, b, c.

6. Simple verb-stem (Ḳăl), § 58. 1.

7. Formation and force of the Pī'ēl stem, § 58. 3. a, b, c.

8. Formation and force of the Pŭ'ăl stem, § 58. 4. a, b, c.

9. Formation and force of the Hĭθpă'ēl stem, § 58. 7. a, b, c.

10. Formation and force of Hĭf. and Hŏf. stems, § 58. 5. a, b, c, 6. a, b, c.

11. Formation and force of the Nĭf'ăl stem, § 58. 2. a, b, c.

12. General view of the verb-stems, § 59. R's 1—4.

13. Inflection of Ḳăl Perf. (active), § 60. R's 1—3.

14. Inflection of Ḳăl Perf. (stative), § 61. 1—3.

15. Inflection of remaining Perfects, § 62. 1, 2.

16. Inflection of Ḳăl Imperfect (active) § 63. R's 1—4.

17. Inflection of Ḳăl Imperfect (stative), § 64. 1—3.

18. Inflection of remaining Imperfects, § 65. 1—5.

19. Inflection of the various Imperatives, § 66. 1, 2.

20. The various Infinitives (abs. and const.), § 67. 1, 2.

21. The various Participles, § 68. 1—3.

22. General view of the strong verb, § 72. R's 1—7.

23. Classification of weak verbs, § 77. 1—6.

24. Seğolate nouns, § 89. 1.

4. A REVIEW EXERCISE ON THE STRONG VERB.

[Supply in each case the vowel-points, etc.; the superior figures denote the number of places in the paradigm represented by the accompanying form, e. g., קְטַלְתֶּן ,קְטַלְתֶּן ,יִקְטְלֶהָ ³יִקְטְלֶהָ = יִקְטְלֶהָ]

(5) נקטלתם, (4) ²קטלנה, (3) תתקטלי³, (2) ³תתקטלי, (1) יקטלתן

(10) ²התקטלת, (9) התקטלנה, (8) יקטיל, (7) יהקטלת, (6) ²יהקטלו

(14) אקטיל, (13) הקטלה, (12) ²קטול, (11) ²התקטלת

(18) ³התקטל, (17) יתקטל, (16) ⁷הקטל, (15) ²הקטלתם

(22) ¹²תקטלנה, (21) הקטלי, (20) הקטילה, (19) יקטילו

(27) ³קטלנו, (26) ²הקטילו, (25) ³מקטל, (24) ¹⁰יתקטל, (23) ²הקטל, התקטלה,

(31) מקטיל, (30) תתקטלו, (29) ²תתקטל, (28) תתקטל, (27) נקטיל

(36) אתקטל, (35) ⁵אקטל, (34) ⁵קטלו, (33) נקטלה, (32) ²הקטיל, יהקטיל

(40) נתקטל, (39) ⁵תתקטלו, (38) ²נקטלת, (37) תקטילי, (36) ³תקטילי

(44) ²הקטלנה, (43) התקטלתם, (42) תקטילו, (41) מתקטל

(48) ⁷נקטל, (47) ⁵יקטל, (46) ³קטלתי, (45) נקטלו, ²תתקטלנה,

(53) ²קטלי, (52) הקטלנו, (51) נקטלתי, (50) ²הקטלו, (49) התקטלו

(57) הקטלתן, (56) הקטילי, (55) ⁶קטלת, (54) נקטלת, ²יהקטלתן,

(62) נקטלנו, (61) ³קטלה, (60) ¹⁰קטל, (59) יתקטלו, (58) יתקטלו

(66) התקטלי, (65) התקטלתי, (64) ³קטלתם, (63) ²הקטלתי, התקטלי

(68) התקטלתן, (67) ²תתקטיל, תתקטלי.

LESSON XXXI.—GENESIS III. 1-2.

1. NOTE-REVIEW.

(5) (171;) הַשָּׂדֶה (4) (128); חַיַּת (3 (108); כֹּל (2) (49); מ. (1)

מִמֶּנּוּ (9) (41;) בְּתוֹךְ (8) (189); הַגָּן (7) (70); עֵץ (6) (255); אִשָּׁה

(229).

2. NOTES.

273. וְהַנָּחָשׁ—*and-the-serpent:* §§ **49.** 1; **45.** 1; **90.** 1. *a.*

274. הָיָה—Ḳăl Perf. 3 m. sg. of the 'פּ laryng. and ל"ה verb הָיָה *be;* meaning, *he-was;* corresponding form of the strong verb, קָטַל, § **82.** 1. *a.*

275. עָרוּם—*cunning:* a passive formation, § **91.** 1. *c.*

276. עָשָׂה—Ḳăl Perf. 3 m. sg. of the 'פּ laryng. and ל"ה verb עָשָׂה *make;* meaning, *he-made;* corresponding form of the strong verb, קָטַל, § **82.** 1. *a.*

277. אַף—*'ăf—also, even:* an adverb.

278. אָמַר—Ḳăl Perf. 3 m. sg. of the פ"א verb אָמַר; meaning, *he-said;* cor. form of strong verb, קָטַל, § **77.** 2.

279. תֹּאכְלוּ—θô'-x⁴lû—*ye-shall-eat;* cf. וַיֹּאמֶר:
a. תּ = *you,* and with the affix וּ (plur.) indicates Impf. 2 pl. m.
b. The א, as in וַיֹּאמֶר, loses its force, and preform. has ô, § **79.** 1.
c. The ־ֵ under כּ is for ־ֵ or ־ֶ, §§ **79.** 2; **63.** R. 3.

280. וַתֹּאמֶר—wăt-tô"-měr—*and-she-said:*
a. On the form of Wăw Conversive with Impf. see § **70.** 2. *a.*
b. On the retrocession of the accent, § **70.** 3. *a.* (3).
c. On the vowel after תּ (ô), and the vowel under מ (ĕ), § **79.** 1, 2.
d. Ḳăl Impf. 3 f. sg. of the פ"א verb אָמַר *say;* meaning, *she-will-say;* corresponding form of the strong verb, תִּקְטֹל.

281. נֹאכֵל—nô'-xēl—*we-may-eat;* cf. וַיֹּאמֶר:
a. נ, as in נַעֲשֶׂה (130), is connected with אֲנַחְנוּ.
b. א loses its force, and the preformative has ô, § **79.** 1, 2.
c. Ḳăl Impf. 1 pl. com., of the פ"א verb אָכַל; meaning, *we may-eat;* corresponding form of strong verb נִקְטֹל, § **63.** 10.

3. FORMS FOR SPECIAL STUDY.

וַיֹּאמֶר	הָיָה	תֵּאכְלוּ	וַיֹּאמֶר
וַתֹּאמֶר	עָשָׂה	תֹּאמְרוּ	וַתֹּאמֶר
נֹאכַל	בָּרָא	עֵץ־הַגָּן	וַיִּקְרָא
תֵּאכְלוּ	קָרָא	בְּתוֹךְ־הַגָּן	וַיַּבְדֵּל

4. OBSERVATIONS.

123. In verbs פ״א, the א, in Ḳāl Impf., loses its consonantal force, and the preceding vowel is always ô.

124. In verbs ל״ה, where the ה is merely a vowel-letter, and in verbs ל״א, where the א has lost its consonantal force, the ultimate ־ַ of the root form (cf. קָטַל) is rounded in the open syllable to ־ָ.

125. The prefix תּ with the affix וּ indicates an Impf. 2 m. pl.

126. Méθěǧ is found with a long vowel in a closed syllable before Mäḳḳēf, and especially with an unchangeable long vowel.

127. Wâw Conversive with the Imperfect draws the accent from the ultima to the penult, provided the penult is not a *closed* syllable.

5. GRAMMAR-LESSON.

1. § 70. 1. a. b,   Use of Impf. and Perf. with Wâw Conv.

2. § 70. 2. a. b,   The form of the Conjunction.

3. § 70. 3. a. b,   The verbal form employed.
   1, 2,

4. § 70. 3. R. and Note.   Special cases.

5. § 73. 1—3. R, and   Laryngeal Verbs.
   Note.

6. § 84. 1, 2,   Bi-literal Verbs.

6. WORD-LESSON.

1. In the Word-Lists, under List VI., nouns numbered 46—60.
2. Make out a list of the new words in Genesis III. 1—2.

7. PRINCIPLES OF SYNTAX.—COMPARISON.

וְהַנָּחָשׁ הָיָה עָרוּם מִכֹּל חַיַּת הַשָּׂדֶה—*And the serpent was*
cunning from every (= more cunning than any) *beast of the field.*

Principle 6.—Comparison is expressed by means of the prep. מִן.

8. EXERCISES.

1. To be translated into Hebrew:—(1) *The sun is larger than*
(Heb., *great from*) *the moon;* (2) *The man is better than the wo-*
man; (3) *The woman is better than the man;* (4) *We may eat of all*
good fruit; (5) *She may eat from the fruit of the tree which is in*
the midst of the garden; (6) *We may say, ye* (m.) *may say, she will*
say, I will say.

2. To be translated into Hebrew:—(1) *God created the heavens,*
and made the luminaries; (2) *He made* (the) *man in the sixth*
day, and rested in the seventh day; (3) *He will sanctify the*
seventh day, and will rest in it; (4) *The man will give food to the*
cattle, and to the fowl of the heavens, and will give (Heb., *call*) *to*
them names.

3. To be translated into English:—(1) עָשָׂה וַיִּשְׁבֹּת; (2) שָׁבַת;
(3) וַיְקַדֵּשׁ; (4) הָלַכְתִּי וָאֵשֵׁב; (5) יַעֲלֶה וְאָמַר; תִּשְׁבֹּת
(6) וְאָמַרְתָּ; (7) יִפְרוּ וּמָלְאוּ; הַנָּהָר יִפָּרֵד וְהָיָה לְאַרְבָּעָה
רָאשִׁים.

4. To be written in English letters:—*The new words of Genesis*
III. 1—2.

5. To be written with points and vowel-signs:—*Genesis III. 1, 2.*
from the unpointed text.

6. To be described:[1]—The forms שָׁרָצוּ (1:21),[2]יִסְגֹּר (2:21), יִתֵּן
(1:17), יִקְרָא (2:23), יַבְדֵּל (1:4), יְקַדֵּשׁ (2:3).

9. TOPICS FOR STUDY.

(1) Wâw Conversive with the Impf. (2) Wâw Conversive with
the Perfect. (3) First radical of verbs פ"נ. (4) Hif'îl Impf. with
Wâw Conversive. (5) The הַ_ of ל"ה Impf's with Wâw Conversive. (6) Change of accent with Wâw Conversive. (7) D. l. after
a disjunctive accent. (8) The use of Méθëğ before Măkkēf.

LESSON XXXII. GENESIS III. 3-5.

1. NOTE-REVIEW.

(1) מוֹת (231); (2) תִּמְתּוּן (231); (3) מִמֶּנּוּ (229); (4) וְרַע (199);
(5) הוּא (Principle 5).

2. NOTES.

282. תִּגְּעוּ—θïg-g⁽e⁾û—ye-shall-touch, for תִּנְגְּעוּ :

a. ת, with וּ, indicates Impf. 2 m. pl.

b. נ, the first radical, is assimilated, §§ 78. 2. a.

c. A new disjunctive accent called Tîfḥâ; §§ 22. 10; 24. 6.

d. Kăl Impf. 2 m. pl. of the פ"נ and ל׳ laryng. verb נָגַע touch;
meaning, ye-shall-touch; corresponding form of strong verb,
תִּקְטְלוּ .

---

[1] The description of a verb includes a statement of (1) the stem, (2)
tense, (3) pers., gen., num., (4) class, (5) root, with its meaning, (6) meaning of the form, (7) corresponding form of קְטֹל ; this order is to be followed rigidly.

[2] These figures refer to the chapter and verse of the text in which the
form occurs.

283. פֶּן בּוֹ תִּגְּעוּ—The D. l. in בּ and פ, § **12.** 3.

284. תְּמֻתוּן—t'mû-θûn—*ye-shall-die;* cf. תִּגְּעוּ:

a. ת, with ן (וּן archaic § **63.** R. 3). indicates Impf. 2 m. pl.

b. The root is מוּת *die;* ־ֻ is defective for וּ, § **6.** 4. N. 2.

285. יֹדֵעַ—yô-dē(ă)'—*knowing,* = *knows;* cf. זֹרֵעַ:

a. Ķăl act. part. sg. masc. of the פ"וֹ and ל laryngeal verb יָדַע, *know* meaning, *knowing;* corresponding form, קֹטֵל.

b. The ־ֵ under עַ is Pắθăḥ-*furtive,* §§ **76.** 1. c. (3).

286. אֲכָלְכֶם—'ăxŏl-xĕm—*your-eating;* cf. אָכְלְךָ:

a. The ־ֲ under כ is ŏ deflected from original ŭ, § **71.** 3. a. (1)

b. Ķăl Inf. const., with pronominal suffix כֶם.

287. וְנִפְקְחוּ—*and-will-be-opened:*

a. The וְ is Wâw Conversive with the Perfect, § **70.** 2. b.

b. The נ is the characteristic of the Nĭf'ăl, § **59.** 2.

c. Nĭf'ăl Perf. 3 c. plur. of the ל laryng. verb פָּקַח *open;* meaning, *they-were-opened;* corresponding form, נִקְטְלוּ.

288. עֵינֵיכֶם—'ê-nê-xĕm—*your eyes:*

a. Eye עַיִן [two] *eyes* עֵינַיִם; [two] *eyes-of* עֵינֵי־, § **107.** 6.

b. The grave suffix כֶם, always accented, § **51.** 1. a.

289. וִהְיִיתֶם—wĭh-yî-θĕm—*and-ye-shall-be:*

a. וִ, so written before a consonant with Š'wâ, is Wâw Conversive.

b. תֶם is the personal termination of the Perf. 2 m. plur.

c. First radical ה, second י, third י; ־ִ under ה silent.

290. כֵּאלֹהִים—kê'-lô-ḥîm—*like-God:*

a. For כֵּאֱלֹהִים according to § **47.** 3; but א is weak and loses its consonantal force, and Š'wâ disappears with it. The vowel under כ then becomes ־ֵ in compensation for the quiescent א. § **47.** R. 1.

291. יֹדְעֵי—yô-d'ʿê—*knowers-of;* cf. יֹדֵעַ (285):

a. The m. plur. const. of יֹדֵעַ; note the ending י ־ֵ.

3. FORMS FOR SPECIAL STUDY.

| עֵינַיִם | יִהְיֶה | נִפְקְחוּ | לֵאמֹר | יֹאכַל | יִתֵּן |
| עֵינֵיכֶם | וִהְיִיתֶם | נִקְטַל | כֵּאלֹהִים | תֹּאכַל | תִּתֵּן |

4. OBSERVATIONS.

128. The ending וֵֹ is the construct ending of *dual* as well as of plural nouns.

129. The letter הִ, of הָיָה *be*, always takes simple (silent) šʻwâ, unless it is initial.

130. The Nif'äl Perfect and Participle have the prefix נִ.

131. When a consonant is elided after a short vowel, that vowel is strengthened in compensation and becomes unchangeable.

132. Any 3 *masc.* sg. verbal form, of the Imperfect may be made 3 *fem.* sg. by change of וֹ to תּ.

5. GRAMMAR-LESSON.

1. § **74.** Tabular view,   Inflection of עָטַל in Ḳäl, Nif'äl and Hif'îl
                               stems.
2. § **74.** 1,   Rejection of D. f. by the laryngeal.
3. § **74.** 2. *a, b,*   Preference of laryngeals for *a*-class vowels.
4. § **74.** 3. *a—d,*   Preference of laryngeals for comp'd šʻwâ.
5. § **42.** 1—3,   Peculiarities of laryngeals (*to be read*).

Note 1.—In the study of this class of verbs, (1) examine closely the synopses, noting the variations from the strong verb, (2) analyze exhaustively all forms given under § **74.** with which you are familiar, (3) master thoroughly the sections indicated to be learned, (4) write *without help* a complete paradigm of the Ḳäl, Nif'äl and Hif'îl stems, (5) compare the result with the paradigm given in the grammar.

Note 2.—In the study of 'פ laryng. verbs use for practice (1) עָמַד *stand*, (2) עָבַד *serve*, (3) חָזַק *be strong*.

6. WORD-LESSON.

1. In the Word-Lists, under List VI., nouns numbered 61-76.
2. Make out a list of the new words in Genesis III. 3—5.

7. PRINCIPLES OF SYNTAX.

כִּי יֹדֵעַ אֱלֹהִים—*For God* (is) *knowing*=For God knows.

בְּיוֹם אֲכָלְכֶם מִמֶּנּוּ וְנִפְקְחוּ עֵינֵיכֶם—*In the day of your eating from it,* THEN *will be opened your eyes.*

Principle 7.—The participle is often used for the present tense.

Principle 8.—The conjunction וְ is frequently used "to connect a statement of time with the clause to which it relates."

8. EXERCISES.

1. To be translated into Hebrew:—(1) *She caused to serve;* (2) *He will be strong;* (3) *She was served;* (4) *I caused to stand;* (5) *They will cause to stand;* (6) *Thou* (f.) *wilt be served;* (7) *It will be said;* (8) *She will abandon;* (9) *Ye* (m.) *did abandon;* (10) *I shall be served;* (11) *Be thou served;* (12) *To be abandoned;* (13) *We shall serve;* (14) *Ye* (m.) *shall stand;* (15) *Be strong.*

2. To be translated into Hebrew:—(1) *Serving thou shalt serve God;* (2) And the man saw the good fruit; (3) And the woman saw that the fruit was good; (4) Their eyes were opened; (5) In the day of your ruling the earth; (6) The woman will eat the fruit, and of (= from) it she will give to her husband, who will eat with her.*

3. To be translated into English:—(1) לָקְחָה הָאִשָּׁה אֶת־הַפְּרִי

(3) ;מִי יִתֵּן אֶת־הַפְּרִי הַזֶּה לְאִשָּׁה הַזֹּאת (2) וַתִּתֵּן לָאִישׁ

(5) ;הָאִישׁ יֹאכַל אֶת־פְּרִי הָעֵץ (4) וַיַּעֲמֹד הָאִישׁ בַּגָּן

אֱלֹהִים אָמַר יְהִי־אוֹר.

4. To be written in English letters:—*The new words of Genesis III. 3—5.*

5. To be written with points and vowel-signs:—*Genesis III. 3-5, from the unpointed text.*

6. To be described:—The forms תִּרְאֶה, יַעֲלֶה־, יַעֲזֹב־, עֲשׂוֹת,
עָבַד, נַעֲשֶׂה, אֶעֱשֶׂה.

9. TOPICS FOR STUDY.

(1) Dual abs. affix. (2) Dual const. affix. (3) ה with ָ. (4)
And-he-saw, and-she-saw. (5) Formation of feminine nouns. (6)
Synopsis in Ḥif. of שָׂכַל. (7) The א of verbs פ״א. (8) The
vowel of the Preformative in Ḳăl Impf. of verbs פ״א. (9) The
stem-vowel of verbs פ״א in the Ḳăl Impf.

LESSON XXXIII. GENESIS III. 6-8.

1. NOTE-REVIEW.

(1) הָיָה (274); (2) תִּגְּעוּ (282); (3) וַיִּהְיוּ (269); (4) וַיַּעַשׂ (87);
(5) וַיְבָרֶךְ (114); (6) יַעֲלֶה (179); (7) נִשְׁמַת (186).

2. NOTES.

292. וַתֵּרֶא—wăt-tē'-rĕ'—*and-*(she)*-saw;* cf. וַיַּרְא *and-*(he)*-saw:*

a. Full form תִּרְאֶה (cf. יִהְיֶה), but ה_ never stands with Wăw
conversive (§ 82. 5. *b*);—ָ standing under the tone, becomes_
(§ 82. 5. *b*. (4)); and a helping ָ is inserted after ר (§ 29. 4. *b*.)

293. תַּאֲוָה—(a) *delight:* a noun formed by prefix ת, § 93.

294. לָעֵינַיִם—*to-the-*[two]*-eyes:* §§ 45. R. 3; 106. 5. *a.*

295. נֶחְמָד—nĕḥ-măd—*desirable:*

a. Nĭf. part. of the פ׳ laryng. verb חָמַד *desire;* meaning, *desired* or *desirable;* corresponding form נִקְטָל, but the ־ has become ־ִ

before ה, § **74. 2.** *b.*

b. The strong laryngeal ח has simple (silent) š⁽ᵉ⁾wâ, § **74. 3.** *b.*

296. לְהַשְׂכִּיל—lᵉhăś-kîl—*to-make-wise:*

a. Hîf. Inf. const. of שָׂכַל *be wise;* corresponding form הַקְטִיל.

b. Synopsis: מַשְׂכִּיל; הִשְׂכִּיל, יַשְׂכֵּל, הַשְׂכֵּל, הַשְׂכִּיל, הַשְׂכִּיל

—note the ־ַ under preformative, except in Perfect.

297. מִפִּרְיוֹ—*from-its-fruit:* (1) מִן, (2) פְּרִי, (3) וֹ.

298. וַתִּתֵּן—*and-she-gave:* feminine of וַיִּתֵּן (94).

299. עִמָּהּ—ʽim-mâh—*with-her;* preposition עִם:

c. הָ_ַ, arising from הָ_ָ, is âh, not åh.

300. וַתִּפָּקַחְנָה—*and-*(they, f.)*-were-opened;* cf. יָקוּן:

a. Nîfʽăl (note D. f. in and ־ַ *under* פ), Impf. 3 fem. ·(נָה) plur. of

the פ"ל laryngeal root פָּקַח; corresponding form תִּקָּטַלְנָה.

301. עֵינֵי—ʽê-nê—*eyes-of;* cf. עֵינֵיכֶם (288), עֵינַיִם (294).

302. וַיֵּדְעוּ—wăy-yê-dⁱʽ⁽ᵉ⁾û—*and-they-knew:*

a. Ḳăl Impf. 3 m. plur. of the פ"י and פ"ל laryng. verb יָדַע *know.*

b. Corresponding form, יִקְטְלוּ; the first radical י, being weak,

drops out, and ־ַ now standing in an open syl., becomes ־ֵ,

§ **80. 2.** *a.* (1).

c. Mé₍θ₎ĕğ with long vowel before vocal š⁽ᵉ⁾wâ pretonic, § **18. 2.**

303. עֵירֻמִּים—ʽê-rŭm-mîm—*naked:* irregular plural of עֵירֹם.

304. הֵם—hêm—*they* (m.): cf. the other form הֵמָּה, pron. suf.הֶם.

305. וַיִּתְפְּרוּ—wăy-yĭθ-p⁽ᵉ⁾rû—*and-they-sew⁽e⁾d:*

a. Ḳăl Impf. 3 m. sg. ofתָּפַר *sew;* cor. form, יִקְטְלוּ; 3 m. *sg.*יִתְפֹּר.

b. Synopsis: תָּפוּר, תָּפֹר ,תָּפוֹר ,יִתְפֹּר ,תִּתְפֹּר ,תָּפַר.

306. עֲלֵה—⁽ᵉ⁾lé(h)—*leaf-of:* abs. sg. עָלֶה.

307. תְּאֵנָה—θ⁽ᵉ⁾ê-nå(h)—*fig-tree:* note the Zåḳēf-ḳåtōn.

308. וַיִּעֲשׂוּ—wăy-yă'-ăśû—and-they-made; cf. וַיַּעַשׂ and-he-made.

309. וַיִּשְׁמְעוּ—and-they-heard; cf. וַיִּתְפְּרוּ (305).

310. קוֹל—ḳôl—voice; cf. כָּל (kōl) all.

311. מִתְהַלֵּךְ—walking: Hĭθpä'ēl participle of הָלַךְ walk.

312. וַיִּתְחַבֵּא—and-(he)-hid-himself; cf. מִתְהַלֵּךְ.

3. FORMS FOR SPECIAL STUDY.

יִשְׁמְעוּ	יִתְפְּרוּ	יֵדְעוּ	יִשְׁמְעוּ

4. OBSERVATIONS.

133. Of two šᵉwâs in the middle of a word the first is silent, the second is vocalized.

134. Where a closed syllable would have ĭ, an open syllable has ē.

5. GRAMMAR-LESSON.

1. § **74.** Tabular View, Synopses of עָטַל in Pĭ'ēl, Pŭ'ăl, Hĭθpä'ēl, and Hŏf'äl.

2. § **74.** 2. a—b.   Preference of the laryngeal for ă.

3. § **74.** 3. a—d.   Preference of the laryng. for comp'd šᵉwâ.

4. § **42.** 1—3,   Peculiarities of laryngeals (to be read).

Note 1.—In the study of this class of verbs (1) examine closely the synopses, noting the variations from the strong verb, (2) analyze exhaustively all familiar forms given under § 74. 1-3, (3) master thoroughly the sections indicated to be learned, (4) write without help a complete paradigm of the verb, and (5) compare the result with the paradigm given in the grammar.

Note 2.—In this study of 'פ laryng. verbs, use for practice (1) חָמַד desire, (2) עָזַב forsake, (3) עָלַם conceal, (4) הָפַךְ turn.

6. WORD-LESSON.

1. In the Word-Lists, under List VII., the nouns numbered 77—84.
2. Make out a list of the new words in Genesis III. 6—8.

7. EXERCISES.

1. To be translated into Hebrew:—(1) *He will desire;* (2) *He was caused to turn;* (3) *She was abandoned* (Pŭ'äl עֻזַּב); (4) *She will conceal herself* (Hiθp.); (5) *They will be caused to stand;* (6) *We shall be forsaken* (Nif.); (7) *Thou* (f.) *wilt be desired* (Nif.) (8) *She will be caused to turn;* (9) *Be thou* (f.) *desirable* (Nif.); (10) *Cause ye* (m.) *to forsake;* (11) *Be ye* (m.) *caused to forsake.*

2. To be translated into Hebrew:—(1) *And the woman saw that the fruit was good and she desired it;* (2) *She took the fruit and gave it to the man;* (3) *I caused the man to serve God;* (4) *The man was forsaken in the garden;* (5) *The woman turned herself and saw the man who was standing under the tree.*

3. To be translated into English: — (1) לָקְחָה הָאִשָּׁה מִפְּרִי

(2) הָעֵץ וַתֵּרֶא כִּי טוֹב וַתֹּאכַל מִמֶּנּוּ יַעֲזֹב הָאִישׁ אָבִיו; (3) וְאִמּוֹ וְדָבַק בְּאִשְׁתּוֹ וַיִּתֵּן אֶת הָאִישׁ לַעֲבֹד אֶת־הָאֲדָמָה; (6) מִתְהַלֵּךְ אֱלֹהִים בַּגָּן (5) נֶחְמָד הַפְּרִי לְהַשְׂכִּיל (4) וַתִּתְחַבֵּא הָאִשָּׁה וַתַּעַשׂ לָהּ חֲגוֹרָה.

4. To be written in English letters:—*The new words of Genesis III.* 6—8.

5. To be written with points and vowel-signs:—*Genesis III.* 6—8.

6. To be written out:—*Synopses of* עָמַד and חָמַד *in all stems.*

7. To be described : — The forms וַתֵּרֶא, יֵעָשֶׂה, נֶחְמָד יֵהָפֵךְ, יַחְמֹד.

8. TOPICS FOR STUDY.

(1) The peculiarities of laryngeals as seen in verbs פ laryng. (2) The meanings of Nîf'äl and Hiθpä'ēl stems. (3) The two ways of vocalizing Imperfect Ķäl in פ laryng. verbs. (4) The differing grades of strength in the various laryngeals. (5) Compensation for the failure to double a laryngeal. (6) The common element in the Imperfect, Imperative and Infinitive Construct.

LESSON XXXIV. GENESIS III. 9-11.

1. *NOTE-REVIEW.*

(1) שְׁנֵיהֶם (88,270); (2) רוּחַ (15); (3) אִשְׁתּוֹ (268); (4) פְּנֵי (13);

(5) בְּתוֹךְ (41); (6) הַגָּן (189); (7) וַיִּקְרָא (29); (8) אָדָם (131).

2. *NOTES.*

313. אַיֶּכָּה—'ăy-yĕ′k-kâ(h)—*where-*(art)*-thou?:*

a. אַי *where*, with union syllable יָ‗ , § **71**. 2. *c.* (3).

b. כָה, a fuller writing for ךְ, the pronominal suffix.

314. שָׁמַעְתִּי—*I-heard;* corresponding form קָטַלְתִּי; cf. נָתַתִּי.

315. וָאִירָא—wâ-'î-râ'—*and-I-was-afraid:*

a. וָ‍, the Wâw Convers., before a laryngeal, loses D. f. and becomes וָ.

b. א indicates the first person *I;* the root is יָרֵא *be-afraid.*

c. The accent Tᵉvîr (ָ), and that under שָׁמַעְתִּי, Tifḥâ (ָ), are disjunctives of the third class, § **22**. 10, 11.

316. וָאֵחָבֵא—wâ-'ē-ḥâ-vē'—*and-I-hid-myself:*

a. On וָ and א see preceding note (315. *a*).

b. Nif'äl Impf. 1 c. sg. of the 'פ laryng. and ל״א verb חָבָא *hide.*

c. D. f. rejected from ח, and preceding vowel lowered, § **74**. 1.

317. הִגִּיד—(he) *made-known;* cf. יָפַח ,יֵטַע ,הַמְטִיר:

a. Hif'îl (הִ) Perfect 3 sg. m. of the פ״ן verb נָגַד *make known.*

b. Cor. form, הַגִּיד ,הַגֵּד ,הַגֵּד ,הַגִּיד; *Synopsis,* הִגִּיד ,יַגִּיד ,הַגֵּד; מַגִּיד; the D. f. in ג is for the assimilated נ, § **78**. 2. *b.*

318. לְךָ—preposition לְ, with suffix ךָ, § **51**. 3.

319. אַתָּה—pausal for אַתָּה, §§ **50**. 2; **38**. 2.

320. הֲמִן—hᵃmĭn—*?-from,* §§ **46**. 1; **48**.

321. צִוִּיתִיךָ—ṣĭw-wî-θî′-xâ—*I-commanded-thee;* cf. וַיְצַו:

a. Pi'ēl Perf. 1 sg. of the ל״ו verb צָוָה *command.* § **82**.

b. Cor. form, קְטַלְתִּיךָ; but instead of לְ‍_, we have י‍_ = ‍ן; § **82.**
3. *b.*

c. תִּי = *I;* ךָ = *thee;* D. f. in ן, characteristic of Pī‘ēl.

322. לְבִלְתִּי—*to-not:* prep. לְ, and בִּלְתִּי, the neg. used with Inf's.

323. אֱכָל־—'ᵃxŏl+—(to)-*eat:* Ḳăl Inf. const. before Măḳḳēf, § **17. 2.**

3. *FORMS FOR SPECIAL STUDY.*

וָאִירָא	שָׁמַעְתִּי בַגָּן	יִתְחַבֵּא
וָאֵחָבֵא	וָאִירָא כִּי	אֲחַבֵּא

4. *OBSERVATIONS.*

135. ‍ן‍,. before the *first* person (א), becomes ן.

136. A dăǧ. l. in an initial spirant will stand even when the preceding word closes with a vowel, if that word carries a disjunctive accent.

137. The Hĭθpă‘ēl is generally reflexive; the Nĭf‘ăl was originally reflexive, and in common usage frequently has this force.

5. *GRAMMAR-LESSON.*

1. § **75.** Tabular View,   Synopses of קָאַל in Ḳăl, Nĭf‘ăl, Hĭf‘ĭl and Hŏf‘ăl stems.

2. § **75.** 1. *a, b,* and N. 1-3,   Rejection of D. f. by the laryngeal.

3. § **75.** 2. *a-c,*   Preference of the laryngeal for ă.

4. § **75. 3,**   Preference of the laryngeal for comp'd Š°wâ.

5. § **42. 1-3,**   Peculiarities of laryngeals (*to be read*).

6. *WORD-LESSON.*

1. Make out a list of the new words in Genesis III. 9—11.

7. PRINCIPLES OF SYNTAX.

בָּרָא אֱלֹהִים אֶת הַשָּׁמַיִם—*God created the heavens.*

וַיְבָרֶךְ אֹתָם אֱלֹהִים—*And God blessed them.*

אֶת־קֹלְךָ שָׁמַעְתִּי בַגָּן—*Thy voice I heard in the garden.*

Principle 9.—The object of the verb generally stands *after* both predicate and subject; but if the object is pronominal it stands between the predicate and subject; or, if the object is to be emphasized, it stands *before* both predicate and subject.

8. EXERCISES.

1. To be translated into Hebrew:—(1) *He will redeem;* (2) *Redeem thou* (f.); (3) *They* (m.) *will redeem;* (4) *Thou* (f.) *wilt be redeemed;* (5) *We were redeemed;* (6) *I shall cause to redeem;* (7) *They caused to redeem;* (8) *He was caused to redeem;* (9) *Being caused to redeem;* (10) *To cause to redeem.*

2. To be translated into Hebrew:—(1) *Thou didst hear the voice of God from the heavens;* (2) *Let us make for ourselves large girdles;* (3) *They will hide themselves* (Nif. or Hiθp.) *in the garden;* (4) *This is the day in which God spoke to the man in the midst of the garden of Eden;* (5) *God will redeem the man and his seed;* (6) *The man will be redeemed in that day.*

1. To be translated into English: — (1) נִשְׁמַע קוֹל אֱלֹהִים (2) בָּרוּךְ אֱלֹהָי; (3) מִי הִתְחַבֵּא מִפְּנֵי אֱלֹהִים (2) עַל־הָאָרֶץ; נֶחְמְדָה הָאָרֶץ (4) הַשָּׁמַיִם; (5) בְּכָל־הָאָרֶץ הַמְשֵׁל הָאָדָם; בְּעֵינֵי כָל־הַבָּשָׂר.

4. To be written in English letters:—*The new words of Genesis III., 9—11.*

5. To be written with points and vowel-signs:—*Genesis III., 9—11 from the unpointed text.*

6. To be written out:—Synopses in Ḳäl, Nïf. Hïf. and Hŏf. of

גָּאַל and שָׁחַת ; and of גָּאַל in Pï'ēl, Pŭ'äl and Hïθp.

7. To be described:—יְבְחַר, גָּאֲלִי, נִגְאַלְתֶּם, הַגְאִילָה, יְגָאֲלוּ.

9. TOPICS FOR STUDY.

(1) Wâw Conversive before א. (2) Cases of Nïf. and Hïθp. stems in Gen. III. 7—11; (3) Synopses of the strong verb קָטַל ; (4) The personal pronoun; (5) The inseparable prepositions; (6) Wâw Conversive with Perfect and Imperfect; (7) Synopses of ע׳ laryng. verb in Ḳäl, Nïf. Hïf. and Ḥŏf. stems.

LESSON XXXV. GENESIS III. 12-14.

1. NOTE-REVIEW.

(1) מִמֶּנּוּ (229); (2) הָאָדָם (131); (3) אִשָּׁה (255); (4) מִן (49);

(5) וַתֹּאמֶר (280); (6) הַנָּחָשׁ (273); (7) בְּהֵמָה (125); (8) חַיַּת (128); (9) הַשָּׂדֶה; (10) תֹּאכַל (228).

2. NOTES.

324. נָתַתָּה—nâ-θåt-tâ(h)—*thou-gavest;* cf. קָטַלְתָּ :

a. Ḳäl Perf. 2 sg. m. of the פ״ן verb נָתַן, § 78. 2. R. 3.

b. The vowel-letter ה at the end is not usual; the ending is gen-erally תָּ ,

325. עִמָּדִי—'ïm-mâ-dî—*with-me:* note Zåḳēf ḳåṭon, § 24. 4.

326. הִוא נָתְנָה־לִּי—hî' nâ-θ'nâ(h)l+lî—*she gave+to-me,* § 15. 3:

a. The pronoun used as subject of a verb is expressed whenever, as here, it is emphatic.

327. וָאֹכַל—wå-'ô-χēl—*and-I-ate;* cf. וָאֵירָא, וָאֶחֱבָא:

a. אֹכַל is for אָאֹכַל, of which the radical א is lost, § 79. 1. N.

b. וָ, the form of Wåw Conversive with the Impf., becomes וַ before א, § 70. 2. a. (3).

328. מַה־זֹּאת—mă(h)z+zô(')θ—*what+this?* §§ 54. 2. a; 52. 1. b.

329. עָשִׂית—*thou-*(f.)*-hast-done;* ת =*thou* (f.); on יִ see § 82. 3. b.

330. הִשִּׁיאַנִי—hĭš-śî-'ă-nî—(he) *deceived-me;* cf. הִגִּיד:

a. נִי is the pron. suf. of 1st pers., ־ the so-called connecting vowel.

b. הִשִּׁיא Hif. Perf. 3 m. sg. of נָשָׁא, נ being assim., § 78. 2. b.

331. עָשִׂית זֹאת—'ă-śî-θå-zô(')θ—*thou-*(m.)*-hast-done this:*

a. עָשִׂית = *thou-*(f.)*-hast-done;* עָשִׂיתָ = *thou-*(m.)*-hast-done.*

b. D. f. in זֹ is conj., § 15. 3; accent over זֹאת, S͏eğōltå, § 24. 3.

332. אָרוּר—'å-rûr—*cursed;* Ķål Part. Pass. of אָרַר, § 68. 1. c.

333. גְחֹנְךָ—*thy-belly;* cf. מְאֹרַת, גְדֹלִים:

a. The absolute form is גָּחֹן but with suffix גְחֹן § 109. 1. a.

b. The ô is here written defectively; the suffix is ךָ with ־.

334. תֵּלֵךְ—θē-lēχ—*thou-shalt-go:*

a. The root is הָלַךְ, or יָלַךְ, § 80. 2. R. 3.

b. The prefix ת = *thou* (m.); cor. form of קָטַל is תִּקְטֹל.

335. יְמֵי—*days-of;* sg. יוֹם, plur. יָמִים, plur. const. יְמֵי.

336. חַיֶּיךָ—ḥăy-yě'-χå—*thy-lives;* from the plur. חַיִּים:

a. On the vowel יֶ (ê) see § 30. 5 and b.

3. FORMS FOR SPECIAL STUDY.

אָתָּה	אָכַלְתָּ	נָתְנָה־לִי	עָשִׂיתָ	מִי	הַגִּיד
אָכַלְתְּ	נָתַתָּה	עָשִׂיתָ זֹאת	עָשִׂית	מַה׳	הִשִּׁיא

4. OBSERVATIONS.

138. The radical ג, when it would stand at the end of a syllable, and before a dental consonant is assimilated.

139. The Interrog. pronouns are מִי *who?*, and ·מָה *what?*.

140. תָּ = *thou* (m.), תְּ = *thou* (f.), but both have their soft sound (θ) when a vowel precedes.

141. D. f. conj. may or may not be accompanied by Măḳḳēf.

142. The personal termination תָּ *thou* (m.) is generally written without, though sometimes with, the vowel-letter ה.

5. GRAMMAR-LESSON.

1. § 76. Tabular View, Synopses of קָטַח in Ḳăl, Nĭf. Hĭf. and Hŏf. stems.

2. § 76. 1. *a, b,* Preference of the laryngeal for ă.

3. § 76. 1. *c,* Insertion of Păθăḥ-furtive.

4. § 76. 1. *d,* Insertion of — in Perfects 2 f. sg.

5. § 76. 2, Preference of the laryng. for comp'd Šᵉwâ.

6. 42. 1—3, Peculiarities of laryngeals (*to be learned*).

Note 1.—Treat as directed in former Lessons the familiar forms in § 76. 1, 2.

Note 2.—In the study of ל׳ laryngeal verbs use for practice (1) מָשַׁח *anoint,* (2) שָׁלַח *send,* (3) שָׁבַע *swear,* (4) שָׁמַע *hear.*

6. WORD-LESSON.

1. In the Word-Lists, under List VII., nouns numbered 85—94.
2. Make out a list of the new words in Genesis III. 12—14.

7. EXERCISES.

1. To be translated into Hebrew:—(1) *I will anoint;* (2) *He will cause to anoint;* (3) *Sending, sent;* (4) *Thou* (f.) *didst hear;* (5) *He will send;* (6) *I swore* (Nĭf.); (7) *I will swear;* (8) *She caused to send;* (9) *To anoint;* (10) *Cause thou* (m.) *to send;* (11) *To be sent.*

2. To be translated into Hebrew:—(1) *He told the man that he
was good;* (2) *Hast thou eaten fruit from the tree of lives?* (3)
Who gave the woman to the man? (4) *He gave me fruit and I ate;*
(5) *She gave him fruit and he ate;* (6) *I gave her fruit and we ate.*

3. To be translated into English:—(1) ;יְמוֹת הָאֹכֵל כֹּן־הָעֵץ

(4) ;הִשִּׁיא הַנָּחָשׁ אֶת־הָאִשָּׁה וַתֹּאכַל (3) ;מִי עָשָׂה (2) אֵת זֹאת

מַה־נָּתַנָּה לָקַחַת (5) ;הַמִן־הָעֵץ הַזֶּה אַתָּה מִמֶּנּוּ (6) ;הִגְרִל

הָאִשָּׁה לָאִישׁ.

4. To be written in English letters:—*The new words of Genesis
III. 12—14.*

5. To be written with points and vowel-signs:—*Genesis III.
12—14 from the unpointed text.*

6. To be written out:—Synopses of מָשַׁח, בָּטַח, and שָׁמַע in
Ķāl, Nif., Hīf. and Ḥōf. stems.

7. To be described:—The forms זֶרַע, יָצְמַח, יֶטַע, יִפַּח, יִצְמֶח,

הִשְׁבַּעַת, יָדַעַתָּ, שָׂמַח, הִשְׁלַח, מַזְרִיעַ, יָדַע.

8. *TOPICS FOR STUDY.*

(1) The נ of verbs פ״ן in the Hif. (2) Hē Interrogative. (3)
The negative used with the Infinitive. (4) The peculiarities of the
verb נָתַן. (5) וְ before אֲ. (6) D. f. conjunctive. (7) The Interrogative pronouns. (8) תָּ and תָה (9) P̣ăθăḥ-furtive. (10) The helping-vowel ־ַ in Perfects 2 f. sg. (11) Synopses of the strong verb.

LESSON XXXVI.—GENESIS III. 15-17.

1. *NOTES.*

337. וְאֵיבָה—w'ēvă(h)—*and-enmity:* a fem. noun, from root אָיַב.

338. אָשִׁית—*I-will-put;* א = I, the root being שִׁית (עֵ״יׁ) *put:*

a. Observe the Rᵉvî(ă)', § **24. 5.** *b.*

339. זַרְעֲךָ—*thy-seed;* זַרְעָהּ *her-seed;* cf. זַרְעוֹ *his-seed.*

340. יְשׁוּפְךָ—*he-shall-bruise-thee;* תְּשׁוּפֶנּוּ *thou-shalt-bruise-him.*

a. The Ḳäl Impf. of שׁוּף is יָשׁוּף (3 m. sg.), תָּשׁוּף (2 m. sg.).

b. When the tone is shifted the ā under ׳ and תָ becomes ־ֻ,

c. ךָ with ־ַ = (m.); ־ֶנּוּ is the pron. suffix הוּ *him,* with the connecting syllable נַ־ ; § 71. 2. c. (3) and Note 1.

341. רֹאשׁ—*head,* and עָקֵב *heel* are accusative of specification.

342. הַרְבָּה—*causing-to-be-great:* irreg. for הַרְבֵּה, Hif. Inf.
Abs. of רָבָה *multiply.*

343. אַרְבֶּה—*I-will-cause-to-be-great:* Hif. Impf. 1 sg. of רָבָה,
§ 82. 1. b.

344. עִצְּבוֹנֵךְ—ʿĭṣ-ṣᵉvô-nēẋ—*thy-(f.)-sorrow:*

a. עִצָּבוֹן (root עָצַב, formative addition וֹן, § 103. 3) becomes
עִצְּבוֹן when the tone is shifted, as before the pron. suffix,
§ 109. 1. a.

b. The 2 fem. pron. suf. is ךְ; ־ֵ is the so-called connecting vowel.

345. הֵרוֹנֵךְ—*thy-conception:* הֵרוֹן with ךְ and ־ֵ, see 344. b.

a. Note that ־ֵ in the first syl. is away from the tone and in an
apparently open syl. In reality, dāḡ. f. has been rejected from ר;
hence an original ־ֶ has become ־ֵ in compensation for the loss
of doubling.

346. עֶצֶב—*sorrow:* an a-class Seğolate, § 89. 1.

347. תֵּלְדִי—tē-l·dî—*thou-(f.)-shalt-bring-forth:*

a. For תּוֹלְדִי (cf. תִּקְטְלִי), but וֹ, being weak, drops out and
־ֹ, in an open syllable, becomes ־ֵ, § 80. 2. a.

b. Root יָלַד = וָלַד; Impf. 3 m. sg. יֵלֵד, for יֵוְלֵד.

c. תָ and ׳ are fragments of אַתִּי, the older form of אַתְּ, § 50.
3. c.

348. בָּנִים—vă-nîm—*sons:* irreg. plur. of בֵּן *son.*

349. תְּשׁוּקָתֵךְ—t°šû-ḳâ-θēx—*thy-*(f.)-*desire:*

a. Abs. תְּשׁוּקָה, a feminine formation, § **98**. R.

b. Const. תְּשׁוּקַת, suf. ךְ with ־ֵ; cf. הֶרְנֵךְ (345), עִצְּבוֹנֵךְ (344).

c. Before ־ֵ ךְ, ־ַ in an open syllable becomes ־ָ, § **108**. 2.

350. יִמְשָׁל־בָּךְ—yĭm-šŏl+bâx—*he-shall-rule+in-thee* (f.):

a. יִמְשָׁל for יִמְשֹׁל before Măḳḳēf, § **17**. 2; cf. כֹּל, כָּל־.

b. בָּךְ = *in-thee* (f.); cf. בְּךָ *in-thee* (m.), § **51**. 3.

351. אִשְׁתֶּךָ—'ĭš-tē'-xâ—*thy-wife;* pausal for אִשְׁתְּךָ, § **38**. 1. N.:

a. תְּ indicates the feminine, here attached to אֵשׁ; cf. const אֵשֶׁת.

b. S°ḡōltâ repeated according to § **23**. 6.

c. Another case of a short-vowel (ĕ) in an open syl. under the tone; cf. וַיְבָאֶהָ (256) and הִשִּׁיאַנִי (330).

352. אֲרוּרָה—fem. sg. of אָרוּר (332), Ḳăl Part. pass. of אָרַר *curse.*

353. בַּעֲבוּרֵךְ—bä'-vû-rĕ-xâ—*on-account-of-thee:*

a. A compound preposition, בַּעֲבוּר = *on-account-of, for-the-sake-of.*

b. ךְ with the preceding ־ֵ changed to ־ֵ as in אִשְׁתֶּךָ, § **38**. 1. N.

c. D. l. in בּ because of preceding disjunctive, Tĭfḥâ (ɩ), § **22**. 10

354. תֹּאכֵלֶנָּה—tô'-x•lĕn-nâ(h)—*thou-*(m.)-*shalt-eat-it:*

a. תֹּאכֵל is Ḳăl Impf. 2 sg. masc. of אָכַל eat, § **79**. 1.

b. ־ֶנָּה is for ־ֶנְהָ, just as ־ֶנּוּ (in תְּשׁוּפֶנּוּ) was for ־ֶנְהוּ; note carefully § **71**. 2. c. (3) and N. 1, 2.

2. FORMS FOR SPECIAL STUDY.

תְּשׁוּפֶנּוּ	עִצְּבוֹנֵךְ	יִמְשָׁל־בָּךְ	אִשְׁתֶּךָ	אָרוּר
תֹּאכֵלֶנָּה	תְּשׁוּקָתֵךְ	יַעֲזָב־אִישׁ	בַּעֲבוּרֵךְ	אֲרוּרָה

3. OBSERVATIONS.

144. In pausal forms there stands between the verb and the pronominal suffix a syllable, נ‍ָ‍‍; instead of נְ‍ה‍וּ and נְ‍ה‍ָ , we find נ‍וּ‍ and נ‍ָ‍ה .

145. Between the usual form of the noun and the 2 fem. sing. pron. suffix ך there stands the vowel ־ֵ .This may be called a connecting vowel.

146. The o of the Ḳāl Impf. is changeable (ō), and before Mäḳ-ḳēf ŏ appears instead.

147. The ־ֵ which stands before the suffix ך is a reduction of an original ־ַ , which in pause is restored, and deflected to ĕ.

148. The ־ַ which stands directly before the tone is from an original ä; when the tone is shifted with affixes for gender and number, this ă, if in an open syllable, is reduced to Šᵉwâ.

4. GRAMMAR-LESSON.

1. § **78.** Tabular View,　　Synopses of נָטֵל in various stems.
2. § **78.** 1. a, b,　　　　Loss of נ in Ḳāl Inf. const. and Imv.
3. § **78.** 2. a, b,　　　　Assimilation of נ.
4. § **78.** 2. N. 1,　　　The preformative vowel in Hŏf'äl.
5. § **78.** 2. R's 2, 3,　　The verbs לָקַח and נָתַן.

Note 1.—In the study of this class of verbs, follow the order indicated in previous Lessons, analyzing exhaustively the familiar forms given under § 78. 1, 2 and Remarks 1—3.

Note 2.—Use for practice (1) נָגַד in Hīf=*make known*, (2) נָפַל *fall*, (3) נָגַשׁ *approach*.

5. WORD-LESSON.

1. In the Word-Lists, under List VII., nouns numbered 95—104.
2. Make out a list of the new words in Genesis III. 15—17.

6. EXERCISES.

1. To be translated into Hebrew:—(1) *Approach thou, to approach;* (2) *She will approach, I shall approach;* (3) *They made known* (Hĭ.), *thou* (f.) *wilt make known;* (4) *It will be made known;* (5) *I shall take, to take, take thou, taking;* (6) *Thou shalt give, I shall give, to give, give thou* (m.); (7) *He will fall, he will cause to fall.*

2. To be translated into Hebrew:—(1) *Between thee and between me;* (2) *Between him and between her;* (3) *God made known to the woman that the man should rule over her;* (4) *Thou* (f.) *didst hear the voice of thy husband;* (5) *Cursed is the earth because thou didst eat from this tree;* (6) *I will give thee food all the days of thy lives.*

3. To be translated into English:— (1) ;תְּשׁוּקָתִי אֶל־הָאִישׁ

(2) נָתַתִּי לְךָ כָּל אֲשֶׁר־לִי (3) ;בְּעֶצֶב תֵּלֵד הָאִשָּׁה בָנִים

(4) לָתֵת לֵאלֹהִים הוּא טוֹב (5) ;נֵשׁ אֶל־יְהֹוָה וּבָרֵךְ שְׁמוֹ.

4. To be written in English letters:—*The new words of Genesis III.* 15—17.

5. To be written with points and vowel-signs:—*Genesis III.* 15—17 *from the unpointed text.*

6. To be written out:—Synopses of the verb נגד in the Hĭf. and Hŏf., and of נפך in Ḳăl, Nĭf., Pĭ'ēl, Hĭf., and Hŏf.

7. To be described:— The forms גֶּשֶׁת, גַּע, יִפַּח, יִטַּע, תִּגְּעוּ, הַגֵּיד, הִשִּׁיא, וַיִּפֹּל, יִתֵּן, תֵּת, תֵּן, הֵן, יִקַּח.

7. TOPICS FOR STUDY.

(1) Form of the pronominal suffix הוּ and of the pron. suf. הָ with נְ. (2) The pron. suf. of the 2 f. sg. (3) *Thou* (f.) *shalt bear.* (4) The accent Sⁱ*ğoltâ; its repetition.* (5) *Cursed* (m.), *Cursed* (f.). (6) Change from ־ָ to ĕ. (7) הָ and תָ. (8) Loss of נ.

(9) Assimilation of נ. (10) ־ֵ in sharpened syllables. (11) Synopsis and peculiarities of לָקַח; of נָתַן. (12) Synopses of נָטַל in various stems.

LESSON XXXVII.—GENESIS III. 18-21.

1. NOTES.

355. תַּצְמִיחַ—*she-will cause-to-spring-forth:* Hif. of צָמַח § 76. 1. c. (1).

356. לָךְ—pausal for לְךָ *for-thee* (m.); לָךְ = *for-thee* (f.).

357. וְאָכַלְתָּ—Accent on ultima, because of the Wâw Convers. §§ 21. 4; 70. 3. b.

358. בְּזֵעַת—b*zê-'åθ—*in-sweat-of;* const. of זֵעָה.

359. אַפֶּיךָ—'ăp-pê'-Xå—*thy-nostrils;* from אַף *nose:*
a. Sg. אַף, dual אַפַּיִם, form before ךָ (or הָ) אַפֵּי; cf. חַיֶּיךָ.
b. The Dåḡēš-fŏrtē in פ also serves as Dåḡēš-lēnē, § 13. 2. N. 1.
c. On the disjunctive accent Păštå (׳) see §§ 22. 8; 23. 5, 6.

360. לֶחֶם—*bread;* cf. בֵּית לֶחֶם *Bethlehem.*

361. שׁוּבְךָ—*thy-returning;* Ḳål Inf. const. with pron. suffix: This is a bi-literal verb, with forms differing from the corresponding triliteral forms; § 55. 3.

362. מִמֶּנָּה—*from-her:* for מִמֶּנָה; cf. מִמֶּנּוּ for מִמֶּנָּהוּ, § 51. 5. b.

363. לֻקָּחַתְּ—lŭḳ-ḳå'h-ṭå—*thou-wast-taken,* § 38. 2.

364. תָּשׁוּב—*thou-shalt-return;* cf. תָּמוּת(231) and שׁוּבְךָ(361):
a. Ḳål Impf. 2 m. sg. of the biliteral verb שׁוּב *turn.*
b. תָּקְטֵל is for תַּקְטֵל, the ־ַ being attenuated, and the ־ְ becoming ō under the tone.

c. Note that ă in תָּשׁוּב has been rounded to å in an open syl. before the tone; and that ַ has been lengthened to û.

365. חַוָּה—ẖăw-wå(h)—*Eve;* cf. חִיָה *life.*

366. הוּא—*she.* This is an example of the usage of *Kᵉθív* and *Ḳᵉrî;* see § 19. The consonants here (i. e., the *Kᵉθív*) call for the pointing הוּא; the vowel (i. e., the Ḳᵉrî) requires the reading הִיא. This is the regular way of writing *she* in the Pentateuch; § 50. 3. *a.*

367. הָיְתָה—hå-yᵉθå(h)—*she-was:*

a. Ḳăl Perf. 3 f. sg. of the 'פ laryng., and ל"ה verb הָיָה *be,* § 82. 4.

b. Mёθёǧ with a long vowel before vocal šᵉwâ pretonic, § 18. 2.

368. אִם—but—אִמּוֹ (266): אִם is for אִמֵּם, § 100. 1. *a.*

369. חַי—pausal for חַי; an adjective meaning *living.*

370. כָּתְנוֹת—kõθ-nôθ—*tunics-of;* const. pl. of כְּתֹנֶת.

371. וַיַּלְבִּשֵׁם—wăy-yăl-bî-šēm—*and-he-caused-them-to-put-on:*

a. Hîf. Impf. 3 m. sg. of לָבַשׁ, with suffix ם joined by ֵ.

b. The ַ under בְּ is î, though written defectively.

2. FORMS FOR SPECIAL STUDY.

1. Verbal Forms: — לָקַחַת, שׁוּבְךָ, תֹּאכַל, וְאָכַלְתָּ, תַּצְמִיחַ, וַיַּלְבִּשֵׁם, וַיַּעַשׂ, הָיְתָה, תָּשׁוּב.

2. Nominal Forms:— עֵשֶׂב, לֶחֶם, עָפָר, אָדָם, קוֹץ, עוֹר.

3. PRINCIPLES OF SYNTAX.

בְּזֵעַת אַפֶּיךָ תֹּאכַל לֶחֶם—*In,* or *at the cost of, the sweat of thy nostrils* (=face) *thou shalt eat bread.*

Principle 10.—The preposition בְּ may denote the condition *in* which, or the cost *at* which a thing may be done, i. e., the manner or the price.

4. GRAMMAR-LESSON.

1. § **79.** 1, 2,   The peculiarities of verbs פ״א,

2. § **83.** Tabular View,   Synopses of קָטָא in various stems.

3. § **83.** 1,   Final א in verbs ל״א,

4. § **83.** 2. *a, b,* 3. *a—c,*   Medial א in verbs ל״א,

Note 1.—In the study of verbs פ״א and ל״א, follow the order indicated in previous lessons, analyzing exhaustively the familiar forms given under §§ **79.** 1, 2 and **83.** 1—3, and Remarks.

Note 2.—Use for practice (1) אָמַר *say,* (2) מָצָא *find,* (3) קָרָא *call.*

5. WORD-LESSON.

1. In the Word-Lists, under List VII., nouns numbered 105—115.

2. Make out a list of the new words in Genesis III., 11—21.

6. EXERCISES.

1. To be translated into Hebrew:—(1) *Ye will say, I shall say, she will say, thou* (f.) *wilt say;* (2) *I shall eat, we shall eat, they will eat;* (3) *He will be created, he will cause to call, he was created, he will be caused to call;* (4) *They called, she caused to find, thou* (f.) *wilt find;* (5) *I created, ye were created, thou wast caused to call, we filled* (Pi'ēl); (6) *They* (f.) *will call, ye* (f.) *will be created, call ye* (f.).

2. To be translated into Hebrew:—(1) *The earth caused to sprout forth for man grass and herbs and thorns and thistles;* (2) *We found in the field the fruit which God commanded* (יְוָה) *not to eat;* (3) *The man shall die, and unto the dust he shall return;* (4) *I shall call the name of my wife Eve;* (5) *I have found my mother;* (6) *Eve was the wife of* (אִשֶּׁת) *Adam, and the mother of all living;* (7) *Adam was Eve's husband.*

3. To be translated into English:—(1) מִי הָיָה אִישׁ חַוָּה ;(2)

לָקַח הָאָדָם (3) ;בָּרָא אֱלֹהִים אֶת־הָאָדָם וְאִשְׁתּוֹ וַיַּלְבִּשֵׁם

יָמוּת כֹּל אֲשֶׁר (4) מִן־הֶעָפָר; (5) עָפָר אָנֹכִי וְאֶל־עָפָר אָשׁוּב

בְּאַפָּיו נִשְׁמַת חַיִּים.

4. To be written in English letters:—*The new words of Genesis
III.* 18—21.

5. To be written with points and vowel-signs:—*Genesis III.* 18—
21 *from the unpointed text.*

6. To be written out:—Synopses of אָמַר in the Ḳål and Hīf.
stems, of בָּרָא in Ḳål and Nīf., and of מָצָא in Pī'ēl and Hīf.

7. To be described:—The Forms בָּרָא ,נֹאכַל ,תֹּאכֵל ,וַיֹּאמֶר,

בְּרֵאת ,מָלֵאת ,בְּרָאתִי ,נָשָׁאךְ ,נָשָׂא ,מִלְּאוּ ,יִקְרָא ,תִּדְשָׁא ,יְקָרָא,
תִּקְרֶאנָה.

7. TOPICS FOR STUDY.

(1) The primary form of קָטַל. (2) The form שׁוּב. (3) אֵם,
אִמּוֹ. (4) Peculiarities of verbs פ"א. (5) Inflection of אָטַל in
Ḳål Impf. (6) Peculiarities of verbs ל"א. (7) Synopses of קָטָא
in various stems. (8) Inflection of קָטָא in Ḳål Perf., in other
Perfects, in Impf's and Imv's.

LESSON XXXVIII.—GENESIS III. 22-24.

1. NOTES.

372. הֵן—hēn—*behold:* same as הִנֵּה (145).

373. כְּאַחַד מִמֶּנּוּ—*like-one-of*[*from*]*-us:*

a. אַחַד is the construct of אֶחָד; here followed by a preposition.

b. כִּמֶּנּוּ is the form of כִּן with נוּ *us*, § **51.** 5. *a;* cf. כִּמֶּנּוּ for
כִּמֶנְהוּ,

374. לָדַעַת—*to-know:* Ḳâl Inf. const. of יָדַע *know,* § **80. 2.** (3); לְ, § **47. 5.**

375. וְחָי—wâ-ḥây—*and-*(he-should)-*live:*

a. וְ is Wâw Conversive with Perf., the ָ being pretonic, § **70. 2. b.**

b. חָי is Ḳâl Perf. 3 m. sg. of the ע"ע verb חָיָי *live,* § **85. 1.**

376. וַיִּשְׁלָחֵהוּ — wây-šăl-lᵊḥē-hû — *and-*(= therefore)-(he)-*sent-him:*

a. D. f. of Wâw Convers. omitted from י because it has not a full vowel.

b. Pī‘ēl Impf. 3 m. sg. of the ל' laryngeal verb שָׁלַח *send;* corresponding form, יִקְטְלֵהוּ.

c. The pron. suffix הוּ joined to the verb by the vowel ֵ.

377. לַעֲבֹד—*to-till:* Ḳâl Inf. const., §§ **74. 3.** *a;* **47. 3.**

378. אֲשֶׁר.... מִשָּׁם—*which....from-there,* = *whence.*

379. וַיְגָרֶשׁ—wăy-ḡắ'-rĕš—*and-he-drove-out:*

a. This is for וַיְגַרֵּשׁ, like וַיְקַדֵּשׁ, or וַיִּקְטֵל; but

b. The י, having only a šᵊwâ, drops its D. f., while ר rejects its D. f., and ַ under ג becomes ָ in compensation.

c. The accent being drawn to the penult by וַ, ֶ appears instead of ֵ.

d. Pī‘ēl Impf. 3 masc. sg. of the ע' laryngeal verb גָרֵשׁ *drive out,* § **75. 1.** *a.*

380. וַיַּשְׁכֵּן—wăy-yăš-kēn—*and-he-caused-to-dwell;* cf. וַיַבְדֵּל:

a. Hīf. Impf. 3 m. sg. (with ֵ, not ִ_) from שָׁכֵן *dwell,* § **70. 3.** R.

381. הַכְּרֻבִים—hăk-kᵊrû-vîm—*the-cherubim;* ַ for ן; singular כְּרוּב.

382. הַמִּתְהַפֶּכֶת —hăm-mîθ-hăp-pĕ-xĕθ—*the-*(one)-*turning-itself:* cf. מְרַחֶפֶת, § **106. 2.** *b.*

383. לִשְׁמֹר—lĭš-mōr—*to-keep;* cf. לְשָׁמְרָה (223), and לַעֲבֹד
(377).

2. FORMS FOR SPECIAL STUDY.

1. Verbal Forms:—וַיִּירֶשׁ, לָקַח, וַיְשַׁלְּחֵהוּ, וָחַי, יִשְׁלַח, לָדַעַת,
מִתְהַפֶּכֶת, וַיִּשְׁכֵּן.

2. Nominal Forms:—דֶּרֶךְ, חֶרֶב, לַהַט, כְּרֻבִים, עֵדֶן, עוֹלָם, אֶחָד.

3. PRINCIPLES OF SYNTAX.

וְעַתָּה פֶּן־יִשְׁלַח יָדוֹ וְלָקַח....וְאָכַל....וָחַי—*And now, lest he
put forth his hand and take and eat and live.*

Principle 11.—In the narration of actions which are to occur in
the future, or which can be only conditionally realized, the first
verb is in the Imperfect while those that follow are in the Perfect
and connected with the preceding verb by means of *Wăw Convers.*
(§ 70. 1. *b.*)

4. GRAMMAR-LESSON.

1. § 82. Tabular View, Synopses of קָטָה in Ḳăl, Pī'ēl, Hīθp. and
                      Hīf. stems.

2. § 82. 1. *a—f,*   Treatment of the 3d radical when *final.*

3. § 82. 2,   Treatment of 3d rad. bef. vowel-additions.

4. § 82. 3. *a—e,*   Treatment of 3d rad. bef. cons.-additions.

5. § 82. 4,   The 3 sg. fem. of Perfects.

6. § 82. 5. *a,b*(1)—(8),   Short forms (*to be read*).

Note 1.—In the study of verbs ל״ה, follow the order indicated
in previous Lessons, analyzing exhaustively the familiar forms given
under § 82. 1—5.

Note 2.—Use for practice (1) גָּלָה *reveal,* (2) בָּנָה *build,* (3)
כָּלָה *complete.*

5. *WORD-LESSON.*

1. In the Word-Lists, under List II., verbs numbered 51—60.

2. Make out a list of the new words in Genesis III. 22—24.

6. *EXERCISES.*

1. To be translated into Hebrew:—(1) *He built, he will build, building;* (2) *He commanded* (Pī'ēl), *he will command, commanding, command thou;* (3) *To command* (abs.), *to build, to finish* (Pī'ēl); (4) *I commanded* (Pī'ēl), *we built, thou didst cause to reveal;* (5) *We finished* (Pi'ēl), *ye built, they* (f.) *will build;* (6) *Th'y built, they* (m.) *will command, they caused to build;* (7) *She was, she made, she will finish, they will cause to reveal, thou* (f.) *wilt build.*

2. To be translated into Hebrew:—(1) *I shall put forth my hand and take the fruit and eat;* (2) *The man knew good and evil;* (3) *God drove forth* (Pī'ēl) *the man from Eden because he did that which God had commanded him not to do;* (4) *The man will serve the ground whence he was taken;* (5) *Behold the sword turning itself;* (6) *The cherubim and the sword will keep the way of the tree of life.*

3. To be translated into English: — (1) הִשְׁכִּין אֱלֹהִים מִקֶּדֶם

הִבְדִּיל אֱלֹהִים בֵּין הָרַע וּבֵין הַטּוֹב (2) ;לְגַן־עֵדֶן אֶת־הַכְּרֻבִים

צִוָּה אֱלֹהִים אֶת־הָאָדָם (4) ;לֹא טוֹב הֱיוֹת הָאָדָם לְבַדּוֹ (3)

גֵּרֵשׁ אֱלֹהִים מֵעֵדֶן אֶת־הָאִישׁ וְאֶת־ (5) ;לַעֲבֹד אֶת־הָאֲדָמָה

אִשְׁתּוֹ .

4. To be written in English letters:—*The new words of Genesis III. 22—24.*

5. To be written with points and vowel-signs:—*Genesis 22—24 from the unpointed text.*

6. To be written out:—Synopses of בנה .

7. To be described:—The Forms בָּכֹה, עָשֹׂה, יַעֲלֶה, הִשְׁקָה,

תַּעֲשֶׂינָה, עָשִׂיתָ, הָיוּ, פְּרוּ, יֵרְדוּ, עָשֶׂה, רְאוֹת, עֲשׂוֹת,

הָוָה, הָיְתָה, וַיִּבֶן, וַיְכַל, וַיְצַו.

7. TOPICS FOR STUDY.

(1) The Pī'ēl, Hif'īl, and Hiθpā'ēl stems of קָטָה. (2) The
defective writing of וֹ. (3) Wâw Conversive with the Perfect. (4)
Wâw Conversive with the Imperfect. (5) The form לָדַעַת. (6)
The third radical of verbs called לֹ"ה. (7) The treatment of
this radical when final, before vowel-additions, and before consonant-
additions. (8) The Perf. 3 sg. fem. (9) Short forms. (10) Synopses
of קָטָה in Kāl, Pī'ēl, Hiθp. and Hīf. stems.

LESSON XXXIX.—GENESIS IV. 1-4.

1. NEW WORDS.*

1. הָרָה, (2) קָנָה, (3) אֵת (preposition), (4) יָסַף, (5) אָח,
(6) בְּכוֹרָה, (7) רָעָה, (8) צֹאן, (9) קֵץ, (10) מִנְחָה, (11) הֶבֶל, (6)
(12) שָׁעָה, (13) חֵלֶב.

2. NOTES.

V. 1. וַתַּהַר for תֶּהֱרֶה, §§ 74. 2. a; 74. 3. b, d; 82. 1. b and
5. b. (5).— וַתֵּלֶד, §§ 80. 2. a (1); 70. 3. a. (3).— קָנִיתִי, § 82. 3.
b.—אֶת־יׂ. preposition with.

V. 2. וַתֹּסֶף, for וַתּוֹסֶף, §§ 80. 3. b; 65. 5. b. (1); 70. 3. a.
(2) and (3). — לָלֶדֶת, §§ 47. 5; 80. 2. a. (3). — אָחִיו, §§ 105. 3;
108. 1. b. (2); הוּ = וֹ his, § 44. 4. c.—הֶבֶל, for הֶבֶל, § 38. 2.—
רֹעֵה, abs. רֹעֶה, §§ 82. 1. c; 107. 3.

V. 3. יָמִים, plur. of יוֹם.—וַיָּבָא, § 86. 1. d.—לִיהֹוָה, to be read לַאדֹנָי, § 47. R. 2.

V. 4. הֵבִיא, § 86. 1. d, and 3. c.– מִבְּכֹרוֹת, § 48. 1; 106. 3; sg. בְּכוֹרָה, § 91. 1. a, and 2. — וּמֵחֶלְבֵהֶן (û-mē-ḥĕl-vē-hĕn), §§ 49. 2; 48. 2; חֵלֶב (ĕ defective), const. plur. of חֵלֶב, § 109. 4. e; § 51. 1. c.—וַיִּשַׁע, for יִשְׁעָה, § 82. 5. b. (5).—מִנְחָתוֹ, from מִנְחָה, §§ 106. 2. a. (2); 108. 2.

3. PRINCIPLES OF SYNTAX.

V. 2.—וַתֹּסֶף לָלֶדֶת—And she added to bear=and again she bore.

Principle 12.—when the second of two verbs expresses the principal idea, the first merely modifying it, the second is often an infinitive depending upon the first.

4. GRAMMAR-LESSON.

1. § 82. Tabular View, Synopses of קָטָה in Nif., Pǔ'ăl and Hif. stems.

2. Paradigm Ḳ (pp. Inflection of קָטָה in all stems. 204, 205),

Note:—In the study of these forms use for practice, שָׁנָה change, פָּנָה turn, בָּכָה weep.

5. EXERCISES.

1. To be translated into Hebrew:—It (f.) was built; (2) She was caused to turn; (3) They were completed (Pǔ'ăl); (4) You (f.) were caused to weep; (5) Turning, finishing, being built, being caused to turn; (6) Turn ye (f.), be ye (m.) finished, cause ye (m.) to build.

---

* Consult the Hebrew-English Vocabulary, or a Hebrew Lexicon. Be prepared to pronounce, transliterate, describe and define each word. Let this work be done before proceeding further in the study of the Lesson.

2. To be translated into Hebrew:—(1) *The woman conceived
and bore a son;* (2) *And the woman spoke again;* (3) *Abel was a
shepherd and Cain was a tiller of the ground;* (4) *Cain brought an
offering to God;* (5) *Eve was the wife of Adam and the mother of
Cain and Abel;* (6) *Abel gave to God from the firstlings of his flock.*

3. To be written with points and vowel-signs:—*Gen. IV. 1—4
from the unpointed text.*

4. To be written out:—(1) *Synopses of* בָּכָה *in Ḳȧl, Nȋf., Hȋf.
and Hȯf. stems. and of* כָּלָה *in Pȋʿēl and Puʿȧl stems.*

5. To be described:—The Forms מִשְׁנֶה, בָּנוֹת, כָּלָה, יִבְנוּ,
נִשְׁנִיתֶם, and בְּנִינָה, יִבְנוּ.

6. TOPICS FOR STUDY.

(1) Absence of הַ from לְ״ה forms. (2) The vowel of the
perfect of לְ״ה verbs before consonant-additions. (3) The ־וֹת of
Infin. cst. of verbs לְ״ה. (4) The ־י of אָח before suffixes. (5)
The הַ and הַ of verbs לְ״ה. (6) The preposition לְ before
אֱלֹהִים and יְהֹוָה.

LESSON XL.—GENESIS IV. 5-8.

1. NEW WORDS.

נָשָׂא (6), יָטַב (5), אִם (4), הֲלוֹא (3), לָמָּה (2), חָרָה (1),
פֶּסַח (7), חֲטָאת (8), רָבַץ (9), הוּם (10), הָרַג (11).

2. NOTES.

V. 5. וַיִּחַר, for יְחָרֶה, §§ 82. 5. *b*. (5); 70. 3. (3).—לְקַיִן,
on repeated accent, § 23. 6.— וַיִּפְּלוּ, Méθēǧ with a sharpened syl-

lable; on assim. of נ, § 78. 2. a.— פָּנָיו (pâ-nâw), § 12. 3; on יו‗,
§ 108. 3. d; cf. אָפָיו (185).

V. 6. מָה = לְמָה with לְ, the D. f. being firmative, § 15. 6.—
חָרָה, with accent on penult, § 21. 1.— לְךָ, pausal for לְךָ, § 51.
3 (Tab. View).—פָּנֶיךָ (fâ-né'-χâ), on ‗י (é), § 108. 3. c.

V. 7. הֲלוֹא (h‑lô') = nonne, § 46. 1; this ô is for â, § 30. 6.—
תֵּיטִיב, for תֵּיטִיב (cf. תַּקְטִיל), but ‗ becomes ê (‗י) § 30.
4. b; Hîf. Impf. 2 m. sg. of יָטַב, § 81. 2;—שְׂאֵת, a seemingly
irreg. Ḳâl Inf. const. of נָשָׂא, § 78. 1. a.— וְאֵלֶיךָ, § 23. 6; prep.
אֶל treated as a noun in plur. before the suffix ךָ, cf. פָּנֶיךָ in
v. 6, § 108. 3. c; the ⁻ָ becomes ⁻ָ in an open syl.— תְּשׁוּקָתוֹ,
§§ 108. 2; 18. footnote.— תִּמְשָׁל־בּוֹ, §§ 17. 2; 51. 3. a.

V. 8. אָחִיו, see in v. 2.— בִּהְיוֹתָם (bĭh-yô-θâm), on ⁻, 47. 2;
on Méθĕğ, § 18. 5; on וֹת, § 82. 1. e; ם‗, as in בְּהִבָּרְאָם (167).
— וַיָּקָם (wăy-yâ'-ḳŏm), Ḳâl Impf. 3 m. sg. of קוּם; paradigm-form,
יָקוּם, but see § 86. 1 e. Rm; the ⁻ָ under ק, in an unaccented
closed syl., must be ŏ.— וַיְהַרְגֵהוּ, on ⁻ under י, § 74. 2. a; on
⁻ָ under ה, § 74. 3. d; on ⁻, § 71. 2. b (1); on נ, 16. 2; on ⁻,
§ 71. 2. c. (2).

3. PRINCIPLES OF SYNTAX.

V. 7.— הֲלוֹא אִם תֵּיטִיב שְׂאֵת:—*Is there not a lifting up, if
thou doest well?*

Principle 13.—A question expecting an affirmative answer is
introduced by הֲלֹא (= *nonne?*).

4. *GRAMMAR-LESSON*

1. § **84.**   Bi-literal verbs.

2. § **85.** Tabular View.   Synopses of קָטַט in Ḳāl, Nīf. and Hīf.
                                 stems.

3. § **85.** 1—2.   The doubling of the 2nd radical.

4. § **85.** 3.   The separating vowels.

5. § **85.** 4.   The changes in stem-vowels.

6. § **85.** 5.   The Preformative vowels.

7. Paradigm M.   Inflection of קָטַט in Ḳāl, Nīf, Hīf and
                                Hōf. stems.

Note 1.—Use for practice (1) חָלַל *begin*, (2) סָבַב *encompass*,
(3) קָלַל *be light* (i. e. not heavy).

5. *EXERCISES.*

1. To be translated into Hebrew:—(1) *He began* (Hīf.), *to begin,
beginning;* (2) *Encompassing, he will encompass, he was caused to
encompass, he will be encompassed;* (3) *He will be light, he will
make light;* (4) *Cause to encompass, encompass thou, he caused to
encompass, be thou encompassed.*

2. To be translated into Hebrew:—(1) *The countenance of Cain
fell, because God looked not with favor upon his offering;* (2)
Why was Cain angry (Heb., *why was it kindled to Cain?*); (3) *Did
not God say, let there be light?* (4) *Did not Abel bring to God
from the firstlings of his flock?* (5) *Did not Cain kill Abel?* (6)
Why did Cain kill Abel? (7) *God will bless him who shall do well.*

To be written with points and vowel-signs:—*Genesis IV.* 5—8
from the unpointed text.

4. To be written out:—Inflection of the Ḳāl Perf. and Impf. of
סָבַב and בְּדַד; of the Nīf. Perf. and Impf., of מָרַד, of the
Hīf. Perf., Impf. and Imv. of קָלַל; of the Hōf. Perf. and Impf.
of חלל.

5. To be described: — The Forms תָּבֹזוּ, הָסֵבִּי, הֶחֱלָה, קֵלוּ,

גִּלְגַּלְתִּי, סְבִינָה, תְּסֻבֶּינָה, הֲסִבּוֹת, נְקַלּוֹתָ, סַבּוֹתָ,

6. TOPICS FOR STUDY.

(1) Repetition of post-positive accents. (2) The ending ־ֵינוּ. (3)
D. f. firmative. (4) The ending ־ֵיךְ. (5) הֲלֹא. (6) The ending
וֹת in ל"ה Inf. construct. (7) change of ־ֵ to ־ַ. (8) ע"ע stems
before vowel-additions. (9) ע"ע stems before consonant-additions.

LESSON XLI.—GENESIS IV. 9—12.

1. NEW WORDS.

(1) דָּם, (2) צָעַק, (3) פָּצָה, (4) פֶּה, (5) יָד, (6) כֹּחַ, (7) נָע
(nâ‘), (8) נָד (nâd).

2. NOTES.

V. 9. וַיֹּאמֶר, § 79. 2.— אָחִיךָ, § 108. 1. b. (2).— יָדַעְתִּי, a
פ"י and ל' laryng. verb, cf. קָטַלְתִּי; on the accent ־ִ, § 24. 4.—
הֲשֹׁמֵר, §§ 46. 1; 68. 1. a.

V. 10. מֶה עָשִׂיתָ, §§ 54. d; 82. 3. b.— דְּמֵי, sg. abs., דָּם,
const. דַּם, plur. abs. דָּמִים, const. דְּמֵי, §§ 109. 2. b; 106. 4. b.—
צֹעֲקִים, §§ 68. 1. a; 109. 3. R. 3; plur. in agreement with דְּמֵי,
not אֵלַי—קוֹל, cf. אֵלֶיךָ in v. 7; really a plural noun.

V. 11. אָרוּר אַתָּה, §§ 68. 1. c; 38. 2, 3.— פָּצְתָה, §§ 18. 2;
82. 4. and N.— פִּיהָ, from פֶּה, §§ 105. 3; 108. 1. b. (2).— לָקַחַת
§ 47. 5; Ḳâl Inf. const. of לָקַח, § 78. 2. R. 2; on ־ַ under ח instead of ־ֵ, § 89. 2. a, מִיָּדְךָ, pausal for מִיָּדְךָ, §§ 38. 1. N.; 108.
1. R. 2.

V. 12. תְּעָבֵד, corresponding to הִקְטִיל ; on ־־, § 74. 2. a; on
־־, § 74. 3. b; on ō, § 64. 1.— תֵּסֶף (ộô-sēf), for תּוֹסֵף; on ô,
§ 80. 3. b; on ־־ , § 65. 5. b. (1)— תֵּת־כֹּהָה, on Mêθë̈g̊, § 18. 4; on
־־, lowered from ־־, § 78. 2. R. 3. (1); on הַ_, § 51. 3. a.—
נָע וָנָד (nâʻ wå-nâd,) on the ־ַ (â) under נ in each case, § 86. g;
the roots are נוּעַ and נוּד, and these forms, Ḳăl Part's act.—
תֶּהְיֶה, §§ 74. 3. N.; 18. 5; 82. 1. b.

3. PRINCIPLES OF SYNTAX.

V. 9.— הֲשֹׁמֵר אָחִי אָנֹכִי—Am I keeping my brother, or, my brother's keeper?

Principle 14.—A question asking for information, without neces-
sarily implying the affirmative or negative character of the answer,
is introduced by הֲ.

4. GRAMMAR AND WORD-LESSON.

1. § 85. 6 a—d.   Intensive stems in ע״ע verbs.
2. Paradigm L.   Inflection of Intensive stems in ע״ע verbs.
   (p. 206).
3. § 85. 7.   Place of accent in ע״ע verbs.
4. Word-Lists,   Verbs numbered 61—70 in Lists II and III.

Note:—After a study of the principles here given, write out a
full paradigm of סבב in Ḳăl, Nĭf., Hĭf. and Pôlēl.

5. EXERCISES.

1. To be translated into Hebrew:—(1) *She encompassed, they
caused to encompass, thou (f.) wilt encompass, they will be encompassed;* (2) *Thou didst encompass, I caused to encompass, we were
encompassed, thou wast caused to encompass;* (3) *Thou wast light,
thou shalt encompass, I have encompassed, I shall cause to encompass;* (4) *Cause ye to encompass, they (f.) will encompass, ye (f.)
will cause to encompass, encompass ye (f.).*

2. To be translated into Hebrew:—(1) *I do not know the name of the man;* (2) *Am I a ruler?* (3) *Who did this (f.)?* (4) *Cursed am I from the ground;* (5) *The blood* (pl.) *of thy brother hath cried out to God;* (6) *Thou shalt not till the ground;* (7) *Cain was a wanderer and a fugitive.*

3. To be written with points and vowel-signs:—*Genesis IV. 9—12 from the unpointed text.*

4. To be written out:—Synopses of סבב in Ḳäl, Nif. and Hîf., of חקק in Ḳäl and Pôlēl, and of קלל in Nîf. and Hîf.

5. To be described:—The forms יֵקַל‏ ,הֵסֵב‏ ,יָמַּד‏ ,סֹב‏ ,יָסוֹב‏ ,חַי‏, נָסַב‏ ,הוּחַל‏ ,מֵסֵב‏ ,הֵחֵל.

6. TOPICS FOR STUDY.

(1) The ô in the Ḳäl Impf. of verbs פ״א. (2) The î of אָח‏ ,אָב, and פֶּה before suf. (3) Hē Interrogative. (4) The î of ל״ה Perf's. (5) The Perf. 3 f. sg. of verbs ל״ה. (6) Ḳäl Inf. const. of verbs פ״ן. (7) ־ in pause. (8) Ḳäl Impf. of verbs פ laryngeal. (9) The ô of פ״ו Hîf'îls.

LESSON XLII.—GENESIS IV. 13—17.

1. NEW WORDS.

(1) עָוֹן or עָווֹן, (2) סָתַר, (3) לָכֵן, (4) שְׁבְעָתַיִם, (5) נָקַם, (6) נָכָה, (7) יָשַׁב, (8) עִיר, (9) שֵׁם.

2. NOTES.

V. 13.   גָּדוֹל, pl. גְּדוֹלִים; on formation, § 91. 1. *a.*— עֲוֹנִי, from עָווֹן, of same formation as גָּדוֹל; before י_ָ_yields to _ָ_, § 109. 1. *a.*—מִנְּשׂוֹא, the ō being incorrectly written וֹ; מִן indicates comparison.

V. 14. גֵּרַשְׁתָּ, for גֵּרַשְׁתְּ, § 75. 1. *a;* synopsis?—וּמִפָּנֶיךָ, §§ 49.

2; 48.1; on ◌ֶ, § 108. 3. *c.*—אֶסָּתֵר, §§ 72. 2;65. 1. *a;*synopsis?—

וְהָיִיתִי, § 82. 3. *b;* on וְ, § 70. 2. b.— מֹצְאִי, part. מֹצֵא with ◌ֵ; on

change of ◌ַ to ◌ֵ, § 109. 3. R. 3.— יַהַרְגֵנִי, composed of יַהֲרֹג ◌ֵ,

and נִי; on change of ō to ◌ַ, and on ◌ַ, § 71. 2. *b.* (1), and *c.*

(2); on change of ◌ַ to ◌ַ, § 74. 3. *c.*

V. 15. יָקֻם, pausal for יָקֻם; on D. f. in ק (for נ), § 78. 2. *b;*

on ◌ַ in Hôf., § 78. 2. N. 1.— וַיִּישֶׂם, for וַיָּשֶׂם, § 70. 3. *a.* (3); ◌ַ

for ◌ֶ, § 86. 1. *d;* root, שִׂים (ע״י).—הַכּוֹת־אֹתוֹ; on Méθĕǧ, § 18.

4; on D. f. in כּ (for נ), § 78. 2. *b;* on הַ, § 58. 5. *b;* on וֹת, § 82.

1. *e;* on אֹת, § 51. 2.—מְצָאוֹ, cf. מֹצְאִי in v. 14.

V. 16. וַיֵּצֵא (wăy-yê-ṣē'); for וַיִּצֵא, but ו is dropped and ī be-

comes ê, § 80. 2. *a.* (1); on ◌ַ under צ, § 64. 3; on Méθĕǧ, § 18.

6; on the accented penult, § 21. 3.—מִלְּפָנֵי, (1) מִן, (2)לְ, (3) פְּנֵי

— וַיֵּשֶׁב, for וַיִּשֵׁב, but ו is dropped, and ī becomes ê, § 80. 2. *a.*

(1); on shifting of tone, § 21. 3.

V. 17. וַיֵּדַע, for וַיִּדַע, but ו is dropped, and ī becomes ê, §

80. 2. *a.* (1); on ◌ַ under ע instead of ◌ַ, § 80. 2. *a.* (1).—וַתַּהַר,

see note on v. 1.—וַתֵּלֶד, for וַתִּלֶד, but ו is dropped and ī be-

comes ê, § 80. 2. *a.* (1); on shifting of tone, § 21. 3.—וַיְהִי בֹנֶה עִיר,

on the shifting of tone in the case of בֹנֶה, § 21. 1; on D. l. in כּ,

§ 12. 3.

3. PRINCIPLES OF SYNTAX.

V. 14, גֵּרַשְׁתָּ אֹתִי הַיּוֹם—*thou hast driven me out this day.*

Principle 15.—The article often has its original demonstrative

force.

V. 15.— כָּל־הֹרֵג קַיִן —*Any one killing Cain.*

Principle 16.— כֹּל is used to make prominent a single one from among a plurality.

4. GRAMMAR-LESSON.

1. § **86.** Tabular View.   Synopses of Ḳăl, Nĭf., Hĭf. and Hŏf. stems of Middle-Vowel verb.

2. § **86.** 1. *a, b, d, e, g.*   The treatment of the stem-vowel in Middle-Vowel verbs.

3. § **86.** 2. *a, b, c,*   The separating vowels.

4. § **86.** 3. *a, b, c,* 4.   The Preformative vowels.

5. § **86.** 6.   The place of the tone.

Note:—Use for practice, קוּם *to rise,* שׁוּב *to turn,* and כוּן *to prepare.*

5. EXERCISES.

1. To be translated into Hebrew:—(1) *He will rise, thou shalt turn, turn thou, he will die, we shall die;* (2) *He caused to die, he was caused to turn, he will cause to prepare;* (3) *I caused to rise, ye* (m.) *caused to rise, they caused to rise;* (4) *Thou didst cause to turn, we shall cause to rise, I shall be caused to rise, she rose;* (5) *Ye turned, I rose, they will rise, we shall rise;* (6) *Rise thou* (f.), *rise ye* (f.), *she was risen* (Nĭf.), *they were risen;* (7) *Thou shalt return, she was caused to return.*

2. To be translated into Hebrew:—(1) *God is greater than man;* (2) *I drove him out from the garden of Eden;* (3) *The woman will be hidden from the face of God;* (4) *Any one killing me shall die;* (5) *Any one finding him will kill Cain;* (6) *Cain was avenged seven-fold;* (7) *And Cain went out from Eden, and dwelt in the land of Nod.*

3. To be written with points and vowel-signs:—*Genesis IV.* 13—17 *from the unpointed text.*

4. To be written out:—The inflection in Ḳäl of קוּם , כוּן ; in

Nif., of מוּל ,מוּג; in Hif. and Höf., of שׁוּב ,רוּם.

5. To be described:—The Forms נְקוּמוֹת ,הֲקִימָה ,יְקוּמוּ ,קָמוּ,

תְּשׁוּבֵינָה ,תָּשֵׁבְנָה ,אָשִׁיב ,יָקוּמוּ ,שַׁבְתָּ ,שַׁבְתָּ ,הַשִׁיבוֹת.

6. *TOPICS FOR STUDY.*

(1) Nouns with the original vowels ă—â (= ô). (2) The Pi'ēl of

verbs ע״ laryngeal. (3) The ◌ֶ (= ê) before suffixes ךָ and הָ,

and before the plur. fem. נָה. (4) The ◌ֶ of ל״ה Perfects. (5)

The change of ◌ֵ before ◌ֵ to ◌ֵ. (6) The Höf. of verbs פ״ן. (7)

The וֹת of ל״ה Inf's const. (8) The הֶ (ê) of ל״ה participles.

(9) The Article used as a demonstrative. (10) The separating vowel

of Middle-Vowel verbs in Perfect and Imperfect.

LESSON XLIII.—GENESIS IV. 18-22.

1. *NEW WORDS.*

(1) שְׁתַּיִם (const. שְׁתֵּי), (2) אֹהֶל, (3) מִקְנֶה (4) תָּפַשׂ, (5)

בַּרְזֶל, (5) עוּגָב, (6) לָטַשׁ, (8) חָרָשׁ (9) נְחֹשֶׁת, (10) כִּנּוֹר,

(11) אָחוֹת.

2. *NOTES.*

V. 18.   וַיִּוָּלֵד, root וָלַד (= יָלַד); on D. f. in וָ, §§ 13. 2; 80.

3. *a;* on the form, § 65. 1. *a;* cor. form,יָקְטֵל.—אֶת־עִירָד, the sign

of the def. object with a subject, see Principle 17 (below).

V. 19.   וַיִּקַּח, for וַיִּלְקַח; ל assim. like נ, § 78. 2. R. 2; on ◌ֵ

under קֵ, § 76. 1. *a.*—שְׁתֵּי (štê, *not* š•tê), the š•wâ silent; the only case in the language of a syllable beginning with two consonants without an intervening half-vowel; fem. of שְׁנֵי, const. of שְׁנַיִם —

נָשִׁים, cf. (1) אִישׁ man, (2) אִשָּׁה woman, (3) אֲנָשִׁים men, (4) אֵשֶׁת wife-of, (5) נְשֵׁי wives-of.—הַשֵּׁנִית .... הָאַחַת, cf. the masc. forms הָאֶחָד .... הַשֵּׁנִי.

V. 20.   וַתֵּלֶד, cf. note on v. 17.—אֲבִי, const. of אָב; on יַ, §108. 1. b. (2); on accent, §24. 5. a.—יָשַׁב, like קְטֹל.—אֹהֶל, a u-class

Seğolate, cf. בָּקָר, §89. 1 c; here used collectively.—מִקְנֶה (mĭk-nê(h)), meaning substance, cattle, and governed by some word understood signifying possession; on form, §96. 2; on meaning of form, §97. 2.

V. 21.   אָחִיו, see note on v. 2.—תֹּפֵשׂ, like קְטֹל.—קְנוֹר, on form, §93. 4. c.—עוּגָב, on form, §92. 3.

V. 22.   יָלְדָה, §60. R. 3. b; Synopsis in Ḳal, §80. 2. a.—לְטֹשׁ, like קְטֹל. — חָרָשׁ, like קְטֹל.—וַאֲחוֹת, const. of אָחוֹת, and וְ with ־ְ according to §49. 3.

3. PRINCIPLES OF SYNTAX.

V. 18.   וַיִּוָּלֵד לַחֲנוֹךְ אֶת־עִירָד—And Irad was born to Enoch.

Principle 17.—The subject of a passive verb, which would be the object of the same verb if it were active, is often preceded by אֵת, the sign of the object.

V. 20.—יֹשֵׁב אֹהֶל וּמִקְנֶה—Dwelling in tent(s) and (possessing) cattle.

Principle 18.—Two nouns are sometimes connected with a verb, when, strictly speaking, only the former is applicable in meaning (zeugma).

4. GRAMMAR- AND WORD-LESSON.

1. Paradigm M.	Inflection of Pôlēl and Pôlăl stems of middle-vowels verbs.
2. § **86.** 5. a, b, c, d,	Intensive stems of middle-vowel verbs.
3. § **86.** 8.	Interchange of forms between ע״ן and middle-vowel verbs.
4. Word-Lists,	Verbs numbered 71—80 in List III.

5. EXERCISES.

1. To be translated into Hebrew:—(1) Inflection of קוּם throughout the Pôlēl stem; (2) Synopsis of רוּם in the Hîf. stem; (3) Inflection of קוּם throughout the Hôf. stem; (4) Synopsis of שׁוּב in the Ḳăl stem; (5) Synopsis of מוּל in the Nîf. stem.

2. To be translated into Hebrew:—(1) *I will know the name of that city;* (2) *Cain was building the city Enoch;* (3) *Cain and Abel were born to Adam;* (4) *Lamech had* (= *to Lamech were*) *two wives;* (5) *Adam was the father of Cain, and Eve was his mother;* (6) *Abel was the son of Eve, and Tubal Cain was the son of Zillah;* (7) *Father, father-of, mother, son, daughter, husband, wife, wife-of, brother, brother-of, sister, sister-of.*

3. To be written with points and vowel-signs:—*Genesis IV. 18-22 from the unpointed text.*

4. To be described.—וַיֵּשֶׁב, תָּקְמָנָה, הַשִּׁיבוֹת, נָכוֹן, נְקוּמוֹת, תְּשׁוּבֶינָה.

6. TOPICS FOR STUDY.

(1) אֶת with the subject. (2) Assim. of ל. (3) The pronunciation of שֶׁתִי. (4) The words meaning *man, men, woman, women, wife-of, wives-of.* (5) Separating vowels in ע״ן and middle-vowel verbs. (6) The ô of Ḳăl act. Part's. (7) U-class Seğolates. (8) Nouns formed by means of preformative מ. (9) The meanings of nouns with pref. מ.

LESSON XLIV.—GENESIS IV. 23-26.

1. *NEW WORDS.*

(1) נָשִׁים, irreg. plur. of אִשָּׁה, (2) אָזַן, (3) אָמְרָה, (4) פָּצַע,

(5) יֶלֶד, (6) חַבְּרָה or חַבּוּרָה, (7) שִׁבְעִים, (8) שִׁבְעָה, (9) עוֹד,

(10) בֵּין, (11) שִׁית, (12) אַחֵר, (13) חָלָל.

2. *NOTES.*

V. 23. לְנָשָׁיו (lᵉnâ-šâw); on יו ָ, § 108. 3. *d.* (cf. פָּנָיו, אַפָּיו

(v. 5)).—שְׁמַעַן, irreg. for שְׁמַעְנָה, ה ָ_ having been dropped

and _ inserted, § 37. •2; Ḳal Imv. 2 f. pl., like קְטֹלְנָה; on _ under

מ, § 76. 1. *a.*—נָשַׁי, const. of נָשִׁים, cf. נָשָׁיו above.—הַאֲזֵנָה,

for הַאֲזֵנָּה like הַקְטֵלְנָה; on הַ ַ § 58. 5. *a. b;* on _, § 74.

3. *b;* root, אָזַן—אִמְרָתִי, cf. מְנֻחָתוֹ in v. 4; on formation, § 89.

4; on ת ָ, § 108. 2.—הָרַגְתִּי, from הָרַג; synopsis in Ḳal? on

repetition of accent, § 23. 6.—חַבֻּרָתִי, with _ for וּ; cf. מְנֻחָתוֹ

in v. 4, and אִמְרָתִי above; on formation, § 93. 6.

V. 24. יֻקַם (for יֻנְקַם), see on v. 15.—שִׁבְעָה, the sing.

form, is *seven,* while שִׁבְעִים, the plur. form is *seventy.*

V. 25. וַיֵּדַע, see on v. 17.—וַתֵּלֶד, see on v. 20,—שָׁת - לִי

(šâθ), on Méθëǧ, § 18. 4; the _ is á, § 86. 1. *a:*— הָרֵגוּ =

הָרַג + וּ; in the open syl. *before* the tone an original ă is rounded

to å, but in the open syl. *away* from the tone, ă is reduced to šᵉwâ,

§ 71. 1. *b.* (1), (2).

V. 26. גַּם־הוּא, the pronoun inserted thus to emphasize the

preceding noun.—הוּחַל, from the root חָלַל ; § 85. 5. *d;* what

stem?—לִקְרֹא, cf. לִמְשֹׁל, לִשְׁכֹּר; Ḳal Inf. const.

3. PARALLELISM IN HEBREW POETRY.

(1) עָדָה וְצִלָּה שְׁמַעַן קוֹלִי

(2) נְשֵׁי לֶמֶךְ הַאְזֵנָּה אִמְרָתִי

(3) כִּי אִישׁ הָרַגְתִּי לְפִצְעִי

(4) וְיֶלֶד לְחַבֻּרָתִי:

(5) כִּי שִׁבְעָתַיִם יֻקַּם־קָיִן

(6) וְלֶמֶךְ שִׁבְעִים וְשִׁבְעָה

Note 1.—The characteristic external feature of Hebrew poetry is parallelism.

Note 2.—In this song there are six lines or members; the second line is, in the main, a repetition of the thought expressed in the first; the fourth, a repetition of the third; hence the parallelism in the case of the first and second, and of the third and fourth members is called *synonymous*.

Note 3.—The same relation, however, does not exist between the fifth and sixth, the latter being necessary to complete the thought of the former; such parallelism is called *synthetic*.

Note 4.—Another kind of parallelism not illustrated in this passage is the *antithetic*, in which the second member is in contrast with the first.

4. GRAMMAR-LESSON.

1. § **80.** Tabular View, Synopses of יִטַל (= וְטַל) in various stems.

2. § **80.** 1.   The treatment of original ו when initial.

3. § **80.** 2. *a, b,*   The two treatments in the Ḳäl Impf., Imv., and Inf. const.

4. § **80.** 3. *a-c,*   The treatment of ו when medial.

Note 1.—In the study of verbs פ״ו , follow the order indicated in previous Lessons, analyzing exhaustively the familiar forms given under § 80. 1—3.

Note 2.—Use for practice (1) יֵשֵׁב *sit. dwell*, (2) יָלַד *bring forth*, and (3) יָבֵשׁ (with ă in Ḳăl Impf.) *be dry.*

5. EXERCISES.

1. To be translated into Hebrew:—(1) *He will dwell,¹ I shall dwell, thou* (f.) *shalt dwell, dwell thou* (f.) *to dwell, to bring forth,¹ thou* (f.) *shalt bring forth;* (2) *He will know,¹ to know, we shall know;* (3) *He will sleep,² I shall sleep, we shall sleep;* (4) *He will be brought forth, thou wilt be known, he will be feared;* (5) *He will cause to dwell, I shall cause to know, to cause to bring forth, he was brought forth;* (6) *He was caused to know, she will be caused to bring forth.*

2. To be translated into Hebrew:—(1) *Hear ye* (m.) *my voice, and give ear to that which* (אֶת־אֲשֶׁר) *I shall say;* (2) *Adah and Zillah were the wives of Lamech;* (3) *Why didst thou kill the man whom I sent to thee?* (4) *Cain was avenged seven-fold;* (5) *He gave him to God;* (6) *They began* (Hĭf.) *to call on the name of God.*

3. To be written with points and vowel-signs:—*Genesis IV. 23-26 from the unpointed text.*

4. To be written out:—Synopses of the verbs יָרַד in Ḳăl, Hĭf. and Hŏf., of יָבַל in Hĭf. and Hŏf., and of יָבֵשׁ in Ḳăl, Pĭ'ēl and Hĭf.

5. To be described:—The forms יִישַׁן, יָדְעוּ, תֵּלְדִי, יֵשֵׁב, יֵצֵא, הוּרַד, הוֹלִיד, נוֹדַע, יֻלַּד, דֵּעַת, לֶדֶת.

6. TOPICS FOR STUDY.

(1) The ending וֹן ָ. (2) The form of the fem.-ending before suffixes. (3) The Hŏf. of verbs פ״ן. (4) The â in the Middle-Vowel Ḳăl Perfects. (5) The Hŏf. of verbs ע״ע. (6) Synonymous parallelism. (7) Synthetic parallelism. (8) Antithetic parallelism.

LESSON XLV.—REVIEW.

1. *WORD-REVIEW.*

1. Arrange in alphabetical order the roots of all verbal forms both old and new, occurring in the third and fourth chapters.

2. Arrange in alphabetical order the nominal forms of these chapters, using in each case the form of the absolute state.

3. Arrange in alphabetical order the various particles, prepositions and adverbs occurring in these chapters.

2. *VERSE-REVIEW.*

1. Pronounce the pointed text of each verse until it can be read aloud rapidly and without hesitation.

2. Write out on paper the unpointed text, one verse at a time, and then, without the aid of either pointed text or translation, insert the necessary points and vowel-signs. Compare the result with the pointed text, and note the mistakes; repeat the exercise till each verse can be pointed without mistake.

3. *GRAMMAR-REVIEW.*

1. Compare the forms of the Ḳăl Perf. (3 m. sg.) as they appear in the strong verb and in the various other classes of verbs, § **87. 1.** (Perfect.)

2. Compare the forms of the Ḳăl Impf. stem yăḳ-ṭŭl (3 m. sg.) as they appear in the strong verb and in the various other classes cf verbs, § **87. 1.** (Impf. with ō).

3. Compare the same of the stem yăḳ-ṭăl, and of yăḳ-ṭĭl, § **87. 1.**

4. Compare the forms of the Hĭf'îl Perf. and Impf. (3 m. sg.) as they appear in the strong verb, and in the various other classes of verbs, § **87. 3.**

---

[1] This verb forms its Kal as described in § **80. 2. a.**
[2] This verb forms its Kal as described in § **80. 2. b.**

5. Compare the forms of the Nif'âl Perf. and Impf. (3 m. sg.) as they appear in the strong verb and in the various other classes of verbs, § **87. 4.**

Note.—This includes (1) the statement of the forms, and (2) an explanation of the vowel-changes which are seen in each form.

4. *EXERCISES.*

To be translated into Hebrew:—

1. *He made man in the sixth day, and rested in the seventh day.*
2. *He will sanctify the seventh day, and will rest in it.*
3. *The woman will eat the fruit, and of it she will give to her husband who will eat with her.*
4. *In the day of your ruling the earth.*
5. *This is the day in which God spoke to the man.*
6. *Let us make for ourselves large girdles.*
7. *I gave her fruit, and we ate.*
8. *She gave him fruit, and he ate.*
9. *Cursed is the earth, because thou didst eat from this tree.*
10. *God made known to the woman that the man should rule over her.*
11. *I shall call the name of my wife Eve.*
12. *We found in the field the fruit which God commanded not to eat.*
13. *The man will serve the ground whence he was taken.*
14. *I shall put forth my hand and take the fruit and eat.*
15. *The woman conceived and bare a son.*
16. *Did not Abel bring to God from the firstlings of his flock?*
17. *The blood of thy brother hath cried out to God.*
18. *And Cain went out from Eden, and dwelt in the land of Nod.*
19. *Abel was the son of Eve, and Tubal Cain was the son of Zillah.*
20. *Why didst thou kill the man whom I sent to thee?*

LESSON XLVI.—GENESIS V. 1—16.

1. NEW WORDS.

שְׁמֹנֶה (1), סֵפֶר (2), חָיָה (3), שְׁלֹשִׁים (4), מֵאָה (5), אַחַר (6) שְׁמֹנֶה
שְׁתַּיִם,¹ (12), שֶׁבַע (11), חָמֵשׁ (10), תֵּשַׁע (9), בַּת (8), (7)
שִׁשִּׁים, (15) עֶשֶׂר (14), אַרְבָּעִים (13), תִּשְׁעִים.

2. NOTES.

V. 1. זֶה סֵפֶר *This* (is the) *book-of; this book* would be

הַסֵּפֶר הַזֶּה.—תּוֹלְדוֹת (for tăw-lᵉḏôθ), § 98. 3; used only in pl.,

from וָלַד.—"אֹ² בְּרֹא בְּיוֹם, *in the day of the creating of God;*

"אֹ being definite, בְּרֹא is definite, and consequently יוֹם is definite,

Principle 4.—בְּרֹא, Ḳǎl Inf. const. of בָּרָא.

V. 2. בְּרָאָם, on _, § 71. 1. b. (1); on _ under ר, § 71. 1. b.

(2); on _ under אָ, § 71. 1. c. (3.)—וַיְבָרֶךְ, §§ 75. 1. a; 21. 3;

הַבָּרְאָם, the first _=Mĕθĕğ, the second = Sillûḳ; on D. f. § 72. 2;

the בְּ _, same as in בְּרָאָם.

V. 3. וַיְחִי, for וַיִּחְיֶה from חָיָה *live*, as וַיְהִי for וַיִּהְיֶה from

הָיָה *be.*—שְׁלֹשִׁים וּמְאַת שָׁנָה lit., *thirty and a hundred of year;*

note that (1) the word for *thirty* is the plural of *three* (שָׁלֹשׁ), (2)

the word for *hundred* is const., (3) the word for *year* is sg.— וַיּוֹלֶד,

Hif. of וָלַד (יָלַד), § 80. 3. b; on _ for _, §§ 21. 3; 36. 4. a; on

_ for י _, § 70. 3. R.

V. 4. יְמֵי, § 116. 12.—אַחֲרֵי, noun in plur. const. used as a

preposition, § 119. 3. a.—הוֹלִידוֹ. Hif. Inf. const. (for hăw-lîḏ)

with suffix וֹ.—בָּנִים וּבָנוֹת, see the various forms of these words,

§ 116. 9, 10.

---

¹ *Twelve*, not given in the Vocabulary in this form.
² "אֹ is the abbreviation of אֱלֹהִים.

Vs. 5, 6. וַיְחִי, Ḳâl Perf. 3 m. sg. of the ע״ע root חָיָי, § 85.

1.—וַיָּמָת (wăy-yâ-mōθ), pausal for וַיָּמָת, § 86. 1. e. R.—חָמֵשׁ

שָׁנִים, the numeral sg. in form, the subst. plural.

Vs. 8—10. שְׁתֵּים עֶשְׂרֵה lit., two ten = twelve; שְׁתֵּים, a contraction of שִׁתַּיִם (cf. שְׁתֵּי, ch. IV. 19), and עֶשְׂרֵה, a form of

עֶשֶׂר ten.—תִּשְׁעִים, pl. of תִּשְׁעָה or תֵּשַׁע nine.—חֲמֵשׁ עֶשְׂרֵה

lit., five ten = fifteen, cf. above.

Vs.13, 16. אַרְבָּעִים, plur. of אַרְבָּעָה or אַרְבַּע four.—שֵׁשִׁים,
plur. of שִׁשָּׁה or שֵׁשׁ six.

3. PRINCIPLES OF SYNTAX.

V. 4.—אַחֲרֵי הוֹלִידוֹ—After his begetting = after he had begotten.

Principle 19.—Where the Hebrew uses a preposition and an Infinitive, the English prefers a conjunction and a finite verb.

V. 6.—חֲמֵשׁ שָׁנִים: שֶׁבַע שָׁנִים; עֶשֶׂר שָׁנִים;—

Five years; seven years; ten years.

Principle 20.—With the numerals 3—10 the noun is put in the
plural.

Principle 21.—The numerals 3—10 assume the secondary or
masculine form, when the noun is feminine. [שָׁנִים is feminine,
though it has a masculine ending.]

V. 5.—שְׁלשִׁים שָׁנָה; תִּשְׁעִים שָׁנָה; שִׁבְעִים
שָׁנָה.—Thirty years; ninety years; seventy years.

Principle 22.—The tens, formed by changing ה_ of the units
to ים_ (except עֶשְׂרִים twenty, from עֶשֶׂר ten), have the accompanying noun in the singular.

4. GRAMMAR- AND WORD-LESSON.

1. § 117. General view, The numerals 1—10, 11, 12, 20—90, 100,
1,000
2. § 117. 1—8, The formation and use of the Cardinals.
3. § 117. 9—12, The formation and use of the Ordinals.
4. Word-Lists, Verbs numbered 81—90 in List III.

5. *EXERCISES.*

1. To be translated into Hebrew:—(1) *Seven years;* (2) *Nine years;* (3) *Forty years;* (4) *Sixty years;* (5) *Three sons;* (6) *Three daughters;* (7) *Thirty sons and thirty daughters;* (8) *Forty days and forty nights;* (9) *Four heads;* (10) *Fifty days;* (11) *The seven stars;* (12) *Seven of*[1] *the stars;* (13) *Four seasons;* (14) *Twenty-seven days;* (15) *One hundred and fifty-nine years.*

2. To be translated into Hebrew:—(1) *This (is) a good book;* (2) *This good book was given to me;* (3) *In his own likeness God created man;* (4) *In the day that God made earth and heaven* (Heb. order, *In day of making of God*); (5) *In the day that God created man* (Heb. order, *In day of creating of God man*); (6) *After he had begotten a son* (Heb., *after his begetting a son*); (7) *And the man lived three hundred and forty-eight years;* (8) *And he begat four sons and three daughters, and he died;* (9) *And all the days of the man which he lived upon the face of the earth after he had begotten sons, were nine hundred and ninety-nine years.*

3. To be written:—A transliteration of verses 1 and 2 of chapter V.

4. To be written:—A verbal form of the Ḳäl Imperfect 3 m. sg. in each of the classes of verbs.

5. To be written:—The numerals 1—10 in English letters.

6. *TOPICS FOR STUDY.*

(1) Position and agreement of the demonstrative. (2) Nouns formed by prefixing ת. (3) The vowel-changes in קְטָלִם. (4) The short form of ל״ה Imperfects (5) Position and agreement of numerals. (6) פ״י Hif'ils. (7) Prep. with plur. form. (8) ע״ע Ḳäl Perfect 3 m. sg. (9) ע״ו Ḳäl Impf. 3 m. sg. with Wâw convers. in pause. (10) Formation of numerals 20—90. (11) The various forms of the word for *one hundred.* (12) *The form of the numerals 3—10 with fem. nouns, with masc. nouns.*

---

[1] The word *of* after a cardinal must be expressed by מִן.

LESSON XLVII.—GENESIS V. 17-32.

1. *NEW WORDS.*

(1) נַחַם, (2) מַעֲשֶׂה, (3) יָד.

2. *NOTES.*

Vs. 17—21. וַיִּהְיוּ, on Mĕθēğ, § **18.** 5; on _, § **74.** 2. *b.* R. 2;
on omission of third radical, § **82.** 2. חָמֵשׁ, used with a fem. noun;
form with masc. noun, חֲמִשָּׁה; ordinal, חֲמִישִׁי.—שְׁתַּיִם, fem.
of שְׁנַיִם; cf. שְׁתֵּי, ch. IV. 19.—וּמְאַת שָׁנָה lit., *and-*(a)-*hundred-
of year.*—מְתוּשֶׁלַח (v. 21), pausal for מְתוּשֶׁלַח.

Vs. 22—24. וַיִּתְהַלֵּךְ, form and synopsis? force of Hiθpā'ēl
expressed here by the word *live.*—וַיְהִי כָּל-יְמֵי, D. 1. in כ after
disj. accent; verb in sg. agreeing with כָּל, while in v. 17 it was pl.,
agreeing with יְמֵי.—וְאֵינֶנּוּ (wᵉʹê-nĕn-nû); on יְ _, § **111.** 2. R. 1;
on נְ _, §§ **118.** 2. *c;* **71.** 2. *c.* (3) and N. 1; on the D. f. in נ, § **71.**
2. *c.* N. 2; four elements, וְ, אֵין, נ _, הוּ; on ֵ, § **24.** 5.

V. 29. זֶה, these accents need not be considered here.—יְנַחֲמֵנוּ,
Pī'ēl Impf. 3 m. sg. of the פ"ן and ע' laryng. root נָחַם *comfort*, with the suffix נוּ *us;* on D. f. of Pī'ēl in ח, § **75.** 1. *b;* on _,
§ **71.** 2. *c.* (2).—כְּמַעֲשֵׂנוּ, made up of מִן, מַעֲשֶׂה (§ **96.** 1),
and נוּ.—וּמֵעִצְּבוֹן, made up of וְ (§ **49.** 2), מֵ (§ **48.** 2), and the
const. state of עִצָּבוֹן, the ָ yielding to šᵉwâ, § **109.** 3. a.—יָדֵינוּ, *sg.*
יָד, *dual* יָדַיִם; before suffixes the old construct ending *ay* is used;
this before נוּ is contr. to ê, § **108.** 3. *b.*—אֲרָרָהּ ('ē-rʳrâh), Pī'ēl
Perf. 3. m. sg. of the פ' laryng., and ע"ע verb אָרַר *curse;*
for אָרֲר, but ר refuses D. f. (§ **75.** 1. *a*), hence אָרַר; הָ _ַ *be-*

comes הָ ‎_, § **71.** 1. *c.* N.—‎'י ‎אֲרָרָהּ אֲשֶׁר lit., *which cursed-her the Lord* = *which the Lord cursed.*

3. PRINCIPLES OF SYNTAX.

V. 27. ‎מְתוּשֶׁלַח כָּל־יְמֵי וַיִּהְיוּ— *And* WERE *all the days of Methusaleh.*

‎לֶמֶךְ כָּל־יְמֵי וַיְהִי—*And* WAS *all the days of Lamech.*

Principle 23.—The verb in such cases as these may be placed either in the singular or in the plural

V. 31. ‎יְהֹוָה אֲרָרָהּ אֲשֶׁר—*Which the Lord cursed.*

Principle 24.—‎אֲשֶׁר is a particle indicating the subordinate character of the following clause. The subordinate idea may be relative, temporal, causal, etc. In a relative clause having the relative as object of the verb, that object is expressed by a pronominal suffix attached to the verbal form. In a majority of cases, however, the pronominal suffix is not expressed.

4. GRAMMAR- AND WORD-LESSON.

1. § **88.** 1—4   What is included in inflection of nouns.
2. § **89.** 1,2; **109.** 4. 5.   Strong and weak Segolates.
3. § **90.** 1, 2,   Nouns with two, originally short, vowels.
4. § **91.** 1, 2,   Nouns with one short and one long vowel.
5. § **92.** 1—3,   Nouns with one long and one short vowel.
6. Word-Lists.   The verbs numbered 91—100 in List III.

Note.—In the study of noun-formation, copy promiscuously, on a slip of paper, nouns of various classes, and then take up each noun and classify it, noting (1) its root with the meaning of the same, (2) the original vowels used in its formation, (3) the changes which these original vowels have suffered, (4) the force of the formation, (5) the meaning of the word.

5. *EXERCISES.*

1. Form nouns as follows:—(1) From גְדֹל, a *u*-class Segŏlate, a noun of the third class (ă—â); (2) from חֹרֶשׁ, a *u*-class Segŏlate, a noun of the second class, (ă—ă); (3) from חָרַב, an *a*-class Segŏlate, a *u*-class Segŏlate (masc. and fem.), a noun of the fourth class (â—ĭ), a noun of the second class (ă—ĭ); (4) from עָבַד, an *a*-class Segŏlate, a fem. noun of the third class (ă—â); (5) from אָמַן, a *u*-class Segŏlate, a fem. noun of the third class (ĭ—û), a noun of the third class (ă—â), two nouns of the second class (ă—ă, ă—ĭ); (6) from מָתַק, an *i*-class and a *u*-class Segŏlate, a noun of the third class (ă—â); (7) from קָרֵב, a noun of the second class (ă—ĭ), a noun of the third class (ă—â).

2. To be translated into Hebrew:— (1) *Will Noah comfort Lamech from the work of his hands?* (2) *God cursed* (Pĭ'ēl) *the ground which he had created;* (3) *I will walk* (Hĭθpă'ēl) *with God, who created* (Heb., *the one creating*) *the heavens and the earth;* (4) *The sorrow of Cain was exceedingly great;* (5) *The man whom God cursed will die.*

3. To be written:—A transliteration of verses 28 and 29 of chapter V.

4. To be written:—A verbal form of the Hĭf'ĭl Perf. 3 m. sg. in each of the classes of verbs.

6. *TOPICS FOR STUDY.*

(1) The Ḳăl Impf's of הָיָה, חָיָה. (2) The word שֶׁתַּיִם. (3) Various forms of the word for *one hundred.* (4) Particles with verbal suffixes. (5) Synopsis of נָחַם in Pĭ'ēl. (6) Synopsis of אָרַר in Pĭ'ēl. (7) Măppîḳ. (8) *A*-class, *I*-class, *U*-class Segŏlates. (9) Laryngeal, ע״פ, ע״ע, ע״י, ע״י and ל״ה Segŏlates. (10) Feminine Segŏlates. (11) Meaning of Segŏlates. (12) Nouns with two short vowels. (13) Nouns with one short and one long vowel. (14) Nouns with one long and one short vowel.

LESSON XLVIII.—GENESIS VI. 1-8.

1. NEW WORDS.

(1) רָכַב, (2) בָּחַר, (3) דוּן, (4) שָׁנַם (in the text. שָׁנַם), (5) רַק, (11) לֵב, (10) מַחְשָׁבָה, (9) יֵצֶר, (8) גִבּוֹר, (7) נְפִלִים, (6) חֵן, (14) מָחָה, (13) עֶצֶב, (12) (in Nif.), נָחַם.

V. 1. הֶחֵל, from חָלַל, § 85. 1. a, 4. d; on _ under ה, § 85. 5. c; synopsis ·in Hif.?—לָרֹב, prep. ל with pretonic â; רֹב, inf. const. from רָכַב, § 85. 1. a; synopsis in Ḳâl?

V. 2. וַיִּרְאוּ, Ḳâl Impf. 3 m. pl. of רָאָה; on loss of third radical (ʼ), § 82. 2.—בְּנֵי and בְּנוֹת, constructs of בְּנוֹת.בָּנִים, בָּנוֹת—טַבֹת, cf. טוֹב, טוֹבָה, טוֹבִים טוֹבוֹת; ô written defectively.—הִנֵּה, D. f. firmative, §§ 15. 6; 50. 3. e.—וַיִּקְחוּ from לָקַח take; on assim. of ל, § 78. 2. R. 2; on omission of D. f. and on Râfê, §§ 14. 2; 16. 2; synopsis in Ḳâl?—נָשִׁים, § 116. 7.—בָּחֲרוּ, pausal for בָּחֲרוּ.

V. 3. יָדוֹן, Ḳâl Impf. 3 m. sg. The form looks like that of יָבוֹא, but it may be from דָּנַן, with ō written like ô as sometimes happens. Nothing certain is known as to either form or meaning.— בְּשַׁנַּם, rather to be read בְּשַׁנָּם = in (their) wandering; from שָׁנַג, with ă instead of ŭ in the inf. cst.; the traditional rendering in that also is based on the analysis בְּ in, שֶׁ = that (§ 53. 2), נַם also.—יָמָיו, cf. אַפָּיו, פָּנָיו, § 108. 3. d.

V. 4. אַחֲרֵי־כֵן אֲשֶׁר lit., after so, when=afterwards, when.— יָבֹאוּ, cf. the paradigm-form יִקְטֹלוּ; the ô is for â, the form corresponding to yăḳ-ṭăl not yăḳ-ṭŭl; § 86. 1. c; the Impf. designates habitual action in past time.— הַגִּבֹּרִים, § 93. 4. c.—עוֹלָם, § 92.

1.—אֲנָשֵׁי, const. of אֲנָשִׁים, which is plur. of אִישׁ, § 116. 5.

V. 5. רַבָּה, an adj. fem. sg.[1] from רַב, §§ 100. 1. a; 109. 5.

b.—רָעַת, const. of רָעָה.—יֵצֶר, § 89. 1. b.—מַחֲשֶׁבֶת, const.

pl. of מַחֲשָׁבָה.—לִבּוֹ, an עַ"ע i-class Seğolate; §§ 100. 1. a,
109. 5. b.

Vs. 6—8. וַיִּנָּחֶם, §§ 21. 3; 65. 1. a.— וַיִּתְעַצֵּב, cf. וַיִּתְהַלֵּךְ

in ch. V. 22.—אֶמְחֶה, on הֶ_=é § 82. 1. b.—בְּרָאתִי, on repeated

accent, § 23. 6; on ◌ֵ under ר, § 83. 1.— נִחַמְתִּי, for נִנְחַמְתִּי,

the second נ being assimilated and the D. f. implied in ח; Nîf. Perf.

1 c. sg. of נָחַם; Nîf. = repent, Pî'ēl (ch. V. 29) = comfort.—

עֲשִׂיתִם, on ◌ֵ instead of ◌ֵ, § 71. 1. b. (1); the î with ת, written

defectively.—בְּעֵינֵי, on first י_, § 109. 5. a; on second י_, § 107.

3. PRINCIPLES OF SYNTAX.

V. 4.—בַּיָּמִים הָהֵם.—In the days the those = In those days.

Principle 25.—The 3rd personal pronoun is used as the remote demonstrative (that, those), and as such stands after its noun, agreeing with it in gender, number and definiteness.

4. GRAMMAR- AND WORD-LESSON.

1. § 93. Nouns with second radical reduplicated.
2. §§ 96, 97. Nouns with מ prefixed; their signification.
3. § 98. Nouns with ת prefixed.
4. § 99. Nouns formed by means of affixes.
5. Word-Lists, The verbs numbered 101—110 in List III.

Note.—In the study of noun-formation, copy promiscuously, on a slip of paper, nouns of various classes, and then take up each noun and classify it, noting (1) its root, with the meaning of the same, (2) the original vowels used in its formation, (3) the changes

---

[1] The Kal Perf. 3 f. sg. of רָבַב would be רַבָּה.

which these original vowels have suffered, (4) the force of the
formation, (5) the meaning of the word.

5. EXERCISES.

1. Form nouns as follows:—(1) from לָמַד, a noun with מ prefixed (ă—ă), and one with ת (ă—î); (2) from אָכַל, a fem. *u*-class
Seğolate, a noun with מ prefixed (a—a); (3) from חֹשֶׁךְ, a *u*-class
Seğolate, a noun with מ prefixed (ă—ă); (4) from גָּבַר, an *a*-class
Seğolate, a noun with second radical doubled (ĭ—â); (5) from זָמַר,
an *a*-class Seğolate, a fem. *i*-class Seğolate, a noun with מ prefixed (ĭ—â); (6) from סָפַר, an *i*-class Seğolate, a noun with מ
prefixed (ĭ—ă).

2. To be translated into Hebrew:—*The daughters of men were
exceedingly fair* (טוֹב); (2) *Mankind multiplied;* (3) *We chose
wives from all the daughters of men;* (4) *I have found favor in his
eyes;* (5) *From eternity unto eternity I am God;* (6) *I grieved in
my heart;* (7) *I will not repent that I have made them;* (8) *Those
heroes are the men of renown* (*name*).

3. To be written:—A transliteration of verses 1, 2 of chapter VI.

4. To be written:—A verbal form of the Hif'îl Impf. 2 m. sg.
in each of the classes of verbs.

6. TOPICS FOR STUDY.

(1) ע״ע Hif'îls. (2) The absence of י in verbs ל״ה. (3) The
various forms of the words for *son, daughter.* (4) The personal pronouns. (5) The demonstrative pronouns. (6) The words יָדוֹן and
בְּשַׁגַּם. (7) The words meaning *his faces, his nostrils, his days, his
eyes.* (8) The Impf. of habitual action in past time. (9) ע״ע
i-class Seğolates. (10) The remote demonstratives. (11) Nouns with
second radical reduplicated. (12) Nouns with מ prefixed. (13)
Nouns with ת prefixed. (14) Nouns with affixes.

LESSON XLIX.—GENESIS VI. 9-15.

1. *NEW WORDS.*

(1) צַדִּיק, (2) תָּמִים, (3) דּוֹר, (4) שָׁחַת, (5) חָמָס, (6) תֵּבָה,

(13) אַמָּה, (12) כָּפַר, (11) כֹּפֶר, (10) חוּץ, (9) כָּפַר, (8) קֵן, (7) גֹּפֶר,

אֶרֶךְ, (14) רֹחַב, (15) קוֹמָה.

2. NOTES.

(1) = בְּדֹרֹתָיו, § 98. 1.— תּוֹלְדֹת, § 52. 1. *c.*— אֵלֶּה, **V. 9.**
בְּ, (2) דּוֹר, (3) וֹת, (4) ־ָיו (cf. אָפִיו); on the pl. ending ־ָיו
תָּמִים,—5. § 93, צַדִּיק.—N. and 4 .108 § ,ôθ after the pl. ending
object.
§ 91. 1. *b.* —אֶת־הָֽא", here the prep. *with*, not the sign of the def.

Vs. 10, 11. וַיּוֹלֶד, §§ 80. 3. *b;* 70. 3. *a.* (2), (3).—וַתִּשָּׁחֵת,
Synopsis?—וַתִּמָּלֵא. Synopsis?

Vs. 12, 13. נִשְׁחָֽתָה, pausal for נִשְׁחֲתָה, Nif. Perf. 3 f. of
שָׁחַת; Synopsis?—הִשְׁחִית, Synopsis?— דַּרְכּוֹ, from דֶּרֶךְ; cf.
זֶרַע and זַרְעוֹ, צֶלֶם and צַלְמוֹ — בָּא (bâ'), either Perf. or Part.
in form, § 86. 1. *a, g.*— לְפָנַי, § 108. 3. *a.* (1).— מָלְאָה, Synopsis?
— וְהִנְנִי, the adverbial particle הֵן or הִנֵּה with a verbal suffix,
§ 118. 2. *a.*—מַשְׁחִיתָם Hif. part. of שָׁחַת, with suf. ־ָם.

Vs. 14, 15. עָשֵׂה ("ʻsê(h)), § 82. 1. *f.*—טֵבַת, const. of תֵּבָה,
the ־ being unchangeable.— עֲצֵי, const. of עֵצִים, cf. פְּנֵי from
פָּנִים—קִנִּים, plur. of קֵן, an ע"ע *i*-class Segolate, § 109. 5. *b;*
cf. וְכָפַרְתָּ־לֵב, with accent on ultima, § 70. 3. *b;* cf. change from
ult. to penult in וַיֹּאמֶר.—מִבַּיִת וּמִחוּץ, *from house and from out-*
side = within and without.— תֵּעָשֶׂה, cf. נַעֲשֶׂה (ch. I. 26).—
רָחְבָּה (rôḥ-bâh), on ־ (ŏ) under ר, § 111. 1. R. 1; on ה־
§ 108. 1. R. 1.

3. *PRINCIPLES OF SYNTAX.*

V. 10.—שְׁלֹשָׁה בָנִים—*Three sons.*

Principle 26.—When the substantive is *masculine*, the feminine form of the numeral is employed; and when the numeral is a *unit*, the plural form of the substantive is employed.

V. 15. וְזֶה אֲשֶׁר תַּעֲשֶׂה אֹתָהּ—*And this is how thou shalt make it.*

Principle 27.—The relative particle often introduces subordinate clauses that are not strictly relative clauses.

4. *GRAMMAR- AND WORD-LESSON.*

1. § **100,**   Nouns from bi-literal roots.
2. § **104,**   Various ways of forming noun-stems.
3. § **105,**   The Formation of Cases.
4. Word-Lists,   Verbs numbered 111—120 in Lists III and IV.

5. *EXERCISES.*

1. To be translated into Hebrew:—(1) *Noah had* (Heb., *were to Noah*) *three sons;* (2) *The sons of Noah were not righteous;* (3) *The earth was corrupt, and it was full of violence;* (4) *The way of all flesh was corrupt;* (5) *God will destroy the earth and all who dwell upon it;* (6) *Thou shalt make a house; its length shall be twenty cubits, its breadth, twelve cubits, its height, twenty-four cubits.*

3. To be written:—A transliteration of verses 14 and 15 of chapter VI.

4. To be written:—A verbal form of the Nif'äl Perfect 3 m. sg. in each of the classes of verbs.

6. *TOPICS FOR STUDY.*

(1) The demonstrative pronoun. (2) Nouns formed by reduplication of second radical. (3) אֶת־, a preposition. (4) The ŏ of פ"ו

Hif'ils. (5) The characteristics of the Nif'ăl Impf. (6) Primary form of *u*-class Seğolates. (7) Adverbs with verbal suffixes. (8) The ê of ל"ה Imv's. (9) ע"ע *i*-class Seğolates. (10) Change of accent after Wăw Convers. with Perfect. (11) The form of *u*-class Seğolates before pron. suffixes. (12) Relics of the nominative case-ending. (13) The Hē Directive. (14) Other relics of the accusative case-ending.

LESSON L.—GENESIS VI. 16-22.

1. *NEW WORDS.*

(1) צֹהַר, (2) מִלְמַעְלָה, (3) צַד, (4) תַּחְתִּי, (5) שְׁנַיִם, (6) שְׁלִישִׁים (7) מַבּוּל, (8) גָּוַע, (9) קוּם, (10) בְּרִית, (11) אָסַף .

2. *NOTES.*

V. 16. צֹהַר, § 89. 1. c.—תַּעֲשֶׂה (tă·'śé(h), on ⁻ under ת, § 74. 2. *a;* on the ⁻ under ע, § 74. 3. *b;* on ה_, § 82. 1. *b.*—תִּכְלֶנָּה, made up of (1) תִּכְלֶה, with ה_ lacking, (2) נֶּה_ which is for נֶה_, §§ 72. 3; 71. 2. *c.* (3) and Notes 1, 2; cf. וַיְכַל (ch. II. 2).—מִלְמַעְלָה made up of מִן, לְ, מַעַל and ה_ directive; note (1) the Răfê, (2) Zăḳēf ḳăṭōn, (3) simple š·wâ under ע; on ה_, § 105. 2. *a.*— בְּצִדָּהּ (b·ṣid-dâh), from צַד with suf. ה_, the original ⁻ being attenuated in sharpened syl.— תָּשִׂים Ḳăl Impf. 2 m. sg. of the ע"י verb שִׂים put.—תַּעֲשֶׂה, same as the word above, with pron. suf. ה.

V. 17. וַאֲנִי, §§ 49. 3; 50. 3. *d;* here emphatic, being cut off by R·vî(ă)'.—הִנְנִי, a particle with verbal suffix, § 118. 2. *a.*— מֵבִיא Hif. participle from בּוֹא; on preformative ⁻, § 86. 3. *c;* on stem-vowel, ⁻, § 86. 1. *d.*—לְשַׁחֵת, Pi'ēl Inf. const. of the ע' laryng.

verb שָׁחַת, the D. f. being implied in ח, § 75. 1. *b.*—יָנוּעַ, pausal for יָנוּעַ, Ḳal Impf. of גּוּעַ, § 76. 1. *a.*

V. 18. וַהֲקִמֹתִי, on וְ, §§ 49. 3; 70. 2. *b;* on הֲ, § 86. 3. *a;* — is 1 written defectively; ô is separating vowel, § 86. 2. *a.*

אִתָּךְ, pausal for אִתְּךָ, the prep. אֶת *with;* cf. אֹתְךָ, in which אֹת = אֶת, the sign of the def. object.— וּבָאֽתָ, Ḳal Perf. 2 m. sg. of בּוֹא, with Wâw conversive.

Vs. 19, 20. הָחַי, instead of הַחַי with D. f. implied.— תָּבִיא, Hif. Impf. 2 m. sg.; § 86. 1. *d.* and 3. *a.*— לְהַחֲיוֹת, Hif. Inf. const. of חָיָה; on וֹת, § 82. 1. *e.*— יָבֹאוּ, a seemingly irreg. Ḳal Impf. 3 m. pl. of בּוֹא.

Vs. 21, 22. קַח, Ḳal Imv. of לָקַח, § 78. 2. R. 2.— מַאֲכָל, §§ 96. 1; 97. 2.— יֵאָכֵל, § 74. 1.— וְאָסַפְתָּ, on the shifting of tone, § 70. 3. *b;* on Méθěǧ, § 18. 1.— צִוָּה, Pi'ēl Perf. 3 m. sg. of צָוָה *command;* on ־, § 59. 1. *a;* on ה־, § 82. 1. *a.*

3. PRINCIPLES OF SYNTAX.

V. 17.א—וַאֲנִי הִנְנִי מֵבִיא—*And I, behold I am about to bring.*

Principle 28.—The Participle is often used to designate an action which is to take place in the immediate future.

V. 17.—אֶת־הַמַּבּוּל מַיִם—*The flood,* (that is) *water;* not *the flood of water.*

Principle 29.—A noun in the construct state cannot receive the article; hence, in cases like this, the second noun must be in apposition with the first.

4. GRAMMAR- AND WORD-LESSON.

1. § 106. 1, 4,   The masculine singular and plural.
2. § 106. 2. *a—c,*   The three-fold treatment of the original fem. affix ת.

LESSON 50.   165

3. § **106**. 3, 5,   The fem. plur. and the dual.
4. Word-Lists,   The verbs numbered 121—130 in List IV.

5. *EXERCISES*.

1. To be written:—(1) Masc. and fem. sg., masc. and fem. pl. of טוֹב *good*, of גָּדֹל *great*; (2) Fem. pl. of אוֹת *sign*, מָאוֹר *luminary*; (3) Dual of עַיִן *eye*.

2. To be translated into Hebrew:—(1) *Behold, I am about to rain upon the earth*; (2) *I will destroy all flesh in which is the spirit of lives*; (3) *Thou didst establish* (= *cause to stand*) *a covenant with me*; (4) *Will he keep the covenant which he established with them?* (5) *Male and female they shall enter the ark, and for them thou shalt take food which may be eaten*; (6) *Noah collected food in order to preserve alive the fowl and the beast*(s) *and the cattle, and all that was in the ark.*

3. To be written:—A transliteration of verses 18 and 19 of chapter VI.

4. To be written:—The Nif‘al Perf. 3 m. sg., and Impf. 3 m. sg. of a verb of each of the classes.

6. *TOPICS FOR STUDY*.

(1) The הָ of לְ״ה Impfs. (2) The suffix נָה. (3) Hē directive. (4) Râfé. (5) Zâkēf ḳâṭōn. (6) The Ḳăl Impf. of verbs ע״י. (7) וְ before a laryngeal with Šᵉwâ. (8) The vowel-changes in מֵבִיא. (9) ע laryng. Pī‘ēls. (10) The vowel-points in וְהִקֵמֹתִי. (11) Dif. between אֵת *with*, and אֶת *sign of def. object*. (12) פ laryng. Nif‘āls. (13) The retention of the original fem. ת. (14) A later usage of תִי (15) The origin of הָ. (16) Affixes for plur. fem. and masc., and for the dual.

LESSON LI.—GENESIS VII. 1-8.

1. *NEW WORDS.*

(1) טָהוֹר ,(2) עוֹד ,(3) אַרְבָּעִים ,(4) מָחָה ,(5) יְקוּם .

2. *NOTES.*

V. 1. וַיֹּאמֶר , § 79. 1.—בֹּא , Ḳāl Imv. בֹּיתְךָ , on יְ־ , § 109. 5. *a;* on ־ֵ , § 108. 1. *a.* (2).— רָאִיתִי , the ı̂ being attenuaьed from ê, § 82. 3. *b.*—לְפָנַי *to my faces,* on יַ־ , § 108. 3. *a.* (1).—דּוֹר , on ô, § 30. 6. *c.*

Vs. 2, 3. טָהוֹרָה , § 106. 2. *c.*— הוּא , § 50. 3. *a.*—לַחֲיוֹת , Pī‘ēl Inf. const. of חָיָה ; cf. הַחֲיוֹת in ch. VI. 20.

Vs. 4, 5. מַמְטִיר , synopsis in Hif‘ı̂l; cf. Principle 28.— אַרְבָּעִים יוֹם , the numeral being plur. in form, the subst. is sg.— וּמָחִיתִי , on יַ־ (cf. רָאִיתִי above), § 82. 3. *b;* from מָחָה .— הַיְקוּם , on omission of D. f. from יְ , § 14. 2; on formation, § 95. 2.— עָשִׂיתִי , on ı̂, § 82. 3. *b;* cf. מָחִיתִי , and רָאִיתִי .— צִוָּהוּ , for צִוָּה אֹתוֹ ; = הוּ and צִוָּה אֹתוֹ (VI. 22).

Vs. 7, 8. וַיָּבֹא , § 86. 1. *c;* the ô is rounded from â— וּבָנָיו , on יָו־ , § 108. 3. *d.*— אִתּוֹ *with him;* cf. אֹתוֹ =)(*-him.*— אֵינֶנָּה , for אֵינֶנְ־הָ ; on יְ־ , § 109. 5. *a;* on נֶ־ , § 71. 2. *c.* N. 1; on the contraction, נֶּהָ , § 71. 2. *c.* N. 2; on particle with suff., § 118. 2. *c.*

3. *PRINCIPLES OF SYNTAX.*

V. 2.—שִׁבְעָה שִׁבְעָה —*Seven, seven* = by sevens.

V. 9.—שְׁנַיִם שְׁנַיִם —*Two, two* = by twos, in pairs.

Principle 30.—Words are often repeated in order to express the *distributive* relation.

V. 5.—שָׁנָה מֵאוֹת בֶּן־שֵׁשׁ וְנֹחַ—*And Noah* (was) *the son of six hundred years* = And Noah was six hundred years old.

Principle 31.—The word בֶּן is commonly used to express a characteristic; e. g. a son of wisdom = a wise son.

4. *GRAMMAR- AND WORD-LESSON.*

1. § **107.** 1, 2,   The Absolute and Construct states.
2. § **107.** 3,   Substitution of ה_ for ה_ in the construct.
3. § **107.** 4,   Restoration of original ת_ in the construct.
4. § **107.** 6,   Substitution of י_ for יִם_ and יַם_.
5. § **107.** 6. Rm. 3.   Explanation of the Construct form.
6. Word-Lists,   Verbs numbered 131—140 in List IV.

5. *EXERCISES.*

1. To be written: — The corresponding construct forms of רֹעֶה,
מִקְוֶה, חַיָּה, דָּגָה, עֵינַיִם, תֵּבָה, שִׁבְעָה, פָּנִים.

2. To be translated into Hebrew: — (1) *The shepherd of the flock was a good man;* (2) *What did God call the collection of waters?* (3) *The eyes of the man were opened and he saw;* (4) *Noah's ark was made of gopher wood;* (5) *Noah took into the ark of the clean cattle and of the cattle which were not clean;* (6) *The man was forty years old;* (7) *God rained upon the earth forty days and forty nights.*

3. To be written in English letters:—Verses 1, 2 of chapter VII.

4. To be written:—Synopses of the verb אָרַב in Ḳăl, Pĭ. and Hĭf., of רָעֵשׁ in Ḳăl, Nĭf. and Hĭf., and of חָרֵב in Ḳăl, Nĭf., Pŭ., Hĭf. and Hŏf.

6. *TOPICS FOR STUDY.*

(1) The ŏ of verbs פ״א. (2) Synopsis in Ḳăl of בּוֹא. (3) ע״י Segolates before suffixes. (4) The î of ל״ה Perf's before consonant terminations. (5) Omission of D. f. (6) The vowels in אֵינֶנָּה.

(7) Explanation of the Construct form. (8) The substitution of
ה‎ for הָ‎, of יֹ‎ for יׄם‎ and יׄםָ‎. (9) The restoration of ת‎
in the construct.

LESSON LII.—GENESIS VII. 9-16.

1. *NEW WORDS.*

(1) שֵׁשׁ‎, (2) חֹדֶשׁ‎, (3) שִׁבְעָה־עָשָׂר‎, (4) בָּקַע‎, (5) מַעְיָן‎,
(6) אַרְבֶּה‎, (7) פֶּתַח‎, (8) גֶּשֶׁם‎, (9) צִפּוֹר‎, (10) בְּעַד‎.

2. *NOTES.*

Vs. 9, 10.　בְּאוּ‎,accent, § **36.** 6.—כַּאֲשֶׁר‎, *according as*, the particle introducing a subordinate clause of manner, and the preposition governing that clause.— לְשִׁבְעַת הַיָּמִים‎ lit., *to the heptad of
days*, the numeral being in const. relation with the subst.—מֵי‎, const.
of מַיִם‎.

Vs. 11, 12.　בִּשְׁנַת‎, on ĭ, § **47.** 2; abs., שָׁנָה‎, const., שְׁנַת‎, the
ָ being reduced, and ת‎ restored, § **106.** 2.— שֵׁשׁ־מֵאוֹת‎, on
Mêθĕǧ, § **18.** 4; cardinal for ordinal, § **117.** R. 11.— חַיֵּי‎, const. of
חַיִּים‎, § **107.** 6.— נִבְקְעוּ‎, Nif. Perf. 3 pl. of בָּקַע‎. — מַעְיְנוֹת‎,
const. of מַעְיְנוֹת‎, a denominative from עַיִן‎, § **103.** 2.—רַבָּה‎, fem.
of adj. רַב‎; on the D. f. § **109.** 5. *b*.— נִפְתָּחוּ‎ pausal for נִפְתְּחוּ‎,
§ **38.** 1.— גֶּשֶׁם‎ an *a*-class Seǧolate.

Vs. 13, 14.　בְּעֶצֶם הַיּוֹם הַזֶּה‎ *in the bone of this day* = on this
very day.— אַתָּם‎, the original ĭ being found in a sharpened syl.—
הֵמָּה‎, § **50.** 1; on D. f. firmative, § **15.** 6.— הַחַיָּה‎, §§ **18.** 1; **45.**
2.—לְמִינָה‎, §§ **16.** 1; **108.** 1. *a.* (1) and R. 1.— לְמִינֵהוּ‎, § **108.** 1. *b.*
(1).— צִפּוֹר‎, on formation, § **93.** 4. *c.*

Vs. 15, 16.　שְׁנַיִם שְׁנַיִם‎, repetition giving a distributive sense.

— הַבָּשָׂר, cf. מִבִּשָׂרִי (II. 23).— הַבָּאִים, Ḳăl Part. act. pl. of
בּוֹא; Part. with article = a relative clause: *those that went in*.
וַיִּסְגֹּר, with ĭ atten. from ă, and ō lowered from ŭ, § 63. 1. *a*, and
2. *a.*— בַּעֲדוֹ, prep. בְּעַד *around, behind*, with suff. וֹ *him*.

3. PRINCIPLES OF SYNTAX.

V. 9.—כַּאֲשֶׁר צִוָּה א"— *According as God commanded.*

Principle 32.—When אֲשֶׁר follows a preposition, the preposition governs, not the particle, but the clause.

V. 11.—בִּשְׁנַת שֵׁשׁ־מֵאוֹת שָׁנָה—*In* (the) *year of six hundred years* = in the six hundredth year.

Principle 33.—There are no *ordinals* above *ten;* hence the cardinals must serve as ordinals, whenever the context demands.

V. 13.—בָּא נֹחַ וְשֵׁם־וְחָם וָיֶפֶת—*Went in Noah and Shem and Ham and Japhet.*

Principle 34.—The predicate of several subjects united by *and* may stand either in sing. or plur., but it is generally in sing. when it *precedes*.

4. GRAMMAR- AND WORD-LESSON

1. § **108.** *Tabular View,* The noun סוּם with pron. suffixes.
2. § **108.** 1. *a, b,* and R's, Masc. nouns in the sing. with suffixes.
3. § **108.** 2, Fem. nouns in the sing. with suffixes.
4. § **108.** 3. *a—d,* Masc. nouns in the plur. with suffixes.
5. § **108.** 4, Fem. nouns in the plur. with suffixes.
6. Word-Lists, Verbs numbered 141—153 in List IV.

5. EXERCISES.

1. To be translated into Hebrew:—(1) *His day, her day, your* (m.) *day, thy* (f.) *day, our day, their* (m.) *day, thy* (m.) *day;* (2) *Thy lives, her lives, his lives, thy* (f.) *lives, our lives, my lives, your*

lives; (3) *My saying, her saying, your* (m.) *saying, our saying;* (4)
My signs, your signs, our signs, their signs, thy signs; (5) *My father, thy brother, our father, your father, thy mouth, her mouth.*

2. To be translated into Hebrew:—(1) *Our Father who* (art) *in
heaven;* (2) *Take with thee into the ark thy father and thy sons and
thy daughters;* (3) *The fowl according to his kind and the beast according to her kind shall enter the ark two by two;* (4) *Everything
in which is the spirit of life shall expire;* (5) *I was born in the eigh-
teen hundredth year of our Lord, in the seventh month, on the
twenty-fourth day of the month;* (6) *The waters of the flood were
upon the earth many days.*

3. To be written:—A transliteration of verses 13 and 14 of chapter VII.

4. To be written:—An exact statement of the origin and force
of the following suffixes (including the ending of the stem): (1)
יו‭ ‬ָ‭ ‬, (2) יִךָ‭ ‬ָ‭ ‬, (3) יִךְ‭ ‬ֶ‭ ‬, (4) יֵנוּ‭ ‬ֶ‭ ‬, (5) וֹ, (6) הָ‭ ‬ָ‭ ‬, (7) ךָ‭ ‬ֶ‭ ‬, (8) ךְ‭ ‬ָ‭ ‬,
(9) ם‭ ‬ָ‭ ‬, (10) תִי‭ ‬ָ‭ ‬.

6. TOPICS FOR STUDY.

(1) A preposition with the Relative particle. (2) Use of cardinals for ordinals. (3) Denominatives formed by prefixing מ. (4)
ע״ע stems with affixes. (5) The prep. אֵת with suffixes. (6) The
pronominal suffixes. (7) Ḳăl Part's act. of verbs ע״ו. (8) The original vowels in יִסְגֹּר. (9) Agreement of predicate. (10) Suffixes
attached by the connecting vowel â. (11) Suffixes attached by the
connecting vowel ē. (12) Suffixes attached by ‭ ‬ָ‭ ‬ (13) The various
forms assumed by the old construct ending *ay* before suffixes. (14)
Plural feminines with pronominal suffixes.

LESSON LIII.—GENESIS VII. 17-24.

1. NEW WORDS.

‎שָׁאַר (7), חָרְבָה (6), גְּבֹהַּ (5), הַר (4), כָּסָה (3), גְּבַר (2), רוּם (1).

2. NOTES.

Vs. 17, 18. ‎וַיִּרְבּוּ, on rejection of the third radical ‎ן or ‎י, § 82. 2.—‎וַיִּשְׂאוּ, from ‎נָשָׂא; ‎נ assimilated, but D. f. lost, § 14. 2. —‎וַתָּרָם (wăt-tâ´-rŏm), the second ‎ָ being in an unaccented closed syl., must be ŏ; usual form of Middle-Vowel Ḳăl Impf., is with ‎וּ, c. g., ‎תָּרוּם ; but with Wâw convers. § 86. 1. e. R.— ‎יִגְבְּרוּ, (1) ‎י, (2) ‎גְּבַר, the root, (3) ‎וּ.

Vs. 19, 20. ‎וַיְכֻסּוּ, (1) ‎וַ with D. f. lost from ‎י, § 14. 2; (2) ‎י; (3) ‎ֻ = passive; (4) D. f. in ‎ס = intensive; (5) ‎וּ = plur.; the root being ‎כָּסָה, cf. ‎וַיְכֻלּוּ (ch. II. 1).—‎הֶהָרִים, on the ‎ָ § 45. 4.—‎גְּבֹהִים, from ‎גָּבֹהַּ, § 109. 1. a; but Păθăḥ-furtive disappears when ‎ה ceases to be final, nor is the Măppîḳ any longer necessary.—‎מִלְמַעְלָה, see ch. VI. 16.

Vs. 21, 22. ‎וַיִּגְוַע, § 76. 1. a.—‎נִשְׁמַת, construct of ‎נְשָׁמָה.— ‎אַפָּיו, from ‎אַף = אַנְפּ, dual, ‎אַפַּיִם; on ‎יו ‎ָ , § 108. 3. d. — ‎בֶּחָרְבָה, on ‎ָ § 45. 4; ‎ָ under ‎ח, on account of rejection of D. f. from ‎ר, the formation being according to § 93. 1.—‎מֵתוּ, on ē under ‎מ, § 86. 1. a. R.

Vs. 23, 24. ‎וַיִּמַח, for ‎וַיִּמְחֶה (Ḳăl Impf.); ‎ה ‎ָ lacking, and a helping vowel ‎ַ inserted, § 82. 5. b. (5); Râfê over ‎מ, to show that no D. f. is to be expected.—‎וַיִּמָּחוּ, Nîf. Impf. 3 plur., of same root as ‎וַיִּשָּׁאֶר — יִמַּח, another Nîf.; tone receding to penult, final vowel is ‎ַ, not ‎ָ — ‎אִתּוֹ בַּתֵּבָה, D. l. in ‎ב , because of preceding disjunctive accent.—‎יוֹם, sg., although pl. in sense.

3. PRINCIPLES OF SYNTAX.

V. 19.—מְאֹד מְאֹד—*Mightily, mightily.*

Principle 34.—Words are often repeated to express *intensity* or *emphasis*.

V. 22.—בְּאַפָּיו .... כֹּל אֲשֶׁר—*All in whose nostrils*, etc.

Principle 35.—The אֲשֶׁר which serves as sign of relation for a following pronominal suffix is generally separated from the word to which the suffix is attached by intervening words.

4. GRAMMAR- AND WORD-LESSON.

1. § **109. 1,**	Stem-changes resulting from shifting of tone *one* place.	
2. § **109. 2,**	Stem-changes resulting from shifting of tone *two* places.	
3. § **109. 3,**	Stem-changes in the singular construct.	
4. § **109. 3. R. 3,**	Ḳ̄al act. participles, and nouns with ultimate ē.	
5. Word-Lists,	Verbs numbered 154—166 in List IV.	

5. EXERCISES.

1. In the case of בָּשָׂר *flesh*, עוֹלָם *eternity*, write out (1) the const. sg., (2) the form with suffix for *my*, (3) with suffix for *your* (m.), (4) the plur. abs., (5) the plur. const., (6) the plur. with the suffix for *my*, (7) with the suffix for *your* (m.).

2. To be translated into Hebrew:—(1) *This is my word which I have spoken to you;* (2) *The earth and all which* (is) *in it is God's;* (3) *All the mountains were covered, and the waters prevailed upon the earth;* (4) *Three men were left with him in the ark;* (5) *The man to* (בְּ) *whose word I listened was forty years old;* (6) *And he destroyed man and beast, creeper and cattle from upon the ground.*

3. To be written:—A transliteration of verses 22, 23 of ch. VII.

4. To be written: — Exhaustive analyses of (1) וְהֵמָּה, (2) מֵאָדָם ., (5) וּבַבְּהֵמָה (4) מִלְמַעְלָה (3), הֶהָרִים.

6. TOPICS FOR STUDY.

(1) Absence of יִ or in verbs לְ"הֵ. (2) Assimilation of נ in verbs פ"ן. (3) The vowels in middle-vowel Ḳāl Imperfects. (4) The artile with ־ֵ. (5) The suffix and ending יִ_ָ. (6) Each vowel in וַיִּמָּח and וַיִּמְחוּ. (7) D. l. after a disjunctive accent. (8) When does the tone move *one* place? (9) When does it move *two* places? (10) The vowel-changes in either case. (11) The formation of the singular construct. (12) Nouns with ē in the ultima.

LESSON LIV.—GENESIS VIII. 1-7.

1. NEW WORDS.

(7) חָסַר, (6) כְּלָא, (5) סָכַר, (4) שָׁכַךְ, (3) עָבַר, (2) זָכַר, (1)

יָבֵשׁ, (11) עֹרֵב, (10) חַלּוֹן, (9) הַר, (8) קָצֶה.

2. NOTES.

V. 1. וַיִּזְכֹּר, ī atten. from ă, ō lowered from ŭ; Ḳāl Impf. 3 m. sg.; synopsis?—וַיַּעֲבֵר, on ־ֲ instead of יְ_, § 65. 5. *b.* (1); synopsis? — וַיָּשֹׁכּוּ, from שָׁכַךְ, § 85. 1. *a*, 5. *a;* the ־ֹ rounded from orig. ־ֻ; the ō with first radical as regularly in עַ"עַ verbs; the D. f. for strengthening.

Vs. 2, 3. וַיִּסָּכְרוּ, Nîf. Impf. 3 m. plur. of סָכַר = סָנַר. — וַיִּכָּלֵא, § 72. 2. — וַיָּשֻׁבוּ, for וַיִּשׁוּבוּ: original ŭ is lengthened to û and ă of preformative becomes ā in open syl. § 86. 1. *e*, 3. *a.* —הָלוֹךְ.Inf. abs.; on ō(=â), § 67. 1. *b.* (1).—וְשׁוֹב, on ־ֹ, § 49. 4; on שׁוֹב, Inf. abs., § 86. 1. *g.*—וַיַּחְסְרוּ, on ־ֵ before הֵ, § 74. 2. *a;* on ־ֵ under חֵ, § 74. 3. *c.*— מִקְצֵה, for מִקְצֶה; on omis. of D. f., § 14. 2; on ־ֵ under קֵ, instead of ־ֶ, § 109. 6. *b;* on הֵ־ (ê), § 107. 3

Vs. 4, 5. וַתָּנַח, from נוּחַ (cf. וַיַּנִחֵהוּ ch. II. 15); usual Impf., יָנוּחַ, but the form with Wâw convers. has ŏ, § 86. 1. *e.* R.; but the laryng. prefers ă.— הָרֵי, const. pl. of הַר, which is from הָרַר; hence the ⟂ is unchangeable, and stands in the const., §§ 109. 5. *b;* 31. 4. N. 2.—חָסוֹר, Inf. abs.; on ô (= â), § 67. 1. *b.* (1)— נִרְאוּ, Nif. of רָאָה — רָאשֵׁי, const. plur.; another case of unchangeable ⟂ in const.; irreg. plur. of רֹאשׁ, § 116. 17.— הֶהָרִים on the ⟂ under הַ, § 45. 4.

Vs. 6, 7. וַיִּפְתַּח, § 76. 1. *a.*— וַיְשַׁלַּח, on ⟂ under לְ, § 76. 1. *b.*— וַיֵּצֵא, § 80. 2. *a.* (1).— יָצוֹא, § 67. 1. *b.* (1).— יְבֶשֶׁת, a fem. Inf. const., § 80. 2. *b.* R. 1.

3. *PRINCIPLES OF SYNTAX.*

V. 3.—הָלוֹךְ וָשׁוֹב ... וַיָּשֻׁבוּ—*And they returned, going and returning.*

V. 7.—וַיֵּצֵא יָצוֹא וָשׁוֹב—*And it went forth, going forth and returning.*

V. 5.—וְהַמַּיִם הָיוּ הָלוֹךְ וְחָסוֹר—*And the waters were going on and diminishing.*

Principle 36.—The Infinitive absolute, coming after a finite verb from the same root, gives to the latter the force of *continued and lasting action.* This idea of *continuance* is also expressed by the use of the verb הָלַךְ, in which case the principal idea is added in the form of a second Inf. abs. The thought of the phrases given above is: (1) "They went on going backwards"; (2) "It went repeatedly to and fro"; (3) "And the waters were abating continually."

V. 5.—בָּעֲשִׂירִי בְּאֶחָד לַחֹדֶשׁ—*In the tenth* (month), *on the first* (lit., *one*) (day) *of* (lit., *to*) *the month.*

Principle 37.—In dates (1) the words *day* and *month* are often

omitted, (2) the cardinals are often used instead of ordinals, and
(3) instead of the construct relation, a periphrastic expression by
means of לְ is employed.

4. GRAMMAR- AND WORD-LESSON.

1. § 109. 4. *a—f,*   Stem-changes in the inflection of Segolates.
2. § 109. 5. *a, b,*   Stem-changes in the inflection of middle-vowel
                       and ע״ע Segolates.
3. § 109. 6. *a, b,*   Stem-changes in the inflection of ל״ה nouns.
4. Word-Lists,   Verbs numbered 167—180 in List IV.

5. EXERCISES.

1. In the case of קָצֶה, חֹק, זַיִת, מָוֶת, יֶלֶד, write (1) sg. const.,
(2) sing. form with suffix *your*, (3) plur. abs., (4) plur. const., (5)
plur. form with suffix *my*.

2. To be translated into Hebrew:—(1) *Remember thou the days
in which God blessed thee;* (2) *God caused the waters to return
from upon the earth;* (3) *He died in the sixth year, in the seventh
month, on the fifth day of the month;* (4) *The words of God are
good;* (5) *He will live unto eternities of eternities;* (6) *The kings
of the earth shall return unto their land.*

3. To be written:—A transliteration of verses 2, 3 of ch. VIII.

4. Write a complete analysis of the following forms:—(1)
וַיִּשְׁלַח, (2) מַעֲיְנֹת, (3) לַחְדֹּשׁ, (4) הַגֶּשֶׁם, (5) וּמֵאַת.

6. TOPICS FOR STUDY.

(1) Vowels of the Ḳal Impf. 3 m. sg. of a strong verb. (2) ע״ע
Ḳal Impf. (3) Middle-vowel Ḳal Impf. (4) Nif‘al Impf. 3 m. sg. (5)
Form of Inf. abs. (6) The ô of the Inf. abs. (7) The ê of ל״ה nouns.
(8) Unchangeable ָ in const. plur. (9) Article with ָ . (10) לְ
laryngeal Pi‘ēl Impf. (11) פ״י Ḳal Impf. (12) Various forms assumed by Segolate stems in inflection. (13) Middle-vowel Segolates.
(14) ע״ע Segolates. (15) ל״ה nouns ending in הָ_ .

LESSON LV.—GENESIS VIII. 8-14.

1. *NEW WORDS.*

‎אַחֵר (7), חִיל (6), רֶגֶל (5), כַּף (4), מָנוֹחַ (3), קָלַל (2), יוֹנָה (1),
‎חָרֵב (13), רִאשׁוֹן (12), יָחַל (11), טָרָף (10), זַיִת (9), עֵת (8),
‎מִכְסֶה (15), סוּר (14).

2. *VERBAL FORMS.*

[In the case of each form, state (1) stem, (2) tense, (3) pers., numb., gen., (4) class, (5) root, (6) meaning of root, (7) corresponding form of קְטֹל, (8) the variation, and the section in the "Elements" which explains it. The superior figure indicates the verse in which the word occurs.]

(6) יֵשֵׁב,⁹ (1) יְשַׁלַּח,⁸ (2) לִרְאוֹת,⁸ (3) קַלּוּ,⁸ (4) מָצְאָה,⁹ (5)
(10) שַׁלַּח,¹⁰ (11) וַיֹּסֶף,¹⁰ (10) וַיָּחֶל,¹⁰ (9) יָבֹא,⁹ (8) יִקְחֶהָ,⁹ (7) יְשַׁלַּח,⁹
(17) וַיְהִי,¹³ (16) שׁוּב,¹² (15) וַיָּיַחֶל,¹² (14) וַיָּיַחֶל,¹¹ (13) וַיֵּדַע,¹¹ (12) תָּבֹא,¹¹
(20) וַיִּרָא,¹³ (19) וַיָּסַר,¹³ (18) יָבְשָׁה,¹⁴ חָרְבוּ,¹³

3. *NOMINAL FORMS.*

[In the case of each form, state (1) abs. sg., (2) meaning, (3) formation, (4) const. sg., (5) abs. and const. plur., (6) its form with one or more suffixes in sg. and plur.]

(1) אֲדָמָה,⁸ (2) רַגְלָה,⁹ (3) יָדוֹ,⁹ (4) יָמִים,¹⁰ (5) עֶרֶב,¹¹ (6) זַיִת,¹¹
(7) חֹדֶשׁ,¹³ (8) מִכְסֶה,¹³

4. *PARTICLES, PREPOSITIONS, SUFFIXES, ETC.*

[In the case of each, state all that may be known concerning it.]

(1) אֶת־,⁸ (2) מִן,⁸ (3) אֵת⁸ (*with*), (4) הַ,⁸ (5) הֲ־,⁸ (6) עַל,⁸ (7)
(14) לְ,¹¹ (13) הָ,⁹ (12) וְ,⁹ (11) כִּי,⁹ (10) אֶל־,⁹ (9) לֹא,⁹ (8) וְ,⁹
(15) הִנֵּה,¹¹ יְ,¹²

5. GRAMMAR- AND WORD-LESSON.

1. § **110**. 1—5, Classification of Noun-stems.

2. § **111**. 1. Tab. View and R's, Strong and Laryngeal Seğolates.

3. § **111**. 2. Tab. View and R's, ע״ו, ע״י, ל״ה and ע״ו Seğolates.

4. Word-Lists, Verbs numbered 181—194 in List
IV.

6. EXERCISES.

1. To be written:—A word-for-word translation of verses 8—14
of Genesis VIII.

2. To be written:—A transliteration of verses 9 and 10 of Genesis
VIII.

3. To be written:—Five Hebrew sentences of not less than eight
words each, based on the verses constituting this lesson.

LESSON LVI.—GENESIS VIII. 15-22.

1. NEW WORDS.

(1) דָּבָר, ·(2) מִשְׁפָּחָה (3) מִזְבֵּחַ, (4) עֹלָה, (5) רוּחַ, (6) רֵיחַ,

(7) נִיחֹחַ, (8) נְעוּרִים, (9) קָצִיר, (10) קֹר, (11) חֹם, (12) קַיִץ,

(13) חֹרֶף.

2. VERBAL FORMS.

[In the case of each form, state (1) stem, (2) tense, (3) pers., numb., gen.,
(4) class, (5) root, (6) meaning of root, (7) corresponding form of קָטַל
(8) the variation from the strong form, the reason for the variation, and the
section in the "Elements" which explains it. The superior figure indicates
the verse in which the word occurs.]

(1) יְדַבֵּר,[15] (2) לֵאמֹר,[15] (3) יָצָא[16] (§ **80**. 2. a), (4) הוֹצֵא[17] (acc.

to K'rê, הַיְצֵא; usual form would be הוֹצֵא, §§ **19**. 1, 2, 3; **80**. 3. b),

²⁰וַיַּעַל 10) ²⁰וַיִּקַּח (9) ²⁰וַיִּבֶן (8) ¹⁹יֵצְאוּ (7) ¹⁸וַיֵּצֵא (6) ¹⁷וּפָרוּ, (5

(in Hif., not Ḳäl), (11) ²¹וַיִּרַח (cf. וַתֵּנַח, v. 4), (12) ²¹אָסֹף, (13)

²²יִשְׁבֹּתוּ (16) ²¹עָשִׂיתִי, (15) ²¹לְהַכּוֹר, (14) ²¹לְקַלֵּל,

3. NOMINAL FORMS.

[In the case of each form, state (1) abs. sg., (2) meaning, (3) formation, (4) const. sg., (5) abs. and const. plur., (6) its form with one or more suffixes in sg. and plur.]

¹⁷בְּאֶרֶץ, (1) ¹⁷הַחַיָּה, (2) ¹⁷בָּשָׂר, (3) ¹⁷בְּהֵמָה, (4) ¹⁷רֶמֶשׂ, (5)

²¹לְכוּ, (6) מִשְׁפַּחַת, ¹⁹ (7) ²⁰מִזְבֵּחַ, (8) ²⁰טָהוֹר, (9) ²⁰עֹלֹת, (10)

²²חֹרֶף. (11) ²¹יֵצֶר, (12) ²¹נְעָרָיו, (13) ²²זֶרַע, (14) ²²קַיִץ, (15)

4. PARTICLES, PREPOSITIONS, IRREGULAR FORMS.

[In the case of each, state all that may be known concerning it.]

¹⁶אִתָּךְ, (1) ¹⁶אִשְׁתְּךָ, (2) ¹⁶בָּנֶיךָ, (3) ¹⁶נְשֵׁי, (4) ¹⁶אִתָּךְ, (5) מִן, (6)

¹⁸אִתּוֹ, (7) ²¹לֹא, (8) ²¹בַּעֲבוּר, (9) ²¹כַּאֲשֶׁר, (10) ²²יְמֵי,

5. GRAMMAR- AND WORD-LESSON.

1. § **112.** Tab. View and R's,   Nouns of the Second Class.
2. § **113.** Tab. View and R's,   Nouns of the Third Class.
3. § **114.** Tab. View and R's,   Nouns of the Fourth and Fifth Classes.
4. Word-Lists,   Verbs numbered 195—208 in List IV.

6. EXERCISES.

1. To be written:—A word-for-word translation of verses 15-22 of Genesis VIII.

2. To be written:—A transliteration of verses 17, 18 of Genesis VIII.

3. To be written:—Five Hebrew sentences of not less than ten words each, based on the verses constituting this Lesson.

MANUAL.

EXPLANATION OF SIGNS

USED IN THE TRANSLATION AND TRANSLITERATION.

---

1. *Parentheses* ( ) enclose words for which there is no equivalent in the Hebrew.

2. *Brackets* [ ] enclose words which are in the Hebrew, but are not to be rendered into English.

3.)(stands for 'ēθ, the sign of the definite object.

4. The *Hyphen* (-) connects those English words which, in Hebrew, form a single word.

5. The sign of *Addition* (+) stands for Măḳḳēf.

6. The *Asterisk* (*) stands for the 'Aθnâḥ (⌐); the *Dagger* (†), for Sᵉġōltâ (⫶); the *Period* (.), for Sôf Pâsûḳ (⫶⊤) preceded by Sillûḳ.

180

GENESIS I–IV.

THE HEBREW TEXT.

CHAPTER I.

א בְּרֵאשִׁית בָּרָא אֱלֹהִים אֵת הַשָּׁמַיִם וְאֵת הָאָרֶץ:

2 וְהָאָרֶץ הָיְתָה תֹהוּ וָבֹהוּ וְחֹשֶׁךְ עַל־פְּנֵי תְהוֹם וְרוּחַ
אֱלֹהִים מְרַחֶפֶת עַל־פְּנֵי הַמָּיִם:

3 וַיֹּאמֶר אֱלֹהִים יְהִי־אוֹר וַיְהִי־אוֹר:

4 וַיַּרְא אֱלֹהִים אֶת־הָאוֹר כִּי־טוֹב וַיַּבְדֵּל אֱלֹהִים בֵּין הָאוֹר
וּבֵין הַחֹשֶׁךְ:

ה וַיִּקְרָא אֱלֹהִים לָאוֹר יוֹם וְלַחֹשֶׁךְ קָרָא לָיְלָה וַיְהִי־עֶרֶב
וַיְהִי־בֹקֶר יוֹם אֶחָד:

6 וַיֹּאמֶר אֱלֹהִים יְהִי רָקִיעַ בְּתוֹךְ הַמָּיִם וִיהִי מַבְדִּיל בֵּין
מַיִם לָמָיִם:

7 וַיַּעַשׂ אֱלֹהִים אֶת־הָרָקִיעַ וַיַּבְדֵּל בֵּין הַמַּיִם אֲשֶׁר מִתַּחַת
לָרָקִיעַ וּבֵין הַמַּיִם אֲשֶׁר מֵעַל לָרָקִיעַ וַיְהִי־כֵן:

8 וַיִּקְרָא אֱלֹהִים לָרָקִיעַ שָׁמָיִם וַיְהִי־עֶרֶב וַיְהִי־בֹקֶר יוֹם
שֵׁנִי:

9 וַיֹּאמֶר אֱלֹהִים יִקָּווּ הַמַּיִם מִתַּחַת הַשָּׁמַיִם אֶל־מָקוֹם
אֶחָד וְתֵרָאֶה הַיַּבָּשָׁה וַיְהִי־כֵן:

י וַיִּקְרָא אֱלֹהִים לַיַּבָּשָׁה אֶרֶץ וּלְמִקְוֵה הַמַּיִם קָרָא יַמִּים
וַיַּרְא אֱלֹהִים כִּי־טוֹב:

11 וַיֹּאמֶר אֱלֹהִים תַּדְשֵׁא הָאָרֶץ דֶּשֶׁא עֵשֶׂב מַזְרִיעַ זֶרַע
עֵץ פְּרִי עֹשֶׂה פְּרִי לְמִינוֹ אֲשֶׁר זַרְעוֹ־בוֹ עַל־הָאָרֶץ
וַיְהִי־כֵן:

12 וַתּוֹצֵא הָאָרֶץ דֶּשֶׁא עֵשֶׂב מַזְרִיעַ זֶרַע לְמִינֵהוּ וְעֵץ
עֹשֶׂה־פְּרִי אֲשֶׁר זַרְעוֹ־בוֹ לְמִינֵהוּ וַיַּרְא אֱלֹהִים כִּי־טוֹב:

13 וַיְהִי־עֶרֶב וַיְהִי־בֹקֶר יוֹם שְׁלִישִׁי:

14 וַיֹּאמֶר אֱלֹהִים יְהִי מְאֹרֹת בִּרְקִיעַ הַשָּׁמַיִם לְהַבְדִּיל
בֵּין הַיּוֹם וּבֵין הַלָּיְלָה וְהָיוּ לְאֹתֹת וּלְמוֹעֲדִים וּלְיָמִים
וְשָׁנִים:

ט וְהָיוּ לִמְאוֹרֹת בִּרְקִיעַ הַשָּׁמַיִם לְהָאִיר עַל־הָאָרֶץ וַיְהִי־כֵן:

16 וַיַּעַשׂ אֱלֹהִים אֶת־שְׁנֵי הַמְּאֹרֹת הַגְּדֹלִים אֶת־הַמָּאוֹר
הַגָּדֹל לְמֶמְשֶׁלֶת הַיּוֹם וְאֶת־הַמָּאוֹר הַקָּטֹן לְמֶמְשֶׁלֶת
הַלַּיְלָה וְאֵת הַכּוֹכָבִים:

17 וַיִּתֵּן אֹתָם אֱלֹהִים בִּרְקִיעַ הַשָּׁמָיִם לְהָאִיר עַל־הָאָרֶץ:

18 וְלִמְשֹׁל בַּיּוֹם וּבַלַּיְלָה וּלְהַבְדִּיל בֵּין הָאוֹר וּבֵין הַחֹשֶׁךְ
וַיַּרְא אֱלֹהִים כִּי־טוֹב:

19 וַיְהִי־עֶרֶב וַיְהִי־בֹקֶר יוֹם רְבִיעִי:

כ וַיֹּאמֶר אֱלֹהִים יִשְׁרְצוּ הַמַּיִם שֶׁרֶץ נֶפֶשׁ חַיָּה וְעוֹף יְעוֹפֵף
עַל־הָאָרֶץ עַל־פְּנֵי רְקִיעַ הַשָּׁמָיִם:

21 וַיִּבְרָא אֱלֹהִים אֶת־הַתַּנִּינִם הַגְּדֹלִים וְאֵת כָּל־נֶפֶשׁ הַחַיָּה
הָרֹמֶשֶׂת אֲשֶׁר שָׁרְצוּ הַמַּיִם לְמִינֵהֶם וְאֵת כָּל־עוֹף כָּנָף
לְמִינֵהוּ וַיַּרְא אֱלֹהִים כִּי־טוֹב:

22 וַיְבָרֶךְ אֹתָם אֱלֹהִים לֵאמֹר פְּרוּ וּרְבוּ וּמִלְאוּ אֶת־הַמַּיִם
בַּיַּמִּים וְהָעוֹף יִרֶב בָּאָרֶץ:

23 וַיְהִי־עֶרֶב וַיְהִי־בֹקֶר יוֹם חֲמִישִׁי:

24 וַיֹּאמֶר אֱלֹהִים תּוֹצֵא הָאָרֶץ נֶפֶשׁ חַיָּה לְמִינָהּ בְּהֵמָה
וָרֶמֶשׂ וְחַיְתוֹ־אֶרֶץ לְמִינָהּ וַיְהִי־כֵן:

כה וַיַּעַשׂ אֱלֹהִים אֶת־חַיַּת הָאָרֶץ לְמִינָהּ וְאֶת־הַבְּהֵמָה
לְמִינָהּ וְאֵת כָּל־רֶמֶשׂ הָאֲדָמָה לְמִינֵהוּ וַיַּרְא אֱלֹהִים
כִּי־טוֹב:

26 וַיֹּאמֶר אֱלֹהִים נַעֲשֶׂה אָדָם בְּצַלְמֵנוּ כִּדְמוּתֵנוּ וְיִרְדּוּ
בִדְגַת הַיָּם וּבְעוֹף הַשָּׁמַיִם וּבַבְּהֵמָה וּבְכָל־הָאָרֶץ וּבְכָל־
הָרֶמֶשׂ הָרֹמֵשׂ עַל־הָאָרֶץ:

27 וַיִּבְרָא אֱלֹהִים אֶת־הָאָדָם בְּצַלְמוֹ בְּצֶלֶם אֱלֹהִים בָּרָא
אֹתוֹ זָכָר וּנְקֵבָה בָּרָא אֹתָם:

28 וַיְבָרֶךְ אֹתָם אֱלֹהִים וַיֹּאמֶר לָהֶם אֱלֹהִים פְּרוּ וּרְבוּ
וּמִלְאוּ אֶת־הָאָרֶץ וְכִבְשֻׁהָ וּרְדוּ בִּדְגַת הַיָּם וּבְעוֹף
הַשָּׁמַיִם וּבְכָל־חַיָּה הָרֹמֶשֶׂת עַל־הָאָרֶץ:

29 וַיֹּאמֶר אֱלֹהִים הִנֵּה נָתַתִּי לָכֶם אֶת־כָּל־עֵשֶׂב זֹרֵעַ זֶרַע
אֲשֶׁר עַל־פְּנֵי כָל־הָאָרֶץ וְאֶת כָּל־הָעֵץ אֲשֶׁר־בּוֹ פְרִי־
עֵץ זֹרֵעַ זָרַע לָכֶם יִהְיֶה לְאָכְלָה:

ל וּלְכָל־חַיַּת הָאָרֶץ וּלְכָל־עוֹף הַשָּׁמַיִם וּלְכֹל רוֹמֵשׂ עַל־
הָאָרֶץ אֲשֶׁר־בּוֹ נֶפֶשׁ חַיָּה אֶת־כָּל־יֶרֶק עֵשֶׂב לְאָכְלָה
וַיְהִי־כֵן:

31 וַיַּרְא אֱלֹהִים אֶת־כָּל־אֲשֶׁר עָשָׂה וְהִנֵּה־טוֹב מְאֹד וַיְהִי־
עֶרֶב וַיְהִי־בֹקֶר יוֹם הַשִּׁשִּׁי:

CHAPTER II.

א   וַיְכֻלּוּ הַשָּׁמַיִם וְהָאָרֶץ וְכָל־צְבָאָם:

2 וַיְכַל אֱלֹהִים בַּיּוֹם הַשְּׁבִיעִי מְלַאכְתּוֹ אֲשֶׁר עָשָׂה וַיִּשְׁבֹּת
בַּיּוֹם הַשְּׁבִיעִי מִכָּל־מְלַאכְתּוֹ אֲשֶׁר עָשָׂה:

3 וַיְבָרֶךְ אֱלֹהִים אֶת־יוֹם הַשְּׁבִיעִי וַיְקַדֵּשׁ אֹתוֹ כִּי בוֹ שָׁבַת
מִכָּל־מְלַאכְתּוֹ אֲשֶׁר־בָּרָא אֱלֹהִים לַעֲשׂוֹת:

4 אֵלֶּה תוֹלְדוֹת הַשָּׁמַיִם וְהָאָרֶץ בְּהִבָּרְאָם בְּיוֹם עֲשׂוֹת
יְהוָֹה אֱלֹהִים אֶרֶץ וְשָׁמָיִם:

ה   וְכֹל שִׂיחַ הַשָּׂדֶה טֶרֶם יִהְיֶה בָאָרֶץ וְכָל־עֵשֶׂב הַשָּׂדֶה
טֶרֶם יִצְמָח כִּי לֹא הִמְטִיר יְהוָֹה אֱלֹהִים עַל־הָאָרֶץ
וְאָדָם אַיִן לַעֲבֹד אֶת־הָאֲדָמָה:

6 וְאֵד יַעֲלֶה מִן־הָאָרֶץ וְהִשְׁקָה אֶת־כָּל־פְּנֵי הָאֲדָמָה:

7 וַיִּיצֶר יְהוָֹה אֱלֹהִים אֶת־הָאָדָם עָפָר מִן־הָאֲדָמָה וַיִּפַּח
בְּאַפָּיו נִשְׁמַת חַיִּים וַיְהִי הָאָדָם לְנֶפֶשׁ חַיָּה:

8 וַיִּטַּע יְהוָֹה אֱלֹהִים גַּן בְּעֵדֶן מִקֶּדֶם וַיָּשֶׂם שָׁם אֶת־הָאָדָם
אֲשֶׁר יָצָר:

9 וַיַּצְמַח יְהוָֹה אֱלֹהִים מִן־הָאֲדָמָה כָּל־עֵץ נֶחְמָד לְמַרְאֶה
וְטוֹב לְמַאֲכָל וְעֵץ הַחַיִּים בְּתוֹךְ הַגָּן וְעֵץ הַדַּעַת טוֹב
וָרָע:

ה׳ זְעִירָא .v. 4 ◦

י וְנָהָר יֹצֵא מֵעֵדֶן לְהַשְׁקוֹת אֶת־הַגָּן וּמִשָּׁם יִפָּרֵד וְהָיָה
לְאַרְבָּעָה רָאשִׁים:

11 שֵׁם הָאֶחָד פִּישׁוֹן הוּא הַסֹּבֵב אֵת כָּל־אֶרֶץ הַחֲוִילָה
אֲשֶׁר־שָׁם הַזָּהָב:

12 וּזֲהַב הָאָרֶץ הַהִוא טוֹב שָׁם הַבְּדֹלַח וְאֶבֶן הַשֹּׁהַם:

13 וְשֵׁם־הַנָּהָר הַשֵּׁנִי גִּיחוֹן הוּא הַסּוֹבֵב אֵת כָּל־אֶרֶץ
כּוּשׁ:

14 וְשֵׁם הַנָּהָר הַשְּׁלִישִׁי חִדֶּקֶל הוּא הַהֹלֵךְ קִדְמַת אַשּׁוּר
וְהַנָּהָר הָרְבִיעִי הוּא פְרָת:

טו וַיִּקַּח יְהוָֹה אֱלֹהִים אֶת־הָאָדָם וַיַּנִּחֵהוּ בְגַן־עֵדֶן לְעָבְדָהּ
וּלְשָׁמְרָהּ:

16 וַיְצַו יְהוָֹה אֱלֹהִים עַל־הָאָדָם לֵאמֹר מִכֹּל עֵץ־הַגָּן אָכֹל
תֹּאכֵל:

17 וּמֵעֵץ הַדַּעַת טוֹב וָרָע לֹא תֹאכַל מִמֶּנּוּ כִּי בְּיוֹם אֲכָלְךָ
מִמֶּנּוּ מוֹת תָּמוּת:

18 וַיֹּאמֶר יְהוָֹה אֱלֹהִים לֹא־טוֹב הֱיוֹת הָאָדָם לְבַדּוֹ אֶעֱשֶׂה־
לּוֹ עֵזֶר כְּנֶגְדּוֹ:

19 וַיִּצֶר יְהוָֹה אֱלֹהִים מִן־הָאֲדָמָה כָּל־חַיַּת הַשָּׂדֶה וְאֵת
כָּל־עוֹף הַשָּׁמַיִם וַיָּבֵא אֶל־הָאָדָם לִרְאוֹת מַה־יִּקְרָא־לוֹ
וְכֹל אֲשֶׁר יִקְרָא־לוֹ הָאָדָם נֶפֶשׁ חַיָּה הוּא שְׁמוֹ:

כ וַיִּקְרָא הָאָדָם שֵׁמוֹת לְכָל־הַבְּהֵמָה וּלְעוֹף הַשָּׁמַיִם וּלְכֹל
חַיַּת הַשָּׂדֶה וּלְאָדָם לֹא־מָצָא עֵזֶר כְּנֶגְדּוֹ:

21 וַיַּפֵּל יְהוָֹה אֱלֹהִים תַּרְדֵּמָה עַל־הָאָדָם וַיִּישָׁן וַיִּקַּח אַחַת
מִצַּלְעֹתָיו וַיִּסְגֹּר בָּשָׂר תַּחְתֶּנָּה:

22 וַיִּבֶן יְהוָֹה אֱלֹהִים אֶת־הַצֵּלָע אֲשֶׁר־לָקַח מִן־הָאָדָם
לְאִשָּׁה וַיְבִאֶהָ אֶל־הָאָדָם:

23 וַיֹּאמֶר הָאָדָם זֹאת הַפַּעַם עֶצֶם מֵעֲצָמַי וּבָשָׂר מִבְּשָׂרִי
לְזֹאת יִקָּרֵא אִשָּׁה כִּי מֵאִישׁ לֻקֳחָה־זֹּאת:

24 עַל־כֵּן יַעֲזָב־אִישׁ אֶת־אָבִיו וְאֶת־אִמּוֹ וְדָבַק בְּאִשְׁתּוֹ וְהָיוּ
לְבָשָׂר אֶחָד:

כה וַיִּהְיוּ שְׁנֵיהֶם עֲרוּמִּים הָאָדָם וְאִשְׁתּוֹ וְלֹא יִתְבֹּשָׁשׁוּ:

CHAPTER III.

א וְהַנָּחָשׁ הָיָה עָרוּם מִכֹּל חַיַּת הַשָּׂדֶה אֲשֶׁר עָשָׂה
יְהוָֹה אֱלֹהִים וַיֹּאמֶר אֶל־הָאִשָּׁה אַף כִּי־אָמַר אֱלֹהִים
לֹא תֹאכְלוּ מִכֹּל עֵץ הַגָּן:

2 וַתֹּאמֶר הָאִשָּׁה אֶל־הַנָּחָשׁ מִפְּרִי עֵץ־הַגָּן נֹאכֵל:

3 וּמִפְּרִי הָעֵץ אֲשֶׁר בְּתוֹךְ־הַגָּן אָמַר אֱלֹהִים לֹא תֹאכְלוּ
מִמֶּנּוּ וְלֹא תִגְּעוּ בּוֹ פֶּן תְּמֻתוּן:

4 וַיֹּאמֶר הַנָּחָשׁ אֶל־הָאִשָּׁה לֹא־מוֹת תְּמֻתוּן:

ה כִּי יֹדֵעַ אֱלֹהִים כִּי בְּיוֹם אֲכָלְכֶם מִמֶּנּוּ וְנִפְקְחוּ עֵינֵיכֶם
וִהְיִיתֶם כֵּאלֹהִים יֹדְעֵי טוֹב וָרָע:

מי ברגש v. 25. ○

6 וַתֵּרֶא הָאִשָּׁה כִּי טוֹב הָעֵץ לְמַאֲכָל וְכִי תַאֲוָה־הוּא
לָעֵינַיִם וְנֶחְמָד הָעֵץ לְהַשְׂכִּיל וַתִּקַּח מִפִּרְיוֹ וַתֹּאכַל
וַתִּתֵּן גַּם־לְאִישָׁהּ עִמָּהּ וַיֹּאכַל׃

7 וַתִּפָּקַחְנָה עֵינֵי שְׁנֵיהֶם וַיֵּדְעוּ כִּי עֵירֻמִּם הֵם וַיִּתְפְּרוּ
עֲלֵה תְאֵנָה וַיַּעֲשׂוּ לָהֶם חֲגֹרֹת׃

8 וַיִּשְׁמְעוּ אֶת־קוֹל יְהֹוָה אֱלֹהִים מִתְהַלֵּךְ בַּגָּן לְרוּחַ
הַיּוֹם וַיִּתְחַבֵּא הָאָדָם וְאִשְׁתּוֹ מִפְּנֵי יְהֹוָה אֱלֹהִים
בְּתוֹךְ עֵץ הַגָּן׃

9 וַיִּקְרָא יְהֹוָה אֱלֹהִים אֶל־הָאָדָם וַיֹּאמֶר לוֹ אַיֶּכָּה׃
וַיֹּאמֶר אֶת־קֹלְךָ שָׁמַעְתִּי בַּגָּן וָאִירָא כִּי־עֵירֹם אָנֹכִי
וָאֵחָבֵא׃

11 וַיֹּאמֶר מִי הִגִּיד לְךָ כִּי עֵירֹם אָתָּה הֲמִן־הָעֵץ אֲשֶׁר
צִוִּיתִיךָ לְבִלְתִּי אֲכָל־מִמֶּנּוּ אָכָלְתָּ׃

12 וַיֹּאמֶר הָאָדָם הָאִשָּׁה אֲשֶׁר נָתַתָּה עִמָּדִי הִוא נָתְנָה־
לִי מִן־הָעֵץ וָאֹכֵל׃

13 וַיֹּאמֶר יְהֹוָה אֱלֹהִים לָאִשָּׁה מַה־זֹּאת עָשִׂית וַתֹּאמֶר
הָאִשָּׁה הַנָּחָשׁ הִשִּׁיאַנִי וָאֹכֵל׃

14 וַיֹּאמֶר יְהֹוָה אֱלֹהִים אֶל־הַנָּחָשׁ כִּי עָשִׂיתָ זֹּאת אָרוּר
אַתָּה מִכָּל־הַבְּהֵמָה וּמִכֹּל חַיַּת הַשָּׂדֶה עַל־גְּחֹנְךָ תֵלֵךְ
וְעָפָר תֹּאכַל כָּל־יְמֵי חַיֶּיךָ׃

<hr>

מלעיל v. 10. º

טו וְאֵיבָה אָשִׁית בֵּינְךָ וּבֵין הָאִשָּׁה וּבֵין זַרְעֲךָ וּבֵין זַרְעָהּ
הוּא יְשׁוּפְךָ רֹאשׁ וְאַתָּה תְּשׁוּפֶנּוּ עָקֵב:

16 אֶל־הָאִשָּׁה אָמַר הַרְבָּה אַרְבֶּה עִצְּבוֹנֵךְ וְהֵרֹנֵךְ בְּעֶצֶב
תֵּלְדִי בָנִים וְאֶל־אִישֵׁךְ תְּשׁוּקָתֵךְ וְהוּא יִמְשָׁל־בָּךְ:

17 וּלְאָדָם אָמַר כִּי שָׁמַעְתָּ לְקוֹל אִשְׁתֶּךָ וַתֹּאכַל מִן־הָעֵץ
אֲשֶׁר צִוִּיתִיךָ לֵאמֹר לֹא תֹאכַל מִמֶּנּוּ אֲרוּרָה הָאֲדָמָה
בַּעֲבוּרֶךָ בְּעִצָּבוֹן תֹּאכֲלֶנָּה כֹּל יְמֵי חַיֶּיךָ:

18 וְקוֹץ וְדַרְדַּר תַּצְמִיחַ לָךְ וְאָכַלְתָּ אֶת־עֵשֶׂב הַשָּׂדֶה:

19 בְּזֵעַת אַפֶּיךָ תֹּאכַל לֶחֶם עַד שׁוּבְךָ אֶל־הָאֲדָמָה כִּי
מִמֶּנָּה לֻקָּחְתָּ כִּי־עָפָר אַתָּה וְאֶל־עָפָר תָּשׁוּב:

כ וַיִּקְרָא הָאָדָם שֵׁם אִשְׁתּוֹ חַוָּה כִּי הוּא הָיְתָה אֵם
כָּל־חָי:

21 וַיַּעַשׂ יְהוָה אֱלֹהִים לְאָדָם וּלְאִשְׁתּוֹ כָּתְנוֹת עוֹר
וַיַּלְבִּשֵׁם:

22 וַיֹּאמֶר יְהוָה אֱלֹהִים הֵן הָאָדָם הָיָה כְּאַחַד מִמֶּנּוּ
לָדַעַת טוֹב וָרָע וְעַתָּה פֶּן־יִשְׁלַח יָדוֹ וְלָקַח גַּם
מֵעֵץ הַחַיִּים וְאָכַל וָחַי לְעֹלָם:

23 וַיְשַׁלְּחֵהוּ יְהוָה אֱלֹהִים מִגַּן־עֵדֶן לַעֲבֹד אֶת־הָאֲדָמָה
אֲשֶׁר לֻקַּח מִשָּׁם:

24 וַיְגָרֶשׁ אֶת־הָאָדָם וַיַּשְׁכֵּן מִקֶּדֶם לְגַן־עֵדֶן אֶת־הַכְּרֻבִים
וְאֵת לַהַט הַחֶרֶב הַמִּתְהַפֶּכֶת לִשְׁמֹר אֶת־דֶּרֶךְ עֵץ
הַחַיִּים:

CHAPTER IV.

א וְהָ֣אָדָ֔ם יָדַ֖ע אֶת־חַוָּ֣ה אִשְׁתּ֑וֹ וַתַּ֙הַר֙ וַתֵּ֣לֶד אֶת־קַ֔יִן
וַתֹּ֕אמֶר קָנִ֥יתִי אִ֖ישׁ אֶת־יְהֹוָֽה׃

2 וַתֹּ֣סֶף לָלֶ֔דֶת אֶת־אָחִ֖יו אֶת־הָ֑בֶל וַֽיְהִי־הֶ֙בֶל֙ רֹ֣עֵה צֹ֔אן
וְקַ֕יִן הָיָ֖ה עֹבֵ֥ד אֲדָמָֽה׃

3 וַֽיְהִ֖י מִקֵּ֣ץ יָמִ֑ים וַיָּבֵ֨א קַ֜יִן מִפְּרִ֧י הָֽאֲדָמָ֛ה מִנְחָ֖ה
לַֽיהֹוָֽה׃

4 וְהֶ֨בֶל הֵבִ֥יא גַם־ה֛וּא מִבְּכֹר֥וֹת צֹאנ֖וֹ וּמֵֽחֶלְבֵהֶ֑ן וַיִּ֣שַׁע
יְהֹוָ֔ה אֶל־הֶ֖בֶל וְאֶל־מִנְחָתֽוֹ׃

ה וְאֶל־קַ֥יִן וְאֶל־מִנְחָת֖וֹ לֹ֣א שָׁעָ֑ה וַיִּ֤חַר לְקַ֙יִן֙ מְאֹ֔ד
וַֽיִּפְּל֖וּ פָּנָֽיו׃

6 וַיֹּ֥אמֶר יְהֹוָ֖ה אֶל־קָ֑יִן לָ֚מָּה חָ֣רָה לָ֔ךְ וְלָ֖מָּה נָֽפְל֥וּ פָנֶֽיךָ׃

7 הֲל֤וֹא אִם־תֵּיטִיב֙ שְׂאֵ֔ת וְאִם֙ לֹ֣א תֵיטִ֔יב לַפֶּ֖תַח חַטָּ֣את
רֹבֵ֑ץ וְאֵלֶ֙יךָ֙ תְּשׁ֣וּקָת֔וֹ וְאַתָּ֖ה תִּמְשָׁל־בּֽוֹ׃

8 וַיֹּ֥אמֶר קַ֖יִן אֶל־הֶ֣בֶל אָחִ֑יו וַֽיְהִי֙ בִּֽהְיוֹתָ֣ם בַּשָּׂדֶ֔ה וַיָּ֥קָם
קַ֛יִן אֶל־הֶ֥בֶל אָחִ֖יו וַיַּֽהַרְגֵֽהוּ׃

9 וַיֹּ֤אמֶר יְהֹוָה֙ אֶל־קַ֔יִן אֵ֖י הֶ֣בֶל אָחִ֑יךָ וַיֹּ֙אמֶר֙ לֹ֣א יָדַ֔עְתִּי
הֲשֹׁמֵ֥ר אָחִ֖י אָנֹֽכִי׃

י וַיֹּ֖אמֶר מֶ֣ה עָשִׂ֑יתָ ק֚וֹל דְּמֵ֣י אָחִ֔יךָ צֹעֲקִ֥ים אֵלַ֖י מִן־
הָֽאֲדָמָֽה׃

11 וְעַתָּ֖ה אָר֣וּר אָ֑תָּה מִן־הָֽאֲדָמָה֙ אֲשֶׁ֣ר פָּֽצְתָ֣ה אֶת־פִּ֔יהָ
לָקַ֛חַת אֶת־דְּמֵ֥י אָחִ֖יךָ מִיָּדֶֽךָ׃

כִּי תַעֲבֹד אֶת־הָאֲדָמָה לֹא־תֹסֵף תֵּת־כֹּחָהּ לָךְ נָע וָנָד 12
תִּהְיֶה בָאָרֶץ:

וַיֹּאמֶר קַיִן אֶל־יְהֹוָה גָּדוֹל עֲוֺנִי מִנְּשֹׂא: 13

הֵן גֵּרַשְׁתָּ אֹתִי הַיּוֹם מֵעַל פְּנֵי הָאֲדָמָה וּמִפָּנֶיךָ אֶסָּתֵר 14
וְהָיִיתִי נָע וָנָד בָּאָרֶץ וְהָיָה כָל־מֹצְאִי יַהַרְגֵנִי:

וַיֹּאמֶר לוֹ יְהֹוָה לָכֵן כָּל־הֹרֵג קַיִן שִׁבְעָתַיִם יֻקָּם וַיָּשֶׂם טו
יְהֹוָה לְקַיִן אוֹת לְבִלְתִּי הַכּוֹת־אֹתוֹ כָּל־מֹצְאוֹ:

וַיֵּצֵא קַיִן מִלִּפְנֵי יְהֹוָה וַיֵּשֶׁב בְּאֶרֶץ־נוֹד קִדְמַת־עֵדֶן: 16

וַיֵּדַע קַיִן אֶת־אִשְׁתּוֹ וַתַּהַר וַתֵּלֶד אֶת־חֲנוֹךְ וַיְהִי בֹּנֶה 17
עִיר וַיִּקְרָא שֵׁם הָעִיר כְּשֵׁם בְּנוֹ חֲנוֹךְ:

וַיִּוָּלֵד לַחֲנוֹךְ אֶת־עִירָד וְעִירָד יָלַד אֶת־מְחוּיָאֵל וּמְחִיָּיאֵל 18
יָלַד אֶת־מְתוּשָׁאֵל וּמְתוּשָׁאֵל יָלַד אֶת־לָמֶךְ:

וַיִּקַּח־לוֹ לֶמֶךְ שְׁתֵּי נָשִׁים שֵׁם הָאַחַת עָדָה וְשֵׁם הַשֵּׁנִית 19
צִלָּה:

וַתֵּלֶד עָדָה אֶת־יָבָל הוּא הָיָה אֲבִי יֹשֵׁב אֹהֶל וּמִקְנֶה: כ

וְשֵׁם אָחִיו יוּבָל הוּא הָיָה אֲבִי כָּל־תֹּפֵשׂ כִּנּוֹר וְעוּגָב: 21

וְצִלָּה גַם־הִוא יָלְדָה אֶת־תּוּבַל קַיִן לֹטֵשׁ כָּל־חֹרֵשׁ 22
נְחֹשֶׁת וּבַרְזֶל וַאֲחוֹת תּוּבַל־קַיִן נַעֲמָה:

וַיֹּאמֶר לֶמֶךְ לְנָשָׁיו 23

עָדָה וְצִלָּה שְׁמַעַן קוֹלִי
נְשֵׁי לֶמֶךְ הַאֲזֵנָּה אִמְרָתִי

○ v. 18. יתיר י׳

כִּי אִישׁ הָרַגְתִּי לְפִצְעִי

וְיֶלֶד לְחַבֻּרָתִי:

24 כִּי שִׁבְעָתַיִם יֻקַּם־קָיִן

וְלֶמֶךְ שִׁבְעִים וְשִׁבְעָה:

הכ וַיֵּדַע אָדָם עוֹד אֶת־אִשְׁתּוֹ וַתֵּלֶד בֵּן וַתִּקְרָא אֶת־שְׁמוֹ

שֵׁת כִּי שָׁת־לִי אֱלֹהִים זֶרַע אַחֵר תַּחַת הֶבֶל כִּי הֲרָגוֹ

קָיִן:

26 וּלְשֵׁת גַּם־הוּא יֻלַּד־בֵּן וַיִּקְרָא אֶת־שְׁמוֹ אֱנוֹשׁ אָז הוּחַל

לִקְרֹא בְּשֵׁם יְהוָה:

GENESIS I—IV.

A LITERAL TRANSLATION.

CHAPTER I.

1. In-beginning created God*)(the-heavens and-)(the-earth.

2. And-the-earth was desolation and-waste; and-darkness (was) upon+faces-of abyss;* and-(the)-spirit-of God (was) brooding upon+faces-of the-waters.

3. And-said God: Shall-be+(or, let-be)+light;* and-(there)-was+light.

4. And-saw God)(+the-light that+good;* and-caused-a-division God between the-light and-between the-darkness.

5. And-called God to-the-light day, and-to-the-darkness called-he night;* and-(it)-was+evening, and-(it)-was+morning, day one.

6. And-said God: Let-be (an) expanse in-(the)-midst-of the-waters;* and-let-it-be dividing between waters to-waters.

7. And-made God)(+the-expanse,†and-caused-a-division between the-waters which (were) from-under to-the-expanse and-between the-waters which (were) from-upon to-the-expanse;* and-(it)-was+so.

8. And-called God to-the-expanse heavens;* and-(it)-was+evening, and-(it)-was+morning, day second.

9. And-said God: Let-be-collected the-waters from-under the-heavens unto+place one, and-let-be-seen the-dry (land);* and-(it)-was+so.

10. And-called God to-the-dry (land) earth, and-to-(the)-collection-of [the]-waters he-called seas;* and-saw God that+good.

11. And-said God: Let-cause-to-spring-forth the-earth grass, herb causing-to-seed seed, tree-of fruit making fruit to-kind-his which seed-his+in-him (*i. e.,* whose seed is in it) upon+the-earth;* and-(it)-was+so.

12. And-caused-to-come-forth the-earth grass; herb causing-to-seed seed to-kind-his, and-tree making+fruit which seed-his+in-him to-kind-his;* and-saw God that+good.

13. And-(it)-was+evening, and-(it)-was+morning, day third.

14. And-said God: Let-be luminaries in-(the)-expanse-of the-heavens, to-cause-a-division between the-day and-between the-night;* and-thcy-shall-be for-signs, and-for-seasons, and-for-days and-years.

15. And-they-shall-be for-luminaries in-(the)-expanse-of the-heavens to-cause-light upon+the-earth;* and-(it)-was+so.

16. And-made God)(+(the)-two-[of] [the]-luminaries the-great;*)(+the-luminary the-great, for-ruling-of the-day; and-)(+the-luminary the-small, for-ruling-of the-night, and-)(the-stars.

17. Anc-gave)(-them God in-(the)expanse-of the-heavens;* to-cause-light upon +the-earth[.].

18. And-to-rule in-the-day and-in-the-night, and-to-cause-a-division between the-light and-between the-darkness;* and-saw God that+good.

19. And-(it)-was+evening, and-(it)-was+morning, day fourth.

20. And-said God: Let-swarm the-waters swarm(s), soul-of life;* and-fowl shall-fly upon+the-earth, upon+faces-of (the) expanse-of the-heavens.

21. And-created God)(+the-sea-monsters the-great;* and-)(all+ (the)-soul(s)-of [the]-life the-creeping (*or,* which-creep), (with) which swarmed the-waters to-kinds-their and-)(every+fowl of wing to-kind-his and-saw God that+good.

22. And-blessed)(-them God, to-say (*or*, saying):* Be-ye fruitful and-multiply-ye and-fill-ye)(+the-waters in-the-seas, and-the-fowl let-multiply in-the-earth.

23. And-(it)-was+evening, and-(it)-was+morning, day fifth.

24. And-said God: Shall-cause-to-come-forth the-earth soul-of life to-kind-her, cattle, and-creeper, and-beast-of+(the)-earth to-kind-her;* and-(it)-was+so.

25. And-made God)(+(the)-beast-of the-earth to-kind-her, and-)(+the-cattle to-kind-her, and-)(every+creeper-of the-ground to-kind-his;* and-saw God that+good.

26. And-said God: We-will-(*or*, Let-us)-make man in-image-our, ac-cording-to-likeness-our;* and-they-shall-have-dominion in-(the)-fish-of the-sea, and-in-(the)-fowl-of the-heavens, and-in-the-cattle, and-in-all+the-earth, and-in-all+the-creeper(s) the-creeping (*or*, which-creep) upon+the-earth.

27. And-created God)(+the-man in-image-his; in-(the)-image-of God created-he)(-him;* male and-female created-he)(-them.

28. And-blessed)(-them God,† and-said to-them God: Be-ye-fruitful and-multiply-ye, and-fill-ye)(+the-earth and-subdue-ye-her;* and-have-ye-dominion in-(the)-fish-of the-sea, and-in-(the)-fowl-of the-heavens, and-in-every+beast the-creeping upon+the-earth.

29. And-said God: Behold! I-have-given to-you)(+every+herb seed-ing seed which (is) upon+faces-of all+the-earth, and-)(all +the-tree(s) which+in-him (*i. e.*, in-which) (is the) fruit-of +(a)-tree seeding seed;* to-you it-shall-be for-food.

30. And-to-every+beast-of the-earth, and-to-every+fowl-of the-heav-ens, and-to-every creeping-one upon+the-earth which+in-him (*i. e.*, in-which) (is the) soul-of life, (I have given))(+ every+greenness-of herb for-food;* and-(it)-was+so.

31. And-saw God)(+all+which he-had-done, and-behold+good ex-ceedingly;* and-(it)-was+evening, and-(it)-was+morning, day the sixth.

CHAPTER II.

1. And-were-finished the-heavens and-the-earth and-all+host-their.

2. And-finished God, in-the-day the-seventh, work-his which-he-had-done;* and-he-rested in-the-day the-seventh from-all+work-his which he-had-done.

3. And-blessed God)(+day the-seventh and-sanctified)(-it;* because in-it he-rested from-all+work-his which+created God to-make.

4. These (are) (the) generations-of the-heavens and-the-earth in-being-created-their;* in-(the)-day-of (the) making of Lord God earth and-heavens.

5. And-every shrub-of the-field not-yet had-been (*lit.*, will-be) in-the-earth, and-every+herb-of the-field not-yet had-sprouted-(*lit.*, will-sprout)-forth;* for not had-caused-to-rain Lord God upon+the-earth and-man was-not to-serve)(+the-ground.

6. And-(a)-mist used-to-go-up (*lit.*, will-go-up) from+the-earth,* and-cause-to-drink (*i. e.*, used-to-water))(+all+(the)-faces-of the-ground.

7. And-formed Lord God)(+the-man (out of) dust from+the-ground, and-breathed in-nostrils-his breath-of lives;* and-was the-man for-(a)-soul-of life (*i. e.*, and-became the-man (a) soul-of life).

8. And-planted Lord God (a) garden in-Eden from-east,* and-placed there)(+the-man whom he-formed.

9. And-caused-to-sprout-forth Lord God from+the-ground, every +tree pleasant to-sight and-good for-food,* and-(the)-tree-of [the]-lives in-(the)-midst-of the-garden, and-(the)-tree-of [the]-knowing good and-evil.

10. And-(a)-river goes-forth (*lit.*, going-forth) from-Eden to-water)(+the-garden,* and-from-there it-is-divided and-becomes four heads (*lit.*, and-is for-four heads).

11. (The) name-of the-one (is) Pishon;* it (*lit.*, he) (is) the-(one-encompassing (*or*, which-encompasses))(all+(the)-land-of-[the]-Havilah, which+there (*i. e.*, where) (is) the-gold.

1? And-(the)-gold-of the-land the-that (*lit.*, she) (is) good;* there (is) the-bdellium and-(the)-stone-of [the]-onyx.

13. And-(the)-name-of+the-river the-second (is) Gihon;* it (is) the-(one)-encompassing)(all+(the)-land-of Cush.

14. And-(the)-name-of the-river the-third (is) Tigris; it (is) the-(one)-going eastward-of Assyria;* and-the-river the-fourth is (*lit.*, he) Euphrates.

15. And-took Lord God)(+the-man,* and-caused-to-rest-him (*i. e.*, placed-him) in-garden-of+Eden to-serve-it (*lit.*, her) and-to-keep-it.

16. And-commanded Lord God upon+the-man to-say (*i. e.*, say-ing):* From-every tree-of+the-garden eating thou-mayest eat[.];

17. But-from-(the)-tree-of [the]-knowing good and-evil, not shalt-thou-eat from-it (*lit.*, him);* for, in-(the)-day-of eating-thy from-it, dying shalt-thou-die.

18. And-said Lord God: Not+good (the)-being-of [the]-man to-separation-his;* I-will-make+for-him (a) help as-over-against-him (*or*, as-his-counterpart).

19. And-formed Lord God from+the-ground every+beast-of the-field and-)(every+fowl-of the-heavens, and-caused-to-come (*i. e.*, brought) unto+the-man to-see what+he-will-call+to-it, (*lit.*, him),* and-all which will-call+to-it the-man, soul-of life, is (*lit.*, he) name-its (*lit.*, his).

20. And-called the-man names to-all+the-cattle, and-to-(the)-fowl-of the-heavens and-to-every beast-of the-field;* and-for-man not +did-he-find (*i. e.*, there was not found) (a) help as-over-against-him.

21. And-caused-to-fall Lord God (a) deep-sleep upon+the-man, and-he-slept,* and-he-took one from-sides-his and-closed (the) flesh instead-of-it.

22. And-built Lord God)(+the-side which+he-took from+the-man for-(a)-woman,* and-caused-to-come-her (*i. e.*, brought her) unto+the-man.

23. And-said the-man † : This, the-tread (*i. e.*, now), bone from-bones-my, and-flesh from-flesh-my;* to-this it-shall-be-called woman, for from-man was-taken+this.

24. Upon+so (*i. e.*, therefore) shall-leave+(a)-man)(+father-his and-)(+mother-his,* and-shall-cleave in-wife-his, and-they-shall-be for-flesh one.

25. And-were (the) two-of-them naked, the-man and-wife-his;* and-not were-(*lit.*, will-be)-they-ashamed.

CHAPTER III.

[In the two remaining chapters, the translation of the pronominal suffix is placed *before* instead of *after* the noun which it limits.]

1. And-the-serpent was crafty from-every beast-of the-field which had-made Lord God;* and-he-said unto+the-woman: (Is it) so that+has-said God, not shall-ye-eat from-every tree-of the-garden[.]?

2. And-said the-woman unto+the-serpent:* From-(the)-fruit-of (the)-tree(s)-of+the-garden we-may-eat[.];

3. But-from-(the)-fruit-of the-tree which (is) in-midst-of+the-garden,† has-said God: Not shall-ye-eat from-it, and-not shall-ye-touch in-it,* lest ye-die.

4. And-said the-serpent unto+the-woman:* Not+dying shall-ye-die.

5. For knowing (is) God that in-(the)-day-of your-eating from-it, then-(*lit.*, and)-shall-be-opened your-eyes,* and-ye-shall-be-like-God, knowers-of good and-evil.

6. And-saw the-woman, that good (was) the-tree for-food, and-that (a) delight-(was)+it to-the-eyes, and-desirable (was) the-tree to-make-wise, and-she-took from-his-fruit and-she-ate;* and-she-gave also+to-her-husband with-her and-he-ate[.];

7. And-were-opened (the) eyes-of (the) two-of-them, and-they-knew that naked (were) they,* and-they-sewed leaf-of fig-tree, and-they-made for-them-(selves) girdles.

8. And-they-heard)(+(the)-voice-of Lord God walking in-the-garden to-(or, at)-(the)-breeze-of the-day;* and-hid-himself the-man and-his-wife from-faces-of Lord God in-midst-of (the) tree(s)-of the-garden.

9. And-called Lord God unto+the-man,* and-said to-him: Where-art-thou[.]?

10. And-he-said:)(+thy-voice I-heard in-the-garden,* and-I-was-afraid, because+naked (was) I; and-I-hid-myself.

11. And-he-said: Who caused-to-know (*i. e.*, made known) to-thee, that naked (wert) thou;* ?-from+the-tree, which I-com-manded-thee to-not eat+from it, hast-thou-eaten[.]?

12. And-said the-man:* The-woman whom thou-gave (to be) with-me, she gave+to-me from+the-tree and-I-ate.

13. And-said Lord God to-the-woman: What+(is)+this thou-hast-done?* And-said the-woman: The serpent corrupted-me and-I-ate.

14. And-said Lord God unto+the-serpent: Because thou-hast-done this,† cursed (art) thou from-all+the-cattle, and-from-every beast-of the-field;* upon+thy-belly shalt-thou-go, and-dust shalt-thou-eat all+(the)+days-of thy-lives.

15. And-enmity will-I-put between-thee and-between the-woman, and-between thy-seed and-between her-seed;* it (*lit.*, he) shall-bruise-thee (as to the) head; and-thou shalt-bruise-him (as to the) heel.

16. Unto+the-woman he-said: Causing-to-be-great I-will-cause-to-be-great (*i. e.*, multiplying I will multiply) thy-sorrow and-thy-conception (*i. e.*, the sorrow of thy conception); in-pain thou-shalt-bring-forth sons,* and-unto+thy-husband (shall-be) thy-desire and-he shall-rule+in-(*or*, over)-thee.

17. And-to-man he-said: Because thou hast-hearkened to-(the)-voice-of thy-wife,† and-hast-eaten from+the-tree which I-commanded-thee, to-say: not shalt-thou-eat from-it,* cursed (is) the-ground for-the-sake-of-thee; in-sorrow shalt-thou-eat-(of)-it all (the) days-of thy-lives.

18. And-thorn and-thistle shall-it-cause-to-spring-forth to-thee;* and-thou-shalt-eat)(+(the)+herb-of the-field.

19. In-(the)-sweat-of thy-nostrils, shalt-thou-eat bread, until thy-return unto+the-ground; for from-it (*lit.*, her) wast-thou-taken;* for+dust (art) thou, and-unto+dust thou-shalt-return.

20. And-called the-man (the) name-of his-wife Eve,* for she was mother-of all+living.

21. And-made Lord God for-man and-for-his-wife tunics-of skin, and-caused-to-put-on-them.

22. And-said Lord God: Behold! the-man has-become like-one-of [from]-us to-know good and-evil;* and-now lest+he-put-forth his-hand and-take also from-(the)-tree-of [the]-lives, and-eat and-live for-ever.

23. Therefore-(*lit.*, and)-sent-him Lord God from-(the)-garden-of +Eden,* to-serve)(+the-ground which he-was-taken from-there.

24. And-he-drove-out)(+the-man,* and-caused-to-dwell (*i. e.*, placed) from-east to-(the)-garden-of+Eden,)(+the-Cherubim, and-)((the) flame-of the-sword (*i e.*, the flaming sword) the-(one)-turning-itself to-keep)(+(the)-way-of (the) tree of [the]-lives.

CHAPTER IV.

1. And-the-man knew)(+Eve his-wife;* and-she-conceived, and-she-bore)(+Cain; and-she-said: I-have-gotten (a) man with+ (the) Lord.

2. And-she-added to-bear (*i. e.,* and again she bore))(+his-brother)(+Abel;* and-was+Abel (a) shepherd-of flock(s), and-Cain was (a) tiller-of ground.

3. And-it-was, from-end-of days,* and-caused-to-come (*i. e.,* brought) Cain from-(the)-fruit-of the-ground (an) offering to (the) Lord.

4. And-Abel caused-to-come, also+he, from-(the)-firstlings-of his flock and-from-their-fats;* and-looked-with-favor (the) Lord unto+Abel and-unto+his-offering.

5. And-unto+Cain and-unto+his-offering not did-he-look-with-favor;* and-it-kindled to-Cain (*i. e.,* and Cain was angry), exceedingly, and-fell his-faces (*or,* countenance).

6. And-said (the) Lord unto+Cain: For-what (*or,* why) has-it-kindled to-thee, and-for-what have-fallen thy-faces[.]?

7. (Is there) ?-not, if+thou-makest-(*or,* doest)-good, (a) lifting-up (of the countenance)? and-if not thou-makest-good, at-the-door sin (is) crouching;* and-unto-thee (shall be) his-desire, and-thou shouldst-rule+in-(*or,* over)-him.

8. And-said Cain unto+Abel his-brother;* and-(it)-was in-their-being in-the-field, and-rose Cain unto+Abel his-brother and-killed-him.

9. And-said (the) Lord unto+Cain: Where (is) Abel thy-brother?* And-he-said: Not have-I-known (*i. e.,* do-know); ?-keeper-of my brother (am) I[.]?

10. And-he-said: What hast-thou-done?* (The) voice-of (the) bloods-of thy-brother (are) crying unto-me from+the-ground.

11. And-now cursed (art) thou,* from+the-ground which has-opened)(+her-mouth to-take)(+(the)+bloods-of thy-brother from-thy-hand.

12. When thou-shalt-till (or, serve))(+the-ground, not+will-it-add to-give+her-strength to-thee;* (a) fugitive and-(a)-vagabond shalt-thou-be in-the-earth.

13. And-said Cain unto+(the) Lord:* Great (is) my-iniquity from-bearing.

14. Behold! thou-hast-driven-out)(-me the-day (*i. e.*, to-day) from-upon (the) faces-of the-ground, and-from-thy-faces shall-I-be-hid;* and-I-shall-be (a) fugitive and-(a)-vagabond in-the-earth, and-it-shall-be (that) any+finding-me will-kill-me.

15. And-said to-him (the) Lord: Therefore (*lit.*, to-so) any+killing Cain, seven-fold shall-he-be-avenged;* and-placed (the) Lord for-Cain (a) sign to-not smite+)(-him any+finding-him.

16. And-went-forth Cain from-to-faces-of (*i. e.*, from the presence of) (the) Lord;* and-he-dwelt in-(the)-land-of+Nod, eastward-of+Eden.

17. And-knew Cain)(+his-wife and-she-conceived, and-bore)(+Enoch;* and-he-was building (a) city, and-he-called (the) name-of the-city according-to-(the)-name-of his-son Enoch.

18. And-there-was-born to-Enoch)(+Irad; and-Irad begat)(+Mehujael;* and-Mehujael begat)(+Methusael; and-Methusael begat)(+Lamech.

19. And-took+to-him Lamech two-[of] wives,* (the) name-of the-one Adah, and-(the)-name-of the-second Zillah.

20. And-bore Adah)(+Jabal;* he was (the) father-of (the) inhabitant-of tent(s) and-(the-possessor-of)-cattle.

21. And-(the)-name-of his-brother (was) Jubal;* he was (the) father-of all+performing-on (the) harp and-(the)-flute.

22. And-Zillah, also+she, bore)(+Tubal Cain, hammerer-of every +cutter-of (*i. e.*, cutting-instrument-of) bronze and-iron;* and-(the)-sister-of Tubal+Cain (was) Naamah.

23. And-said Lamech to-his-wives:—
    Adah and-Zillah, hear-ye my-voice,
    Wives-of Lamech hearken-unto my-saying;*
    For (a) man I-have-killed for-my-wounding;
    And-(a)-youth, for-my-hurt.

24. If seven-fold shall-be-avenged+Cain,*
    Then-Lamech seventy and-seven.

25. And-knew Adam again)(+his-wife and-she-bare (a) son; and-
    she-called)(+his-name Seth:* For has-put+to-me God seed
    another instead-of Abel, for slew-him Cain.

26. And-to-Seth, also+he, was-born+(a)-son; and-he-called)(+his-
    name Enosh;* then it-was-commenced to-call on-(the)-name-of
    (the) Lord.

CHAPTER I.

א בראשית ברא אלהים את השמים ואת הארץ:

2 והארץ היתה תהו ובהו וחשך על פני תהום ורוח
אלהים מרחפת על פני המים:

3 ויאמר אלהים יהי אור ויהי אור:

4 וירא אלהים את האור כי טוב ויבדל אלהים בין האור
ובין החשך:

ה ויקרא אלהים לאור יום ולחשך קרא לילה ויהי ערב
ויהי בקר יום אחד:

6 ויאמר אלהים יהי רקיע בתוך המים ויהי מבדיל בין
מים למים:

7 ויעש אלהים את הרקיע ויבדל בין המים אשר מתחת
לרקיע ובין המים אשר מעל לרקיע ויהי כן:

8 ויקרא אלהים לרקיע שמים ויהי ערב ויהי בקר יום
שני:

9 ויאמר אלהים יקוו המים מתחת השמים אל מקום
אחד ותראה היבשה ויהי כן:

י ויקרא אלהים ליבשה ארץ ולמקוה המים קרא ימים
וירא אלהים כי טוב:

11 ויאמר אלהים תדשא הארץ דשא עשב מזריע זרע
עץ פרי עשה פרי למינו אשר זרעו בו על הארץ
ויהי כן:

12 וַתּוֹצֵא הָאָרֶץ דֶּשֶׁא עֵשֶׂב מַזְרִיעַ זֶרַע לְמִינֵהוּ וְעֵץ
עֹשֶׂה פְּרִי אֲשֶׁר זַרְעוֹ בוֹ לְמִינֵהוּ וַיַּרְא אֱלֹהִים כִּי טוֹב:

13 וַיְהִי עֶרֶב וַיְהִי בֹקֶר יוֹם שְׁלִישִׁי:

14 וַיֹּאמֶר אֱלֹהִים יְהִי מְאֹרֹת בִּרְקִיעַ הַשָּׁמַיִם לְהַבְדִּיל
בֵּין הַיּוֹם וּבֵין הַלָּיְלָה וְהָיוּ לְאֹתֹת וּלְמוֹעֲדִים וּלְיָמִים
וְשָׁנִים:

טו וְהָיוּ לִמְאוֹרֹת בִּרְקִיעַ הַשָּׁמַיִם לְהָאִיר עַל הָאָרֶץ
וַיְהִי כֵן:

16 וַיַּעַשׂ אֱלֹהִים אֶת שְׁנֵי הַמְּאֹרֹת הַגְּדֹלִים אֶת הַמָּאוֹר
הַגָּדֹל לְמֶמְשֶׁלֶת הַיּוֹם וְאֶת הַמָּאוֹר הַקָּטֹן לְמֶמְשֶׁלֶת
הַלַּיְלָה וְאֵת הַכּוֹכָבִים:

17 יִתֵּן אֹתָם אֱלֹהִים בִּרְקִיעַ הַשָּׁמַיִם לְהָאִיר עַל הָאָרֶץ:

18 וְלִמְשֹׁל בַּיּוֹם וּבַלַּיְלָה וּלְהַבְדִּיל בֵּין הָאוֹר וּבֵין הַחֹשֶׁךְ
וַיַּרְא אֱלֹהִים כִּי טוֹב:

19 וַיְהִי עֶרֶב וַיְהִי בֹקֶר יוֹם רְבִיעִי:

כ וַיֹּאמֶר אֱלֹהִים יִשְׁרְצוּ הַמַּיִם שֶׁרֶץ נֶפֶשׁ חַיָּה וְעוֹף
יְעוֹפֵף עַל הָאָרֶץ עַל פְּנֵי רְקִיעַ הַשָּׁמָיִם:

21 וַיִּבְרָא אֱלֹהִים אֶת הַתַּנִּינִם הַגְּדֹלִים וְאֵת כָּל נֶפֶשׁ
הַחַיָּה הָרֹמֶשֶׂת אֲשֶׁר שָׁרְצוּ הַמַּיִם לְמִינֵהֶם וְאֵת
כָּל עוֹף כָּנָף לְמִינֵהוּ וַיַּרְא אֱלֹהִים כִּי טוֹב:

22 וַיְבָרֶךְ אֹתָם אֱלֹהִים לֵאמֹר פְּרוּ וּרְבוּ וּמִלְאוּ אֶת הַמַּיִם
בַּיַּמִּים וְהָעוֹף יִרֶב בָּאָרֶץ:

23 וַיְהִי עֶרֶב וַיְהִי בֹקֶר יוֹם חֲמִישִׁי:

24 וַיֹּאמֶר אֱלֹהִים תּוֹצֵא הָאָרֶץ נֶפֶשׁ חַיָּה לְמִינָהּ בְּהֵמָה
וָרֶמֶשׂ וְחַיְתוֹ אֶרֶץ לְמִינָהּ וַיְהִי כֵן:

כה ויעש אלהים את חית הארץ למינה ואת הבהמה
למינה ואת כל רמש האדמה למינהו וירא אלהים
כי טוב :

26 ויאמר אלהים נעשה אדם בצלמנו כדמותנו וירדו
בדגת הים ובעוף השמים ובבהמה ובכל הארץ
ובכל הרמש הרמש על הארץ :

27 ויברא אלהים את האדם בצלמו בצלם אלהים ברא
אתו זכר ונקבה ברא אתם :

28 ויברך אתם אלהים ויאמר להם אלהים פרו ורבו
ומלאו את הארץ וכבשה ורדו בדגת הים ובעוף
השמים ובכל חיה הרמשת על הארץ :

29 ויאמר אלהים הנה נתתי לכם את כל עשב זרע
זרע אשר על פני כל הארץ ואת כל העץ אשר בו
פרי עץ זרע זרע לכם יהיה לאכלה :

ל ולכל חית הארץ ולכל עוף השמים ולכל רומש
על הארץ אשר בו נפש חיה את כל ירק עשב לאכלה
ויהי כן :

31 וירא אלהים את כל אשר עשה והנה טוב מאד ויהי
ערב ויהי בקר יום הששי :

CHAPTER II.

א ויכלו השמים והארץ וכל צבאם :

2 ויכל אלהים ביום השביעי מלאכתו אשר עשה וישבת
ביום השביעי מכל מלאכתו אשר עשה :

3 ויברך אלהים את יום השביעי ויקדש אתו כי בו שבת
מכל מלאכתו אשר ברא אלהים לעשות :

4 אלה תולדות השמים והארץ בהבראם ביום עשות
יהוה אלהים ארץ ושמים:

ה וכל שיח השדה טרם יהיה בארץ וכל עשב השדה
טרם יצמח כי לא המטיר יהוה אלהים על הארץ
ואדם אין לעבד את האדמה:

6 ואד יעלה מן הארץ והשקה את כל פני האדמה:

7 וייצר יהוה אלהים את האדם עפר מן האדמה ויפח
באפיו נשמת חיים ויהי האדם לנפש חיה:

8 ויטע יהוה אלהים גן בעדן מקדם וישם שם את האדם
אשר יצר:

9 ויצמח יהוה אלהים מן האדמה כל עץ נחמד למראה
וטוב למאכל ועץ החיים בתוך הגן ועץ הדעת טוב
ורע:

י ונהר יצא מעדן להשקות את הגן ומשם יפרד והיה
לארבעה ראשים:

11 שם האחד פישון הוא הסבב את כל ארץ החוילה
אשר שם הזהב:

12 וזהב הארץ ההוא טוב שם הבדלח ואבן השהם:

13 ושם הנהר השני גיחון הוא הסובב את כל ארץ
כוש:

14 ושם הנהר השלישי חדקל הוא ההלך קדמת אשור
והנהר הרביעי הוא פרת:

ט ויקח יהוה אלהים את האדם וינחהו בגן עדן לעבדה
ולשמרה:

16 ויצו יהוה אלהים על האדם לאמר מכל עץ הגן
אכל תאכל :

17 ומעץ הדעת טוב ורע לא תאכל ממנו כי ביום
אכלך ממנו מות תמות :

18 ויאמר יהוה אלהים לא טוב היות האדם לבדו
אעשה לו עזר כנגדו :

19 ויצר יהוה אלהים מן האדמה כל חית השדה ואת
כל עוף השמים ויבא אל האדם לראות מה יקרא לו
וכל אשר יקרא לו האדם נפש חיה הוא שמו :

כ ויקרא האדם שמות לכל הבהמה ולעוף השמים
ולכל חית השדה ולאדם לא מצא עזר כנגדו :

21 ויפל יהוה אלהים תרדמה על האדם ויישן ויקח
אחת מצלעתיו ויסגר בשר תחתנה :

22 ויבן יהוה אלהים את הצלע אשר לקח מן האדם
לאשה ויבאה אל האדם :

23 ויאמר האדם זאת הפעם עצם מעצמי ובשר מבשרי
לזאת יקרא אשה כי מאיש לקחה זאת :

24 על כן יעזב איש את אביו ואת אמו ודבק באשתו
והיו לבשר אחד :

כה ויהיו שניהם ערומים האדם ואשתו ולא יתבששו :

CHAPTER III.

א והנחש היה ערום מכל חית השדה אשר עשה
יהוה אלהים ויאמר אל האשה אף כי אמר אלהים
לא תאכלו מכל עץ הגן :

2   ‏ותאמר האשה אל הנחש מפרי עץ הגן נאכל:‏

3   ‏ומפרי העץ אשר בתוך הגן אמר אלהים לא תאכלו‏
‏ממנו ולא תגעו בו פן תמתון:‏

4   ‏ויאמר הנחש אל האשה לא מות תמתון:‏

ה   ‏כי ידע אלהים כי ביום אכלכם ממנו ונפקחו עיניכם‏
‏והייתם כאלהים ידעי טוב ורע:‏

6   ‏ותרא האשה כי טוב העץ למאכל וכי תאוה הוא‏
‏לעינים ונחמד העץ להשכיל ותקח מפריו ותאכל‏
‏ותתן גם לאישה עמה ויאכל:‏

7   ‏ותפקחנה עיני שניהם וידעו כי עירמם הם ויתפרו‏
‏עלה תאנה ויעשו להם חגרת:‏

8   ‏וישמעו את קול יהוה אלהים מתהלך בגן לרוח‏
‏היום ויתחבא האדם ואשתו מפני יהוה אלהים‏
‏בתוך עץ הגן:‏

9   ‏ויקרא יהוה אלהים אל האדם ויאמר לו איכה:‏

י   ‏ויאמר את קלך שמעתי בגן ואירא כי עירם אנכי‏
‏ואחבא:‏

11   ‏ויאמר מי הגיד לך כי עירם אתה המן העץ אשר‏
‏צויתיך לבלתי אכל ממנו אכלת:‏

12   ‏ויאמר האדם האשה אשר נתתה עמדי הוא נתנה‏
‏לי מן העץ ואכל:‏

13   ‏ויאמר יהוה אלהים לאשה מה זאת עשית ותאמר‏
‏האשה הנחש השיאני ואכל:‏

‏מלעיל‏ v. 10, ○

14 ויאמר יהוה אלהים אל הנחש כי עשית זאת ארור
אתה מכל הבהמה ומכל חית השדה על גחנך תלך
ועפר תאכל כל ימי חייך :

טו ואיבה אשית בינך ובין האשה ובין זרעך ובין
זרעה הוא ישופך ראש ואתה תשופנו עקב :

16 אל האשה אמר הרבה ארבה עצבונך והרנך בעצב
תלדי בנים ואל אישך תשוקתך והוא ימשל בך :

17 ולאדם אמר כי שמעת לקול אשתך ותאכל מן העץ
אשר צויתיך לאמר לא תאכל ממנו ארורה האדמה
בעבורך בעצבון תאכלנה כל ימי חייך :

18 וקוץ ודרדר תצמיח לך ואכלת את עשב השדה:

19 בזעת אפיך תאכל לחם עד שובך אל האדמה כי
ממנה לקחת כי עפר אתה ואל עפר תשוב :

כ ויקרא האדם שם אשתו חוה כי הוא היתה אם
כל חי :

21 ויעש יהוה אלהים לאדם ולאשתו כתנות עור
וילבשם :

22 ויאמר יהוה אלהים הן האדם היה כאחד ממנו
לדעת טוב ורע ועתה פן ישלח ידו ולקח גם מעץ
החיים ואכל וחי לעלם :

23 וישלחהו יהוה אלהים מגן עדן לעבד את האדמה
אשר לקח משם :

24 ויגרש את האדם וישכן מקדם לגן עדן את הכרבים
ואת להט החרב המתהפכת לשמר את דרך עץ
החיים :

CHAPTER IV.

א והאדם ידע את חוה אשתו ותהר ותלד את קין
ותאמר קניתי איש את יהוה:

2 ותסף ללדת את אחיו את הבל ויהי הבל רעה צאן
וקין היה עבד אדמה:

3 ויהי מקץ ימים ויבא קין מפרי האדמה מנחה
ליהוה:

4 והבל הביא גם הוא מבכרות צאנו ומחלבהן וישע
יהוה אל הבל ואל מנחתו:

ה ואל קין ואל מנחתו לא שעה ויחר לקין מאד
ויפלו פניו:

6 ויאמר יהוה אל קין למה חרה לך ולמה נפלו
פניך:

7 הלוא אם תיטיב שאת ואם לא תיטיב לפתח
חטאת רבץ ואליך תשוקתו ואתה תמשל בו:

8 ויאמר קין אל הבל אחיו ויהי בהיותם בשדה
ויקם קין אל הבל אחיו ויהרגהו:

9 ויאמר יהוה אל קין אי הבל אחיך ויאמר לא
ידעתי השמר אחי אנכי:

י ויאמר מה עשית קול דמי אחיך צעקים אלי מן
האדמה:

11 ועתה ארור אתה מן האדמה אשר פצתה את פיה
לקחת את דמי אחיך מידך:

12 כי תעבד את האדמה לא תסף תת כחה לך נע
ונד תהיה בארץ:

13 ויאמר קין אל יהוה גדול עוני מנשוא:

14 הן גרשת אתי היום מעל פני האדמה ומפניך
אסתר והייתי נע ונד בארץ והיה כל מצאי יהרגני:

טו ויאמר לו יהוה לכן כל הרג קין שבעתים יקם
וישם יהוה לקין אות לבלתי הכות אתו כל מצאו:

16 ויצא קין מלפני יהוה וישב בארץ נוד קדמת עדן:

17 וידע קין את אשתו ותהר ותלד את חנוך ויהי
בנה עיר ויקרא שם העיר כשם בנו חנוך:

18 ויולד לחנוך את עירד ועירד ילד את מחויאל
ומחייאל ילד את מתושאל ומתושאל ילד את למך:

19 ויקח לו למך שתי נשים שם האחת עדה ושם
השנית צלה:

כ ותלד עדה את יבל הוא היה אבי ישב אהל
ומקנה:

21 ושם אחיו יובל הוא היה אבי כל תפש כנור ועוגב:

22 וצלה גם הוא ילדה את תובל קין לטש כל חרש
נחשת וברזל ואחות תובל קין נעמה:

23 ויאמר למך לנשיו
עדה וצלה שמען קולי
נשי למך האזנה אמרתי
כי איש הרגתי לפצעי
וילד לחברתי:

24   כי שבעתים יקם קין

ולמך ,שבעים ושבעה:

כה ‏ וידע אדם עוד את אשתו ותלד בן ותקרא את שמו

שת כי שת לי אלהים זרע אחר תחת הבל כי

הרגו קין:

26 ‏ ולשת גם הוא ילד בן ויקרא את שמו אנוש אז

הוחל לקרא בשם יהוה:

Transliteration of Genesis I.

1. B‘rē’-šîθ bå-rå’ ’‘lô-hîm* ’ēθ hāš-šå-må-yĭm w‘’ēθ hå-’å’-rěş.

2. W‘hå-’å’-rěş hå-y‘θå(h) θố-hû wå-vố-hû, w‘hố-šěχ ‘ăl+p‘nê θ‘hôm* w‘rû(ă)ḥ ’‘lô-hĭm m‘rā(ḥ)-ḥě-fēθ ‘ăl+p‘nê hăm-må’-yīm.

3. Wăy-yô’’-měr ’‘lô-hîm y‘hî+’ôr;* wăy-hî+ôr.

4. Wăy-yăr’ ’‘lô-hîm ’ēθ+hå-’ôr kî+ṭôv;* wăy-yăv-dēl ’‘lô-hĭm bēn hå-’ôr û-vēn hă(ḥ)-ḥố-šěχ.

5. Wăy-yĭḳ-rå’ ’‘lô-hîm lå-’ôr yôm w‘lă(ḥ)-ḥố-šěχ ḳå’-rå’ lå’-y‘lå(h);* wăy-hî+’é-rěv wăy-hî+vố-ḳěr yôm ’ě(ḥ)-ḥåđ.

6. Wăy-yô’’-měr ‘lô-hîm, y‘hî rå-ḳî(ă)‘ b‘θôχ hăm-må’-yĭm;* wî-hî măv-dîl bēn må-yĭm lå-må’-yĭm.

7. Wăy-yă-‘ăs ’‘lô-hîm ’ēθ+hå-rå-ḳî(ă)‘;† wăy-yăv-dēl bēn hăm-må-yĭm ’‘šěr mĭt-tă-ḥăθ lå-rå-ḳî(ă)‘ û-vēn hăm-må-yĭm ’‘šěr mē-‘ăl lå-rå-ḳî(ă)‘;* wăy-hî+χēn.

8. Wăy-yĭḳ-rå’ ’‘lô-hîm lå-rå-ḳî(ă)‘ šå-må’-yĭm;* wăy-hî+’é-rěv wăy-hî+vố-ḳěr yôm šē-nî.

9. Wăy-yô’’-měr ’‘lô-hîm, yĭḳ-ḳå-wû hăm-må-yĭm mĭt-tă-ḥăθ hăš-šå-må-yĭm ’ěl+må-ḳôm ’ě(ḥ)-ḥåđ, w‘θē-rå-’é(h) hăy-yăb-bå-šå(h);* wăy-hî+χēn.

10. Wăy-yĭḳ-rå’ ’‘lô-hîm låy-yăb-bå-šå(h) ’é-rěş, û-l‘mĭḳ-wê hăm-må-yĭm ḳå-rå’ yăm-mîm;* wăy-yăr’ ’‘lô-hîm kî+ṭôv.

11. Wăy-yô’’-měr ’‘lô-hîm, tăđ-šē’ hå-’å’-rěş dé-šē’, ’é-sěv măz-rî(ă)‘ zé-rå‘, ’ēş p‘rî ’ô-sé(h) p‘rî l‘mî-nô, ’‘šěr zăr-‘ô+vô ‘ăl+ hå-’å’-rěş;* wăy-hî+χēn.

12. Wăt-tô-şē’ hå-’å’-rěş dé-šē, ’é-sěv măz-rî(ă)‘ zé-rå‘ l‘mî-nē-hû, w‘ēş ’ô-sé(h)+p‘rî ’‘šěr zăr-‘ô+vô l‘mî-nē-hû;* wăy-yăr’ ’‘lô-hîm kî+ṭôv.

213

13. Wăy-hî+'ĕ́-rĕv wăy-hî+vṓ-ḳĕr yôm šᵉlî-šî.

14. Wăy-yô''-mĕr 'ᵉlô-hîm, yᵉhî mᵉ'ô-rôθ bĭr-ḳî(ä)' hăš-šă-mắ-yĭm,
    lᵉhäv-dîl bēn hăy-yôm û-vēn häl-lắ'-yᵉlâ(h);* wᵉhă-yû lᵉ'ô-θôθ
    û-lᵉmô-'ᵃđîm û-lᵉyă-mîm wᵉšă-nîm.

15. Wᵉhă-yû lĭm-'ô-rôθ bĭr-ḳî(ä)' hăš-šă-mắ-yĭm, lᵉhă-'îr 'ăl+hă-'ắ'-
    rĕṣ;* wăy-hî+χēn.

16. Wăy-yắ-'äs 'ᵉlô-hîm 'ĕθ+šᵉnê hăm-mᵉ'ô-rôθ hăg-gᵉđô-lîm,* 'ĕθ
    +hăm-mă-'ôr hăg-gă-đôl lᵉmĕm-šĕ-lĕθ hăy-yôm, wᵉ'ĕθ+hăm-mă-
    'ôr hăḳ-ḳă-ṭōn lᵉmĕm-šĕ-lĕθ häl-lä'-yᵉlâ(h), wᵉ'ēθ hăk-kô-χă-vîm.

17. Wăy-yĭt-tēn 'ô-θăm 'ᵉlô-hîm bĭr-ḳî(ä)' hăš-šă-mắ'-yĭm,* lᵉhă-'îr
    'ăl+hă-'ắ'-rĕṣ[.],

18. Wᵉlĭm-šōl băy-yôm û-văl-lắ-yᵉlâ(h), û-lᵃhäv-dîl bēn hă-'ôr û-vēn
    hä(ḥ)-ḫṓ-šèχ;* wăy-yăr' 'ᵉlô-hîm kî+ṭôv.

19. Wăy-hî+'ĕ́-rĕv wăy-hî+vṓ-ḳĕr yôm rᵉvî-'î.

20. Wăy-yô''-mĕr 'ᵉlô-hîm, yĭš-rᵉṣû hăm-mă-yĭm šĕ-rĕṣ,   nĕ-fĕš ḥăy-
    yă(h);* wᵉ'ôf yᵉ'ô-fēf 'ăl+hă-'ắ'-rĕṣ, 'ăl+pᵉnê rᵉḳî(ä)' hăš-šă-
    mắ'-yĭm.

21. Wăy-yĭv-rắ' 'ᵉlô-hîm 'ĕθ+hăt-tăn-nî-nîm hăg-gᵉđô-lîm,* wᵉ'ēθ
    kŏl+nĕ-fĕš hä(ḥ)-ḥăy-yă(h) hă-rô-mĕ-sēθ 'ᵃšĕr šă-rᵉṣû hăm-mă-yĭm
    lᵉmî-nē-hĕm, wᵉ'ēθ kŏl-'ôf kă-năf lᵉmî-nē-hû; wăy-yăr' 'ᵉlô-hîm
    kî+ṭôv.

22. Wăy-vắ'-rĕχ 'ô-θăm 'ᵉlô-hîm, lê'-môr,* pᵉrû û-rᵉvû   û-mĭl-û
    'ĕθ+hăm-mắ-yĭm băy-yăm-mîm, wᵉhă-'ôf yĭ'-rĕv bă-'ắ'-rĕṣ.

23. Wăy-hî+'ĕ́-rĕv wăy-hî+vṓ-ḳĕr yôm ḥᵃmî-šî.

24. Wăy-yô''-mĕr 'ᵉlô-hîm, tô-ṣē' hă-'ắ'-rĕṣ nĕ-fĕš ḥăy-yă(h) lᵉmî-nâh,
    bᵉhē-mă(h) wă-rĕ-mĕś wᵉḥăy-θô+'ĕ́-rĕṣ lᵉmî-nâh;* wăy-hî+χēn.

25. Wăy-yắ-'äs 'ᵉlô-hîm 'ĕθ+ḥăy-yăθ hă-'ắ'-rĕṣ lᵉmî-nâh, wᵉ'ĕθ+hăb·
    bᵉhē-mă(h) lᵉmî-nâh, wᵉ'ēθ kŏl+rĕ-mĕś hă-'ᵃđă-mă(h) lᵉmî-nĕ-hû;*
    wăy-yăr' 'ᵉlô-hîm kî+ṭôv.

26. Wăy-yô''-mĕr 'ᵉlô-hîm, nă'ᵃ-sế(h) 'â-đâm bᵉṣăl-mḗ-nû, kĭđ-mû-θḗ-nû;* wᵉyĭr-đû vĭđ-ğäθ hăy-yâm û-vᵉ'ôf häš-šâ-mắ-yĭm û-văb-bᵉhē-mâ(h) û-vᵉxŏl+hâ-'å'-rĕṣ, û-vᵉχŏl+hâ-rḗ-mĕś hâ-rô-mēś 'äl+hâ-'å'-rĕṣ.

27. Wăy-yĭv-râ' 'ᵉlô-hîm 'ëθ+hâ-'å-đâm bᵉṣăl-mô, bᵉṣḗ-lĕm 'ᵉlô-hîm bâ-râ' 'ô-θô;* zâ-χâr û-nᵉḳē-vâ(h) bâ-râ' 'ô-θâm.

28. Wăy-vå'-rĕχ 'ô-θâm 'ᵉlô-hîm,† wăy-yô''-mĕr lâ-hĕm 'ᵉlô-hîm, pᵉrû û-rᵉvû û-mĭl-'û 'ëθ+hâ-å'-rĕṣ wᵉxĭv-šû'-hâ* û-rᵉđû bĭđ-ğäθ hăy-yâm û-vᵉ'ôf häš-šâ-mắ-yĭm, û-vᵉxŏl+ḥăy-yâ(h) hâ-rô-mḗ-śëθ 'äl+hâ-'å'-rĕṣ.

29. Wăy-yô''-mĕr 'ᵉlô-hîm, hĭn-nē(h) nâ-θắt-tî lâ-χĕm 'ëθ+kŏl+'ḗ-sĕv zô-rē(ä)' zế-rä' 'ᵃšĕr 'äl+pᵉnê χŏl+hâ-'å'-rĕṣ, wᵉ'ēθ kŏl+hâ-'ēṣ 'ᵃšĕr+bô fᵉrî+'ēṣ zô-rē(ä)' zå'-rä',* lâ-χĕm yĭh-yế(h) lᵉ'ŏχ-lâ(h).

30. û-lᵉxŏl+ḥăy-yäθ hâ-'å'-rĕṣ û-lᵉxŏl +'ôf häš-šâ-mắ-yĭm û-lᵉxōl rô-mēś 'äl+hâ-'å'-rĕṣ 'ᵃšĕr+bô nế-fĕš ḥăy-yâ(h) 'ëθ+kŏl+ yế-rĕḳ 'ē-śĕv lᵉ'ŏχ-lâ(h);* wăy-hî+χēn.

31. Wăy-yăr' 'ᵉlô-hîm 'ëθ+kŏl+'ᵃšĕr 'â-sâ(h) wᵉhĭn-nē(h)+ṭôv mᵉ'ôđ;* wăy-hî+ḗ-rĕv wăy-hî+vố-ḳĕr yôm häš-šĭš-šî.

CHAPTER V.

א זֶה סֵפֶר תּוֹלְדֹת אָדָם בְּיוֹם בְּרֹא אֱלֹהִים אָדָם בִּדְמוּת
אֱלֹהִים עָשָׂה אֹתוֹ:

2 זָכָר וּנְקֵבָה בְּרָאָם וַיְבָרֶךְ אֹתָם וַיִּקְרָא אֶת־שְׁמָם אָדָם
בְּיוֹם הִבָּרְאָם:

3 וַיְחִי אָדָם שְׁלֹשִׁים וּמְאַת שָׁנָה וַיּוֹלֶד בִּדְמוּתוֹ כְּצַלְמוֹ
וַיִּקְרָא אֶת־שְׁמוֹ שֵׁת:

4 וַיִּהְיוּ ׀ יְמֵי אָדָם אַחֲרֵי הוֹלִידוֹ אֶת־שֵׁת שְׁמֹנֶה מֵאֹת
שָׁנָה וַיּוֹלֶד בָּנִים וּבָנוֹת:

ה וַיִּהְיוּ כָּל־יְמֵי אָדָם אֲשֶׁר־חַי תְּשַׁע מֵאוֹת שָׁנָה וּשְׁלֹשִׁים
שָׁנָה וַיָּמֹת:

6 וַיְחִי־שֵׁת חָמֵשׁ שָׁנִים וּמְאַת שָׁנָה וַיּוֹלֶד אֶת־אֱנוֹשׁ:

7 וַיְחִי־שֵׁת אַחֲרֵי הוֹלִידוֹ אֶת־אֱנוֹשׁ שֶׁבַע שָׁנִים וּשְׁמֹנֶה
מֵאוֹת שָׁנָה וַיּוֹלֶד בָּנִים וּבָנוֹת:

8 וַיִּהְיוּ כָּל־יְמֵי־שֵׁת שְׁתֵּים עֶשְׂרֵה שָׁנָה וּתְשַׁע מֵאוֹת
שָׁנָה וַיָּמֹת:

9 וַיְחִי אֱנוֹשׁ תִּשְׁעִים שָׁנָה וַיּוֹלֶד אֶת־קֵינָן:
וַיְחִי אֱנוֹשׁ אַחֲרֵי הוֹלִידוֹ אֶת־קֵינָן חֲמֵשׁ עֶשְׂרֵה שָׁנָה
וּשְׁמֹנֶה מֵאוֹת שָׁנָה וַיּוֹלֶד בָּנִים וּבָנוֹת:

217

11 וַיִּהְיוּ כָּל־יְמֵי אֱנוֹשׁ חָמֵשׁ שָׁנִים וּתְשַׁע מֵאוֹת שָׁנָה
וַיָּמֹת:

12 וַיְחִי קֵינָן שִׁבְעִים שָׁנָה וַיּוֹלֶד אֶת־מַהֲלַלְאֵל:

13 וַיְחִי קֵינָן אַחֲרֵי הוֹלִידוֹ אֶת־מַהֲלַלְאֵל אַרְבָּעִים שָׁנָה
וּשְׁמֹנֶה מֵאוֹת שָׁנָה וַיּוֹלֶד בָּנִים וּבָנוֹת:

14 וַיִּהְיוּ כָּל־יְמֵי קֵינָן עֶשֶׂר שָׁנִים וּתְשַׁע מֵאוֹת שָׁנָה וַיָּמֹת:

טו וַיְחִי מַהֲלַלְאֵל חָמֵשׁ שָׁנִים וְשִׁשִּׁים שָׁנָה וַיּוֹלֶד אֶת־יָרֶד:

16 וַיְחִי מַהֲלַלְאֵל אַחֲרֵי הוֹלִידוֹ אֶת־יֶרֶד שְׁלֹשִׁים שָׁנָה
וּשְׁמֹנֶה מֵאוֹת שָׁנָה וַיּוֹלֶד בָּנִים וּבָנוֹת:

17 וַיִּהְיוּ כָּל־יְמֵי מַהֲלַלְאֵל חָמֵשׁ וְתִשְׁעִים שָׁנָה וּשְׁמֹנֶה
מֵאוֹת שָׁנָה וַיָּמֹת:

18 וַיְחִי־יֶרֶד שְׁתַּיִם וְשִׁשִּׁים שָׁנָה וּמְאַת שָׁנָה וַיּוֹלֶד
אֶת־חֲנוֹךְ:

19 וַיְחִי־יֶרֶד אַחֲרֵי הוֹלִידוֹ אֶת־חֲנוֹךְ שְׁמֹנֶה מֵאוֹת שָׁנָה
וַיּוֹלֶד בָּנִים וּבָנוֹת:

כ וַיִּהְיוּ כָּל־יְמֵי־יֶרֶד שְׁתַּיִם וְשִׁשִּׁים שָׁנָה וּתְשַׁע מֵאוֹת
שָׁנָה וַיָּמֹת:

21 וַיְחִי חֲנוֹךְ חָמֵשׁ וְשִׁשִּׁים שָׁנָה וַיּוֹלֶד אֶת־מְתוּשָׁלַח:

22 וַיִּתְהַלֵּךְ חֲנוֹךְ אֶת־הָאֱלֹהִים אַחֲרֵי הוֹלִידוֹ אֶת־מְתוּשֶׁלַח
שְׁלֹשׁ מֵאוֹת שָׁנָה וַיּוֹלֶד בָּנִים וּבָנוֹת:

23 וַיְהִי כָּל־יְמֵי חֲנוֹךְ חָמֵשׁ וְשִׁשִּׁים שָׁנָה וּשְׁלֹשׁ מֵאוֹת
שָׁנָה:

24 וַיִּתְהַלֵּךְ חֲנוֹךְ אֶת־הָאֱלֹהִים וְאֵינֶנּוּ כִּי־לָקַח אֹתוֹ אֱלֹהִים:

כה וַיְחִי מְתוּשֶׁלַח שֶׁבַע וּשְׁמֹנִים שָׁנָה וּמְאַת שָׁנָה יּוֹלֶד אֶת־לָמֶךְ:

26 וַיְחִי מְתוּשֶׁלַח אַחֲרֵי הוֹלִידוֹ אֶת־לֶמֶךְ שְׁתַּיִם וּשְׁמוֹנִים שָׁנָה וּשְׁבַע מֵאוֹת שָׁנָה וַיּוֹלֶד בָּנִים יּבָנוֹת:

27 וַיִּהְיוּ כָּל־יְמֵי מְתוּשֶׁלַח תֵּשַׁע וְשִׁשִּׁים שָׁנָה וּתְשַׁע מֵאוֹת שָׁנָה וַיָּמֹת:

28 וַיְחִי־לֶמֶךְ שְׁתַּיִם וּשְׁמֹנִים שָׁנָה וּמְאַת שָׁנָה וַיּוֹלֶד בֵּן:

29 וַיִּקְרָא אֶת־שְׁמוֹ נֹחַ לֵאמֹר זֶה יְנַחֲמֵנוּ מִמַּעֲשֵׂנוּ וּמֵעִצְּבוֹן יָדֵינוּ מִן־הָאֲדָמָה אֲשֶׁר אֵרְרָהּ יְהוָֹה:

ל וַיְחִי־לֶמֶךְ אַחֲרֵי הוֹלִידוֹ אֶת־נֹחַ חָמֵשׁ וְתִשְׁעִים שָׁנָה וַחֲמֵשׁ מֵאֹת שָׁנָה וַיּוֹלֶד בָּנִים וּבָנוֹת:

31 וַיְהִי כָּל־יְמֵי־לֶמֶךְ שֶׁבַע וְשִׁבְעִים שָׁנָה וּשְׁבַע מֵאוֹת שָׁנָה וַיָּמֹת:

32 וַיְהִי־נֹחַ בֶּן־חֲמֵשׁ מֵאוֹת שָׁנָה וַיּוֹלֶד נֹחַ אֶת־שֵׁם אֶת־חָם וְאֶת־יָפֶת:

CHAPTER VI.

א וַיְהִי כִּי־הֵחֵל הָאָדָם לָרֹב עַל־פְּנֵי הָאֲדָמָה וּבָנוֹת יֻלְּדוּ לָהֶם:

2 וַיִּרְאוּ בְנֵי־הָאֱלֹהִים אֶת־בְּנוֹת הָאָדָם כִּי טֹבֹת הֵנָּה וַיִּקְחוּ לָהֶם נָשִׁים מִכֹּל אֲשֶׁר בָּחָרוּ:

תרי טעמי ,והקורא יטעים הגרש קודם התלשא   v. 29.

3 וַיֹּ֤אמֶר יְהוָה֙ לֹא־יָד֨וֹן רוּחִ֤י בָֽאָדָם֙ לְעֹלָ֔ם בְּשַׁגַּ֖ם ה֑וּא
בָשָׂ֑ר וְהָי֣וּ יָמָ֔יו מֵאָ֥ה וְעֶשְׂרִ֖ים שָׁנָֽה׃

4 הַנְּפִלִ֞ים הָי֣וּ בָאָרֶץ֮ בַּיָּמִ֣ים הָהֵם֒ וְגַ֣ם אַֽחֲרֵי־כֵ֗ן אֲשֶׁ֨ר
יָבֹ֜אוּ בְּנֵ֤י הָֽאֱלֹהִים֙ אֶל־בְּנ֣וֹת הָֽאָדָ֔ם וְיָֽלְד֖וּ לָהֶ֑ם הֵ֚מָּה
הַגִּבֹּרִ֛ים אֲשֶׁ֥ר מֵעוֹלָ֖ם אַנְשֵׁ֥י הַשֵּֽׁם׃

ה וַיַּ֣רְא יְהוָ֔ה כִּ֥י רַבָּ֛ה רָעַ֥ת הָֽאָדָ֖ם בָּאָ֑רֶץ וְכָל־יֵ֙צֶר֙
מַחְשְׁבֹ֣ת לִבּ֔וֹ רַ֥ק רַ֖ע כָּל־הַיּֽוֹם׃

6 וַיִּנָּ֣חֶם יְהוָ֔ה כִּֽי־עָשָׂ֥ה אֶת־הָֽאָדָ֖ם בָּאָ֑רֶץ וַיִּתְעַצֵּ֖ב
אֶל־לִבּֽוֹ׃

7 וַיֹּ֣אמֶר יְהוָ֗ה אֶמְחֶ֨ה אֶת־הָֽאָדָ֤ם אֲשֶׁר־בָּרָ֙אתִי֙ מֵעַל֙ פְּנֵ֣י
הָֽאֲדָמָ֔ה מֵֽאָדָם֙ עַד־בְּהֵמָ֔ה עַד־רֶ֖מֶשׂ וְעַד־ע֣וֹף הַשָּׁמָ֑יִם
כִּ֥י נִחַ֖מְתִּי כִּ֥י עֲשִׂיתִֽם׃

8 וְנֹ֕חַ מָ֥צָא חֵ֖ן בְּעֵינֵ֥י יְהוָֽה׃

פרשת נח.

9 אֵ֚לֶּה תּֽוֹלְדֹ֣ת נֹ֔חַ נֹ֗חַ אִ֥ישׁ צַדִּ֛יק תָּמִ֥ים הָיָ֖ה בְּדֹֽרֹתָ֑יו
אֶת־הָֽאֱלֹהִ֖ים הִֽתְהַלֶּךְ־נֹֽחַ׃

וַיּ֥וֹלֶד נֹ֖חַ שְׁלֹשָׁ֣ה בָנִ֑ים אֶת־שֵׁ֖ם אֶת־חָ֥ם וְאֶת־יָֽפֶת׃

11 וַתִּשָּׁחֵ֥ת הָאָ֖רֶץ לִפְנֵ֣י הָֽאֱלֹהִ֑ים וַתִּמָּלֵ֥א הָאָ֖רֶץ חָמָֽס׃

12 וַיַּ֧רְא אֱלֹהִ֛ים אֶת־הָאָ֖רֶץ וְהִנֵּ֣ה נִשְׁחָ֑תָה כִּֽי־הִשְׁחִ֧ית
כָּל־בָּשָׂ֛ר אֶת־דַּרְכּ֖וֹ עַל־הָאָֽרֶץ׃

13 וַיֹּאמֶר אֱלֹהִים לְנֹחַ קֵץ כָּל־בָּשָׂר בָּא לְפָנַי כִּי־מָלְאָה
הָאָרֶץ חָמָס מִפְּנֵיהֶם וְהִנְנִי מַשְׁחִיתָם אֶת־הָאָרֶץ׃

14 עֲשֵׂה לְךָ תֵּבַת עֲצֵי־גֹפֶר קִנִּים תַּעֲשֶׂה אֶת־הַתֵּבָה
וְכָפַרְתָּ אֹתָהּ מִבַּיִת וּמִחוּץ בַּכֹּפֶר׃

טו וְזֶה אֲשֶׁר תַּעֲשֶׂה אֹתָהּ שְׁלֹשׁ מֵאוֹת אַמָּה אֹרֶךְ הַתֵּבָה
חֲמִשִּׁים אַמָּה רָחְבָּהּ וּשְׁלֹשִׁים אַמָּה קוֹמָתָהּ׃

16 צֹהַר ׀ תַּעֲשֶׂה לַתֵּבָה וְאֶל־אַמָּה תְּכַלֶּנָּה מִלְמַעְלָה וּפֶתַח
הַתֵּבָה בְּצִדָּהּ תָּשִׂים תַּחְתִּיִּם שְׁנִיִּם וּשְׁלִשִׁים תַּעֲשֶׂהָ׃

17 וַאֲנִי הִנְנִי מֵבִיא אֶת־הַמַּבּוּל מַיִם עַל־הָאָרֶץ לְשַׁחֵת
כָּל־בָּשָׂר אֲשֶׁר־בּוֹ רוּחַ חַיִּים מִתַּחַת הַשָּׁמָיִם כֹּל
אֲשֶׁר־בָּאָרֶץ יִגְוָע׃

18 וַהֲקִמֹתִי אֶת־בְּרִיתִי אִתָּךְ וּבָאתָ אֶל־הַתֵּבָה אַתָּה וּבָנֶיךָ
וְאִשְׁתְּךָ וּנְשֵׁי־בָנֶיךָ אִתָּךְ׃

19 וּמִכָּל־הָחַי מִכָּל־בָּשָׂר שְׁנַיִם מִכֹּל תָּבִיא אֶל־הַתֵּבָה
לְהַחֲיֹת אִתָּךְ זָכָר וּנְקֵבָה יִהְיוּ׃

כ מֵהָעוֹף לְמִינֵהוּ וּמִן־הַבְּהֵמָה לְמִינָהּ מִכֹּל רֶמֶשׂ הָאֲדָמָה
לְמִינֵהוּ שְׁנַיִם מִכֹּל יָבֹאוּ אֵלֶיךָ לְהַחֲיוֹת׃

21 וְאַתָּה קַח־לְךָ מִכָּל־מַאֲכָל אֲשֶׁר יֵאָכֵל וְאָסַפְתָּ אֵלֶיךָ
וְהָיָה לְךָ וְלָהֶם לְאָכְלָה׃

22 וַיַּעַשׂ נֹחַ כְּכֹל אֲשֶׁר צִוָּה אֹתוֹ אֱלֹהִים כֵּן עָשָׂה׃

CHAPTER VII.

א וַיֹּאמֶר יְהוָה לְנֹחַ בֹּא־אַתָּה וְכָל־בֵּיתְךָ אֶל־הַתֵּבָה כִּי־
אֹתְךָ רָאִיתִי צַדִּיק לְפָנַי בַּדּוֹר הַזֶּה׃

2 מִכֹּל ׀ הַבְּהֵמָה הַטְּהוֹרָה תִּקַּח־לְךָ שִׁבְעָה שִׁבְעָה אִישׁ
וְאִשְׁתּוֹ וּמִן־הַבְּהֵמָה אֲשֶׁר לֹא טְהֹרָה הִוא שְׁנַיִם
אִישׁ וְאִשְׁתּוֹ׃

3 גַּם מֵעוֹף הַשָּׁמַיִם שִׁבְעָה שִׁבְעָה זָכָר וּנְקֵבָה לְחַיּוֹת
זֶרַע עַל־פְּנֵי כָל־הָאָרֶץ׃

4 כִּי לְיָמִים עוֹד שִׁבְעָה אָנֹכִי מַמְטִיר עַל־הָאָרֶץ אַרְבָּעִים
יוֹם וְאַרְבָּעִים לָיְלָה וּמָחִיתִי אֶת־כָּל־הַיְקוּם אֲשֶׁר
עָשִׂיתִי מֵעַל פְּנֵי הָאֲדָמָה׃

ה וַיַּעַשׂ נֹחַ כְּכֹל אֲשֶׁר־צִוָּהוּ יְהוָה׃

6 וְנֹחַ בֶּן־שֵׁשׁ מֵאוֹת שָׁנָה וְהַמַּבּוּל הָיָה מַיִם עַל־הָאָרֶץ׃

7 וַיָּבֹא נֹחַ וּבָנָיו וְאִשְׁתּוֹ וּנְשֵׁי־בָנָיו אִתּוֹ אֶל־הַתֵּבָה מִפְּנֵי
מֵי הַמַּבּוּל׃

8 מִן־הַבְּהֵמָה הַטְּהוֹרָה וּמִן־הַבְּהֵמָה אֲשֶׁר אֵינֶנָּה טְהֹרָה
וּמִן־הָעוֹף וְכֹל אֲשֶׁר־רֹמֵשׂ עַל־הָאֲדָמָה׃

9 שְׁנַיִם שְׁנַיִם בָּאוּ אֶל־נֹחַ אֶל־הַתֵּבָה זָכָר וּנְקֵבָה כַּאֲשֶׁר
צִוָּה אֱלֹהִים אֶת־נֹחַ׃

י וַיְהִי לְשִׁבְעַת הַיָּמִים וּמֵי הַמַּבּוּל הָיוּ עַל־הָאָרֶץ׃

11 בִּשְׁנַת שֵׁשׁ־מֵאוֹת שָׁנָה לְחַיֵּי־נֹחַ בַּחֹדֶשׁ הַשֵּׁנִי בְּשִׁבְעָה־
עָשָׂר יוֹם לַחֹדֶשׁ בַּיּוֹם הַזֶּה נִבְקְעוּ כָּל־מַעְיְנוֹת תְּהוֹם
רַבָּה וַאֲרֻבֹּת הַשָּׁמַיִם נִפְתָּחוּ :

12 וַיְהִי הַגֶּשֶׁם עַל־הָאָרֶץ אַרְבָּעִים יוֹם וְאַרְבָּעִים לָיְלָה :

13 בְּעֶצֶם הַיּוֹם הַזֶּה בָּא נֹחַ וְשֵׁם־וְחָם וָיֶפֶת בְּנֵי־נֹחַ וְאֵשֶׁת
נֹחַ וּשְׁלֹשֶׁת נְשֵׁי־בָנָיו אִתָּם אֶל־הַתֵּבָה :

14 הֵמָּה וְכָל־הַחַיָּה לְמִינָהּ וְכָל־הַבְּהֵמָה לְמִינָהּ וְכָל־
הָרֶמֶשׂ הָרֹמֵשׂ עַל־הָאָרֶץ לְמִינֵהוּ וְכָל־הָעוֹף לְמִינֵהוּ
כֹּל צִפּוֹר כָּל־כָּנָף :

טו וַיָּבֹאוּ אֶל־נֹחַ אֶל־הַתֵּבָה שְׁנַיִם שְׁנַיִם מִכָּל־הַבָּשָׂר
אֲשֶׁר־בּוֹ רוּחַ חַיִּים :

16 וְהַבָּאִים זָכָר וּנְקֵבָה מִכָּל־בָּשָׂר בָּאוּ כַּאֲשֶׁר צִוָּה אֹתוֹ
אֱלֹהִים וַיִּסְגֹּר יְהוָה בַּעֲדוֹ :

17 וַיְהִי הַמַּבּוּל אַרְבָּעִים יוֹם עַל־הָאָרֶץ וַיִּרְבּוּ הַמַּיִם וַיִּשְׂאוּ
אֶת־הַתֵּבָה וַתָּרָם מֵעַל הָאָרֶץ :

18 וַיִּגְבְּרוּ הַמַּיִם וַיִּרְבּוּ מְאֹד עַל־הָאָרֶץ וַתֵּלֶךְ הַתֵּבָה עַל־
פְּנֵי הַמָּיִם :

19 וְהַמַּיִם גָּבְרוּ מְאֹד מְאֹד עַל־הָאָרֶץ וַיְכֻסּוּ כָּל־הֶהָרִים
הַגְּבֹהִים אֲשֶׁר־תַּחַת כָּל־הַשָּׁמָיִם :

כ חֲמֵשׁ עֶשְׂרֵה אַמָּה מִלְמַעְלָה גָּבְרוּ הַמָּיִם וַיְכֻסּוּ הֶהָרִים :

21 וַיִּגְוַע כָּל־בָּשָׂר ׀ הָרֹמֵשׂ עַל־הָאָרֶץ בָּעוֹף וּבַבְּהֵמָה
וּבַחַיָּה וּבְכָל־הַשֶּׁרֶץ הַשֹּׁרֵץ עַל־הָאָרֶץ וְכֹל הָאָדָם :

כֹּל אֲשֶׁר נִשְׁמַת־רוּחַ חַיִּים בְּאַפָּיו מִכֹּל אֲשֶׁר בֶּחָרָבָה 22
מֵתוּ :

וַיִּמַח אֶת־כָּל־הַיְקוּם ׀ אֲשֶׁר ׀ עַל־פְּנֵי הָאֲדָמָה מֵאָדָם 23
עַד־בְּהֵמָה עַד־רֶמֶשׂ וְעַד־עוֹף הַשָּׁמַיִם וַיִּמָּחוּ מִן־הָאָרֶץ
וַיִּשָּׁאֶר אַךְ־נֹחַ וַאֲשֶׁר אִתּוֹ בַּתֵּבָה :

וַיִּגְבְּרוּ הַמַּיִם עַל־הָאָרֶץ חֲמִשִּׁים וּמְאַת יוֹם : 24

CHAPTER VIII.

וַיִּזְכֹּר אֱלֹהִים אֶת־נֹחַ וְאֵת כָּל־הַחַיָּה וְאֶת־כָּל־הַבְּהֵמָה א
אֲשֶׁר אִתּוֹ בַּתֵּבָה וַיַּעֲבֵר אֱלֹהִים רוּחַ עַל־הָאָרֶץ וַיָּשֹׁכּוּ
הַמָּיִם :

וַיִּסָּכְרוּ מַעְיְנֹת תְּהוֹם וַאֲרֻבֹּת הַשָּׁמָיִם וַיִּכָּלֵא הַגֶּשֶׁם 2
מִן־הַשָּׁמָיִם :

וַיָּשֻׁבוּ הַמַּיִם מֵעַל הָאָרֶץ הָלוֹךְ וָשׁוֹב וַיַּחְסְרוּ הַמַּיִם 3
מִקְצֵה חֲמִשִּׁים וּמְאַת יוֹם :

וַתָּנַח הַתֵּבָה בַּחֹדֶשׁ הַשְּׁבִיעִי בְּשִׁבְעָה־עָשָׂר יוֹם לַחֹדֶשׁ 4
עַל הָרֵי אֲרָרָט :

וְהַמַּיִם הָיוּ הָלוֹךְ וְחָסוֹר עַד הַחֹדֶשׁ הָעֲשִׂירִי בָּעֲשִׂירִי ה
בְּאֶחָד לַחֹדֶשׁ נִרְאוּ רָאשֵׁי הֶהָרִים :

וַיְהִי מִקֵּץ אַרְבָּעִים יוֹם וַיִּפְתַּח נֹחַ אֶת־חַלּוֹן הַתֵּבָה 6
אֲשֶׁר עָשָׂה :

7 וַיְשַׁלַּח אֶת־הָעֹרֵב וַיֵּצֵא יָצוֹא וָשׁוֹב עַד־יְבֹשֶׁת הַמַּיִם מֵעַל הָאָרֶץ:

8 וַיְשַׁלַּח אֶת־הַיּוֹנָה מֵאִתּוֹ לִרְאוֹת הֲקַלּוּ הַמַּיִם מֵעַל פְּנֵי הָאֲדָמָה:

9 וְלֹא־מָצְאָה הַיּוֹנָה מָנוֹחַ לְכַף־רַגְלָהּ וַתָּשָׁב אֵלָיו אֶל־הַתֵּבָה כִּי־מַיִם עַל־פְּנֵי כָל־הָאָרֶץ וַיִּשְׁלַח יָדוֹ וַיִּקָּחֶהָ וַיָּבֵא אֹתָהּ אֵלָיו אֶל־הַתֵּבָה:

י וַיָּחֶל עוֹד שִׁבְעַת יָמִים אֲחֵרִים וַיֹּסֶף שַׁלַּח אֶת־הַיּוֹנָה מִן־הַתֵּבָה:

11 וַתָּבֹא אֵלָיו הַיּוֹנָה לְעֵת עֶרֶב וְהִנֵּה עֲלֵה־זַיִת טָרָף בְּפִיהָ וַיֵּדַע נֹחַ כִּי־קַלּוּ הַמַּיִם מֵעַל הָאָרֶץ:

12 וַיִּיָּחֶל עוֹד שִׁבְעַת יָמִים אֲחֵרִים וַיְשַׁלַּח אֶת־הַיּוֹנָה וְלֹא־יָסְפָה שׁוּב־אֵלָיו עוֹד:

13 וַיְהִי בְּאַחַת וְשֵׁשׁ־מֵאוֹת שָׁנָה בָּרִאשׁוֹן בְּאֶחָד לַחֹדֶשׁ חָרְבוּ הַמַּיִם מֵעַל הָאָרֶץ וַיָּסַר נֹחַ אֶת־מִכְסֵה הַתֵּבָה וַיַּרְא וְהִנֵּה חָרְבוּ פְּנֵי הָאֲדָמָה:

14 וּבַחֹדֶשׁ הַשֵּׁנִי בְּשִׁבְעָה וְעֶשְׂרִים יוֹם לַחֹדֶשׁ יָבְשָׁה הָאָרֶץ:

טו וַיְדַבֵּר אֱלֹהִים אֶל־נֹחַ לֵאמֹר:

16 צֵא מִן־הַתֵּבָה אַתָּה וְאִשְׁתְּךָ וּבָנֶיךָ וּנְשֵׁי־בָנֶיךָ אִתָּךְ:

17 כָּל־הַֽחַיָּ֞ה אֲשֶׁר־אִתְּךָ֗ מִכָּל־בָּשָׂ֡ר בָּע֧וֹף וּבַבְּהֵמָ֣ה וּבְכָל־
הָרֶ֛מֶשׂ הָרֹמֵ֥שׂ עַל־הָאָ֖רֶץ הוצא אִתָּ֑ךְ וְשָֽׁרְצ֣וּ בָאָ֔רֶץ
וּפָר֥וּ וְרָב֖וּ עַל־הָאָֽרֶץ׃

18 וַיֵּ֣צֵא־נֹ֔חַ וּבָנָ֖יו וְאִשְׁתּ֑וֹ וּנְשֵֽׁי־בָנָ֖יו אִתּֽוֹ׃

19 כָּל־הַֽחַיָּ֗ה כָּל־הָרֶ֙מֶשׂ֙ וְכָל־הָע֔וֹף כֹּ֖ל רוֹמֵ֣שׂ עַל־הָאָ֑רֶץ
לְמִשְׁפְּחֹ֣תֵיהֶ֔ם יָֽצְא֖וּ מִן־הַתֵּבָֽה׃

כ וַיִּ֥בֶן נֹ֛חַ מִזְבֵּ֖חַ לַֽיהוָ֑ה וַיִּקַּ֞ח מִכֹּ֣ל ׀ הַבְּהֵמָ֣ה הַטְּהֹרָ֗ה
וּמִכֹּל֙ הָע֣וֹף הַטָּה֔וֹר וַיַּ֥עַל עֹלֹ֖ת בַּמִּזְבֵּֽחַ׃

21 וַיָּ֣רַח יְהוָה֮ אֶת־רֵ֣יחַ הַנִּיחֹ֒חַ֒ וַיֹּ֨אמֶר יְהוָ֜ה אֶל־לִבּ֗וֹ לֹֽא־
אֹ֠סִף לְקַלֵּ֨ל ע֤וֹד אֶת־הָֽאֲדָמָה֙ בַּֽעֲב֣וּר הָֽאָדָ֔ם כִּ֠י יֵ֣צֶר
לֵ֧ב הָֽאָדָ֛ם רַ֖ע מִנְּעֻרָ֑יו וְלֹֽא־אֹסִ֥ף ע֛וֹד לְהַכּ֥וֹת אֶת־
כָּל־חַ֖י כַּֽאֲשֶׁ֥ר עָשִֽׂיתִי׃

22 עֹ֖ד כָּל־יְמֵ֣י הָאָ֑רֶץ זֶ֡רַע וְ֠קָצִיר וְקֹ֨ר וָחֹ֜ם וְקַ֧יִץ וָחֹ֛רֶף
וְי֥וֹם וָלַ֖יְלָה לֹ֥א יִשְׁבֹּֽתוּ׃

278. עוֹד ('ôd), adv. *still, yet, again*.

279. עוֹלָה [386] ('ôlâ(h)), (const. עוֹלַת) f., *burnt-offering*, pl. עוֹלוֹת.

280. עָוֹן [226] ('âwôn), (const. עֲוֹן) m., *guilt, sin*.

281. עוֹלָם [430] ('ôlâm), m., *age, eternity*.

282. עוּף [32] ('ûf), *fly*, ('פ Lary. and mid-vow.), Pôlēl Impf. יְעוֹפֵף, i. 20.

283. עוֹף [70] ('ôf), m., *bird, fowl*, collective.

284. עוֹר [95] ('ôr), m., *skin*.

285. עָזַב [114] ('âzăv), *leave, forsake*, ('פ Lary.), Impf. יַעֲזָב־, ii. 24.

286. עֵזֶר [21] ('ēzĕr), m., *help*.

287. עַיִן [872] ('ăyĭn), f., *eye*, pl. with suf. עֵינֵיכֶם, iii. 5.

288. עִיר [1074] ('îr), f., *city*, pl. עָרִים.

289. עִירָד ('îrâd), pr. n. *Irad*.

290. עֵירֹם [10] ('êrôm), adj. *naked*, pl. עֵירֻמִּם, iii. 7.

291. עַל ('ăl), prep. *upon, with*, מֵעַל, מִן, *from upon*.

292. עָלָה [862] ('âlâ(h)), *go up*, ('פ Lary. and ל"ה), Impf. יַעֲלֶה, ii. 6, Hif. *offer up*.

293. עָלֶה [18] ('âlê(h)), (const. עֲלֵה) m., *leaf*.

294. עִם ('ĭm), prep. *with, along with*.

294a. עִמָּד prep. *with*.

295. עָפָר [108] ('âfâr), m., *dust*.

296. עֵץ [326] ('ēṣ), m., *tree*.

297. עָצַב [17] ('âṣăv), *suffer pain*, ('פ Lary.), Hiθp. w. Wâw convers. וַיִּתְעַצֵּב, *grieve oneself*, vi. 6.

298. עֶצֶב [7] ('ĕṣĕv), m., *pain, grievance*.

299. עִצָּבוֹן [3] (ĭṣṣâvôn), (const. עִצְּבוֹן) m., *labor, pain*.

300. עֶצֶם [120] ('ĕṣĕm), f., *bone*.

301. עָקֵב [14] ('âḳēv), (const. עֲקֵב) m., heel.

302. עֶרֶב [132] ('érĕv), m., evening.

303. עֹרֵב [10] ('ôrēv), m., raven.

304. עָרוֹם and עָרֹם [16] ('ârōm), adj. naked, pl. עֲרוּמִים, but עֲרוּמִים ('ᵃrŭmmîm), ii. 25.

305. עָרוּם [11] ('ârûm), m., prudent, crafty.

306. עֵשֶׂב [33] ('ēśĕv), m., green herb, plant.

307. עָשָׂה [2521] ('âśâ(h)), do, make, (פ Lary. and ל"ה), Impf. with Wâw convers. וַיַּעַשׂ, i. 7.

308. עֲשִׂירִי [26] ('ᵃśîrî), ordinal num. tenth.

309. עֶשֶׂר [333] ('âśâr), cardinal number ten, used only in compounds with units, as in אַחַד עָשָׂר eleven, fem. עֶשְׂרֵה ('ĕśrē(h)). v. 8.

310. עֶשֶׂר (m. עֲשָׂרָה) [172] ('ēśĕr), f., ten.

311. עֵת [300] ('ēθ), c., time.

312. עַתָּה ('ăttâ(h)), adv. now.

313. פֶּה [480] (pê(h)), mouth, with fem. suf. פִּיהָ, iv. 11.

314. פֶּן־ (pĕn +), conj. lest, with Impf.

315. פָּנִים [2000] (pânîm), m., faces, const. פְּנֵי, i. 2.

316. פַּעַם [110] (pă'ăm), f., tread or step, once.

317. פָּצָה [15] (pâṣâ(h)), rend, open, (ל"ה) iv. 11.

318. פֶּצַע [7] (péṣă'), m., wounding, with suf. פְּצָעִי, iv. 23.

319. פָּקַח [20] (pâḳăḥ), open (the eyes), (ל' Lary.), Nif. נִפְקְחוּ, iii. 5. Impf. with Wâw convers. וַתִּפָּקַחְנָה, iii. 7.

320. פָּרַד [26] (pârăd), separate ('ע Lary.), Nif. Impf. יִפָּרֵד, ii. 10.

321. פָּרָה [28] (pårå(h)), *bear fruit* (לְ"ה), Imv. פְּרוּ, i. 22, 28.

322. פְּרִי [115] (pᵉrî), m., *fruit.*

323. פָּתַח [141] (påθäḥ), *open,* Nïf. *be opened,* in pause נִפְתָּחוּ, vii. 11, (לְ Lary.).

324. פֶּתַח [160] (péθäḥ), m., *opening, door.*

325. צֹאן [268] (ṣô'n), c., *sheep, flock,* collective.

326. צָבָא [13] (ṣåvå'), m., *army, host.*

327. צַד [33] (ṣäd), m., *side,* with prep. and suf. בְּצִדָּה, vi. 16.

328. צַדִּיק [203] (ṣäddîḳ), m., *just, righteous.*

329. צֹהַר [24] (ṣôhär), f., *light,* collective, *lights, windows.*

330. צָוָה [509] (ṣåwå(h)), Ḳäl not used, (לְ"ה), Pï'ēl צִוָּה, *command,* Impf. with Wåw convers. וַיְצַו.

331. צִלָּה (ṣillå(h)), pr. n. *Zillah.*

332. צֶלֶם [16] (ṣélĕm), m., *image, likeness,* i. 26, 27.

333. צֵלָע [42] (ṣēlå'), m., *side, rib,* pl. צְלָעוֹת.

334. צָמַח [31] (ṣåmäḥ), *sprout,* (לְ Lary.), Hïf. *make sprout,* Impf. with Wåw convers. וַיַּצְמַח, ii. 5.

335. צָעַק [54] (ṣå'äḳ), *cry out* (ע Lary.), Part. act. plur. צֹעֲקִים, iv. 10.

336. צִפּוֹר [39] (ṣippôr), c., *little bird.*

337. קֶדֶם [61] (ḳédĕm), m., *front, east,* as adv. *before.*

338. קִדְמָה [4] (ḳidmå(h)), f., *eastward,* const. קִדְמַת, ii. 14.

339. קָדֵשׁ [171] (ḳådäš), *be pure, clean, holy,* Pï'ēl *consecrate,* Impf. with Wåw convers. וַיְקַדֵּשׁ, ii. 3.

340. קָוָה [48] (ḳâwâ(h)), hope,
(ל"ה), Nif. assemble,
gather together, Impf.
יְקַוּוּ, i. 9.

341. קוֹל [500] (ḳôl), m.,
voice, sound.

342. קוּם [450] (ḳûm), rise up,
(mid-vow.), Impf. with
Wâw convers. וַיָּקָם, iv.
8, Hif. הֲקֵמֹתִי, vi. 18.

343. קוֹמָה [45] (ḳômâ(h)),
f., stature, height.

344. קוֹץ [12] (ḳôṣ), m., thorn.

345. קָטֹן [56] (ḳâṭōn), adj.
little.

346. קַיִן (ḳăyĭn), pr. n. Cain.

347. קֵינָן (ḳênân), pr. n. Cainan.

348. קַיִץ [20] (ḳăyĭṣ), m.,
fruit-harvest, summer.

349. קָלַל [82] (ḳâlăl), be light
in weight, be diminished,
(ע"ע), Pĭ'ēl make light
of, curse.

350. קֵן [13] (ḳēn), m., cell.

351. קָנָה [81] (ḳânâ(h)), get,
acquire (ל"ה), iv. 1.

352. קֵץ [65] (ḳēṣ) m., end.

353. קָצֶה [90] (ḳâṣê(h)),
(const. קְצֵה) (= קֵץ),
m., end.

354. קָצִיר [54] (ḳâṣîr) m.,
harvest.

355. קֹר [1] (ḳôr), m., cold.

356. קָרָא [855] (ḳârâ'), call,
(ל"א), Impf. with Wâw
convers. וַיִּקְרָא, i. 5. Nif.
Impf. יִקְרָא, ii. 28.

357. רָאָה [1295] (râ'â(h)), see,
look ('ע Lary. and ל"ה),
Impf. with Wâw convers.
וַיַּרְא, i. 4, vi. 2.

358. רֹאשׁ [600] (rô'š), m.,
head, pl. רָאשִׁים.

359. רִאשׁוֹן [177] (rĭ'šôn),
adj. first.

360. רֵאשִׁית [51] (rē'šîθ), f.,
denom. from רֹאשׁ, be-
ginning.

361. רַב [466] (răv), m., much,
many, fem. רַבָּה.

362. רָבַב [17] (râvăv), multiply, (ע"ע), Inf. const.
רֹב, vi. 1.

363. רָבָה [243] (râvâ(h)), increase (ל"ה), Impf. Jus-
sive יִרֶב, i. 22, Imv. רְבוּ,
i. 22, 28, Hïf. הִרְבָּה,
Inf. abs. הַרְבָּה, iii. 16,
Impf. 1st pers. אַרְבֶּה,
iii. 16.

364. רָבַץ [30] (râvăṣ), lie
down, crouch, Part. act.
רֹבֵץ, iv. 7.

365. רֶגֶל [260] (rěğěl), c., foot,
with suf. רַגְלָהּ, viii. 9.

366. רָדָה [25] (râdâ(h)), have
dominion, rule (ל"ה),
Impf. יִרְדּוּ, i. 26, Imv.
רְדוּ, i. 28.

367. רוּחַ [11] (rû(ă)ḥ), Ḳăl
not used, Hïf. inhale,
smell, 3 m. s. with Wåw
convers. וַיָּרַח, viii. 21.

368. רוּחַ [375] (rû(ă)ḥ), f.,
breath, spirit, wind.

369. רוּם [193] (rûm), be high,
become high, rise, (mid-
vow.) Ḳăl Impf. 3 f. s.
with Wåw convers.
וַתָּרָם, vii. 17.

370. רֹחַב [21] (rôḥăv), m.,
breadth, with suf. רָחְבָּהּ,
vi. 15.

371. רָחַף [3] (râḥăf.), (ע
Lary.), Ḳăl not used, Pï'ēl
רָחַף, brood, hover over,
Part. fem. מְרַחֶפֶת, i. 2.

372. רִיחַ [56] (rê(ă)ḥ), m.,
fragrance.

373. רָמַשׂ [14] (râmăś),
creep, Part. act. with art.
הָרֹמֵשׂ, i. 26, fem.
הָרֹמֶשֶׂת, i. 21.

374. רֶמֶשׂ [17] (rěměś), m.,
creeping thing.

375. רַע (f. רָעָה) [650] (ră'),
adj. bad, evil.

376. רָעָה (râ'å(h)), f., bad-
ness, wickedness.

377. רָעָה [183] (râ'å(h)),
feed, tend, (ע' Lary. and
ל"ה), Part. act. const.
רֹעֵה, iv. 2.

378. רַק (răḳ), adv. only.

379. רָקִיעַ [17] (râḳî(ă)'), m.,
expanse, const. רְקִיעַ, i.
20.

380. שָׁאַר [131] (šå'ăr), remain, ('ע Lary.), Nïf. be
left, vii. 23.

381. שֶׁבַע [96] (šěvă'), (m.
שִׁבְעָה)f., seven, שְׁבִיעִי
seventh, ii. 2, שִׁבְעָתַיִם
sevenfold, iv. 15.

382. שָׁבַת [70] (šåvăθ), rest,
cease, Impf. with Wâw
convers. וַיִּשְׁבֹּת, ii. 2.

383. שֶׁגֶם [1] (šăggăm), only
in vi. 3, with בְּ, (in their)
wandering(?).

384. שֹׁהַם [11] (šōhăm), m.,
onyx, sardonyx.

385. שׁוּב [1100] (šûv), turn,
(mid-vow.), Impf. 2d sg.
תָּשׁוּב, iii. 19.

386. שׁוּף [3] (šûf), bruise,
crush, (mid-vow.), Impf.
יְשׁוּפְךָ, iii. 15.

387. שָׁחַת [151] (šåhăθ), Ķăl
not used, ('ע Lary.),
Pïël destroy, corrupt; Nïf.
Impf. with Wâw convers.
וַתִּשָּׁחֵת, vi. 11.

388. שִׁית [85] (šîθ), put, place,
('ע"י), Perf. שָׁת, iv. 25,
Impf. 1st. sg. אָשִׁית, iii.
15.

389. שָׁכַךְ [5] (šåxăx), subside, ('ע"ע), Impf. 3 m. pl.
with Wâw cons. וַיָּשֹׁכּוּ,
viii. 1.

390. שָׁכַן [127] (šåxăn), abide,
dwell, Hïf. Impf. with
Wâw convers. וַיַּשְׁכֵּן•

391. שָׁלַח [837] (šålăh), send,
put forth ('ל Lary.), Impf.
יִשְׁלַח, Pï'ēl Impf. with
Wâw convers. and suf.
וַיְשַׁלְּחֵהוּ, iii. 23.

392. שָׁלֹשׁ (šålôš), (m.
שְׁלֹשָׁה)f., three; ordinal
שְׁלִישִׁי, third, pl.
שָׁלֹשִׁים; שְׁלִישִׁים
thirty.

393. שָׁם (šåm), adv. there.

394. שֵׁם [850] (šēm), m.,
name.

395. שֵׁם (šēm), pr. n. Shem.

396. שָׁמַיִם [400] (šåmăyïm),
m., only in pl. heavens.

397. שְׁמֹנֶה (šᵉmônê(h)),
(m. שְׁמֹנָה) f., eight,
שְׁמֹנִים, eighty.

398. שָׁמַע [1104] (šâmăʻ),
hear, listen to ('לְ Lary.),
Impf. 3 pl. with Wâw
convers. וַיִּשְׁמְעוּ, iii. 8,
Imv. שְׁמַע, iv. 23.

399. שָׁמַר [460] (šâmăr), keep,
watch, Inf. const. with
prep. and suf. לְשָׁמְרָה,
ii. 15, Part. act. שֹׁמֵר,
iv. 9.

400. שָׁנָה [877] (šânâ(h)), f.,
year, pl. שָׁנִים.

401. שֵׁנִי [150] (šēnî), adj. second, pl. שֵׁנִים, vi. 16.

402. שְׁנַיִם [680] (šᵉnăyĭm),
(const. שְׁנֵי) m., cardinal
two, f. שְׁתַּיִם, const.
שְׁתֵּי, iv. 19.

403. שָׁעָה [15] (šâʻâ(h)), look,
regard ('עַ Lary. and
ה"ל), Impf. with Wâw
convers. וַיִּשַׁע, iv. 4.

404. שָׁקָה [74] (šâḳâ(h)),
Ḳăl not used, Hĭf.

הִשְׁקָה, give to drink,
ii. 6.

405. שָׁרַץ [14] (šârăṣ), swarm,
be many ('עַ Lary.), i. 20.

406. שֶׁרֶץ [15] (šérĕṣ), m.,
swarm, collective, reptiles.

407. שֵׁשׁ [26] (šēš), (m. שִׁשָּׁה)
f., six, ordinal שִׁשִּׁי,
sixth, i. 31.

408. שֵׁת (šēθ), pr. n. Seth.

409. שָׂדֶה [330] (śâdê(h)), m.,
field, open country.

410. שִׂיחַ [4] (śî(ă)ḥ), m.,
shrub, bush.

411. שִׂים [603] (śîm), put,
set, place, (ע"י), Impf.
יָשִׂים, Jussive. יָשֵׂם,
with Wâw convers.
וַיָּשֶׂם, ii. 8.

412. שָׂכַל [76] (śâxăl), look
at, behold, Hĭf. make wise,
Inf. const. הַשְׂכִּיל, iii. 6.

413. תַּאֲוָה [26] (tă'ᵕwâ(h)),
(const. תַּאֲוַת) f., de-
sire.

414. תְּאֵנָה [37] (tᵉʼēnâ(h)),
f., fig, fig-tree.

415. תֵּבָה [28] (tēvå(h)), f.,
ark, chest.

416. תֹּהוּ [20] (tóhû), m.,
wasteness, desolation.

417. תְּהוֹם [35] (tᵉhôm), c.,
abyss, deep.

418. תּוּבַל קַיִן (tûvăl ḳăyĭn),
pr. n. Tubal-cain, iv. 22.

419. תָּוֶךְ [430] (tåwᵉx), m.,
midst, const. תּוֹךְ, i. 6.

420. תּוֹלְדֹת [39] (tôlᵉđôθ), f.
pl., generations, history.

421. תַּחַת (tắḥăθ), prep. under.

422. תַּחְתִּי [20] (tăḥtî), m.,
lowest part, pl. תַּחְתִּים,
vi. 16.

423. תָּמִים [90] (tåmîm),
(const. תְּמִים) m., per-
fect, complete.

424. תַּנִּין [1] (tănnîn), m.,
water-serpent, monster, pl.
תַּנִּינִם, i. 21.

425. תָּפַר [4] (tåfăr), sew
together, Impf. pl. with
Wåw convers. וַיִּתְפְּרוּ,
iii. 7.

426. תָּפַשׂ [54] (tåfăś), catch
(harp strings), play, Part.
act. תֹּפֵשׂ, iv. 21.

427. תַּרְדֵּמָה [7] (tărdē-
må(h)), (const. תַּרְדְּמַת)
f., deep sleep, ii. 21.

428. תְּשׁוּקָה [3] (tᵉšûḳå(h)),
f., desire, longing.

429. תֵּשַׁע [58] (tēšă‘), (const.
תְּשַׁע) (m. תִּשְׁעָה)
nine, תִּשְׁעִים, ninety.

ENGLISH-HEBREW VOCABULARY

OF

GENESIS I.—VIII.*

Abel, 97.
abide, 90.
above, 228.
abyss, 417.
acquire, 351.
Ada, 275.
add, 165.
adhere, 85.
after, 16, 64.
again, 278.
age, 88, 281.
all, 181.
alone, 49.
along with, 294.
also, 80.
altar, 212.
among, 48.
and, 108.
anger, 35.
another, 15.
appearance, 234.
Ararat, 42.
ark, 415.
army, 326.
as, 176.
ashamed, be, 55.
aside, turn, 268.
assemble, 340.
avenge, 261.

Bad, 375.
bdellium, 51.

be, 99.
bear, 162.
bear fruit, 321.
beast, 53, 128.
before, 150, 240, 337.
beget, 162.
begin, 132.
beginning, 360.
begun, be, 132.
behind, 64.
behold, v., 412.
behold! 101.
belly, 78.
bend the knee, 70.
between, 57.
bird, 283, 336.
blade, glittering, 196.
bless, 70.
blood, 89.
low, 256.
bone, 300.
book, 270.
born, be, 162.
both..and, 80.
bread, 197.
breadth, 370.
breath, 259, 264, 368.
breathe, 256.
bring, 54.
bring forth, 162.
bring out, 167.

broken up, be, 65.
bronze, 249.
brood, 371.
brother, 12.
bruise, v., 386.
bruise, 118.
brute, dumb, 53.
build, 62.
bush, 410.
burn, 144.
burnt-offering, 279.
but even, 36.

Cain 346.
Cainan, 347.
call, 356.
cast out, ·83.
catch, 426.
cast, 382.
cell, 350.
change into, 103.
cherub, 190.
chest, 415.
child, 163.
choose, 56.
city, 288.
clean, 148.
clean, be, 339.
cleave, adhere, 85.
cleave, divide, 65.
clothe, 195.

* See last paragraph on page 228.

251

coat, 191.
cold, 355.
collection, 231.
come, 54.
come to pass, 99.
comfort, 247.
command, 330.
complete, v., 183.
complete, 423.
conceive, 106.
conception, 107.
consecrate, 339.
corrupt, 387.
country, open, 409.
covenant, 69.
cover, 187.   [189.
cover (with pitch),
covering, 220.
crafty, 304.
create, 67.
creature, living, 128.
creep, 373.
creeping thing, 374.
crouch, 364.
crush, 386.
cry out, 335.
cubit, 29.
curse, 41, 349.
cut, 67.   [146.
cutting instrument,

Darkness, 147.
daughter, 72.
dawn, 66.
day, 159.
deceive, 263.
deep, 417.
deep sleep, 427.
deluge, 207.
desire, v., 135.
desire, 135, 413, 428.
desolation, 416.
destroy, 213, 387.
devour, 22.

die, 77, 211.   [349.
diminished, be, 140.
divide, 50, 65.
dividing, 50.
do, 307.
dominion, 223.
dominion, have, 366.
door, 324.
dove, 160.
dried up, be, 153.
drink, give, 404.
drive, 83.
dry land, 143, 154.
dry up, 141.
dryness, 143.
dust, 295.
dwell, 174, 390.

Ear, give, 11.
earth, 5, 40.
east, 337.
eastward, 338.
eat, 22.
Eden, 276.
eighty, 397.
elder, 76.
emptiness, 52.
encompass, 266.
end, 352, 353.
ended, be, 183.
enmity, 18.
Enoch, 139.
Enosh, 32.
eternity, 281.
Eve, 122.
even, but, 34.
evening, 302.
every, 181.
evil, 375.
existing, being, 170.
expanse, 379.
expel, 83.
expire, 77.

eye, 287.

Faces, 315.
fail, 140.
fall, 258.
family, 236.
fat,-ness, 130.
father, 1.
favor, 138.
fear, 171.
feed, 377.
female, 260.
field, 409.
fifth, 137.
fig,-tree, 414.
find, 230.
finish, 183.
first, 359.
first-born, 59.
fish, 86.
five, 137.
flame, 196.
flesh, 71.
flock, 325.
flood, 207.
fly, v., 282.
food, 23, 197, 206.
foot, 365.
for, 63, 180, 192.
forge, v., 198.
form, v., 67, 168.
form, 169.
forsake, 285.
fountain, 227.
four, 38.
fowl, 283.
fragrance, 372.
free, set, 132.
fresh, 151.
from, 224.
from upon, 291.
front, 337.
fruit, 322.

fruit, bear, 321.
fugitive, 242.
full, be, 221.

Garden, 81.
gather, 34.
gather together, 340.
gathering, 231.
generation, 88, 420.
get, 351.
giants, 257.
Gihon, 79.
girdle, 119.
give, 265.
give rain, 216.
give rest, 245.
glittering, blade, 196.
glow, 144.
go, 100.
go about, 100.
go in, 54.
go out, 167.
go up, 292.
God, 26.
gold, 110.
good, be, 161.
good, 149.
grace, 138.
grass, tender, 94.
great, 76.
green herb, 306.
greenness, 173.
grievance, 298.
grieve oneself, 297.
ground, 5.
guilt, 280.

Ham, 133.
hammer, v., 198.
hand, 155.
happen, 99.
harp, 185.
harvest, 354.

he, 98.
head, 358.
hear, 398.
heart, 194.
heat, 134.
heavens, 396.
heel, 301.
height, 342.
help, 286.
herb, green, 306.
hero, 74.
Hiddekel, 120.
hide, 117, 271.
hide oneself, 103.
high, 73.
high, be, 369.
history, 420.
hold, 182.
hole, 131.
holy, be, 339.
host, 326.
house, 58.
household, 58.
hover over, 371.
hundred, 204.

I, 33.
if, 28.
image, 90, 332.
imagination, 169.
in, 48.
in behalf of, 63.
in, go, 54.
in presence of, 240.
increase, 363.
inhale, 367.
Irad, 289.
iron, 68.

Jabal, 152.
Japheth, 156.
Jared, 172.
journey, 92.

Jubal, 158.
judge, 87.
just, 328.

Keep, 399.
kill, 105.
kind, 219.
knee, bend the, 70.
know, 156.

Labor, 299.
Lamech, 201.
land, dry, 143, 154.
lattice, 37.
leaf, 293.
leave, 285.
left, be, 380.
length, 39.
lest, 60, 314.
lie down, 364.
life, 126.
lift up, 262.
light, 8, 205, 329.
light (not dark), be, 7.
light, be, 349.
light, give, 7.
lights, 329.
like, 176.
likeness, 90, 332.
listen, 11.
listen to, 398.
little, 343.
live, 127, 129. [170.
living creature, 127,
lo! 101.
longing, 428.
look, v., 357, 403.
look, 234.
look at, 412.
loose, 132.
Lord, 157.
lowest part, 422.
luminary, 205.

lyre, 185.

Mahalaleel, 209.
make, 307.
make sprout, 234.
male, 113.
man, 4, 20.
man of valor, 74.
many, 361.
many, be, 406.
Mehujael, 214.
Methushael, 237.
Methuselah, 238.
midst, 419.
might, 179.
mighty, be, 75.
mist, 3.
monster, 424.
month, 121.
moon, new, 121.
more, yea, 36.
morning, 66.
mother, 27.
mountain, 104.
mouth, 313.
much, 361.
multiply, 362.

Naamah, 254.
naked, 290, 304.
name, 394.
newly plucked, 151.
night, 199.
nine, -ty, 429.
no, 193.
Noah, 246.
Nod, 244.
nose, 35.
not, that, 60.
not, there is, 19.
not yet, 150.
nothing, 19
now, 312.

Offering, 226.
offer up, 292.
olive-tree, 111.
on, 48.
on account of; 184.
once, 316.
one, 14.
one tread or step, 316.
only, 21, 378.
onyx, 384.
open, 317, 319, 323.
open country, 409.
opening, 324.
organ, 277.
out, bring, 167.
out, cast, 83.
out, cry, 335.
out, go, 167.
outside, 124.
over, pass, 273.

Pain, 298, 299.
pain, suffer, 123, 297.
palm, 188.
park, 81.
part, lowest, 422.
pass, come to, 99.
pass over, 273.
perfect, 423.
pipe, 277.
pitch, -wood, 82.
pity, 247.
place, v., 388, 411.
place, 232.
plan, 215.
plant, v., 250.
plant, 306.
play, 426.
pleasantness, 251.
present, 226.
prudent, 304.
pure, be, 339.
purpose, 215.

put, 388, 411.
put forth, 391.
put on, 195.

Rain, 84.
rain, give, 216.
raven, 303.
reed, 277.
regard, 403.
remain, 380.
remember, 112.
rend, 317.
repent, 247.
reptiles, 406.
rest, v., 245, 382.
rest, 251.
rest, give, 245.
resting, a, 225.
resting place, 225.
restrain, 182.
rib, 333.
righteous, 328.
rise up, 342, 369.
river, 243.
rule, v., 87, 235, 366.
rule, 223.
rule over, 235.

Sardonyx, 384.
say, 30.
sea, 164.
season, 210.
second, -story, 400.
seduce, 263.
see, 357.
seed, 116.
seed, yield, 115.
seed-time, 116.
send, 391.
separate, 50, 320.
separation, 49.
serpent, 248.
serpent, water-, 424.

serve, 272.
set, 411.
set free, 132.
set time, 210.
Seth, 408.
seven, -th, -fold, 381.
sew together, 425.
sheep, 325.
Shem, 395.
shine, 7.
show, 239.
shower, 84.
shrub, 410.
shut, 67, 269.
side, 327, 333.
sign, 9.
sin, 125, 280.
sister, 13.
sit, 174.
six, -th, 407.
skin, 284.
slay, 105.
sleep, 175.
sleep, deep, 427.
smell, 367.
smite, 241, 252.
so, 184.
sole, 188.
son, 61.
song, 31.
soul, 259.
sound, 341.
sow, 115.
species, 219.
spirit, 264, 368.
spring, 227.
sprout, 93,. 334.
sprout, make, 334.
star, 178.
stature, 343.
step, one, 316.
still, 278.
stone, 2.

street, 124.
strength, 179.
strike, 252.
strong, be, 75.
subdue, 177.
subside, 389.
substance, 233.
suffer pain, 297.
summer, 348.
surely, 21.
swarm, v., 405.
swarm, 406.
sweat, 114.
sword, 142.

Take, 202.
taken, be, 202.
tell, 239.
ten, 309, 310.
tend, 377.
tender grass, 94.
tent, 6.
tenth, 308.
that, conj., 180.
that not, 60.
the, 95.
then, 10.
there, 393.
therefore, 184.
these, 25.
they, 102.
third, 392.
thirty, 392.
this, 109.
thistle, 91.
thorn, 344.
thorny plant, 91.
thou, 47.
three, 392.
thus, 184.
Tigris, 120.
till, v., 272.
till, 274.

time, 311.
time set, 210.
to, 192.
tool, 146.
totality, 181.
touch, 241.
tread, one, 316.
tread upon, 177.
tree, 296.
true that? is it, 36.
Tubal-Cain, 418.
tunic, 191.
turn, 102, 266, 385.
turn aside, 268.
turning itself, 103.
two, 402.

Under, 241.
until, 274.
unto, 24.
up, go, 292.
upon, 291.
upon, tread, 177.
upwards, 228.
utterance, 31.

Valor, man of, 74.
vapor, 3.
very, 203.
violence, 136.
voice, 341.

Wait, 123.
walk, 100.
wanderer, 253.   (383
wanderings, in their,
wasteness, 416.
watch, 399.
water, 218.
water-serpent, 424.
way, 92.
wealth,. 233.
what? 208.

WORD LISTS—HEBREW.

LIST I.
Verbs occurring 500—5000 times.

1.	אָכַל	8.	יָלַד	15.	עָבַר	22.	רָאָה
2.	אָמַר	9.	יָצָא	16.	עָלָה	23.	שִׂים
3.	בּוֹא	10.	יָשַׁב	17.	עָמַד	24.	שׁוּב
4.	דָּבַר	11.	לָקַח	18.	עָשָׂה	25.	שָׁלַח
5.	הָיָה	12.	מוּת	19.	צָוָה	26.	שָׁמַע
6.	הָלַךְ	13.	נָשָׂא	20.	קוּם		
7.	יָדַע	14.	נָתַן	21.	קָרָא		

LIST II.
Verbs occurring 200—500 times.

27.	אָהַב	37.	יָסַף	47.	מָלַךְ	57.	פָּקַד
28.	אָסַף	38.	יָרֵא	48.	מָצָא	58.	רָבָה
29.	בָּנָה	39.	יָרַד	49.	נָגַד	59.	רוּם
30.	בָּקַשׁ	40.	יָרַשׁ	50.	נָטָה	60.	שָׁכַב
31.	בָּרַךְ	41.	יָשַׁע	51.	נָכָה	61.	שָׁמַר
32.	זָכַר	42.	כּוּן	52.	נָפַל	62.	שָׁפַט
33.	חָזַק	43.	כָּלָה	53.	נָצַל	63.	שָׁתָה
34.	חָטָא	44.	כָּרַת	54.	סוּר		
35.	חָיָה	45.	כָּתַב	55.	עָבַד		
36.	יָכֹל	46.	מָלֵא	56.	עָנָה		

LIST III.
Verbs occurring 100–200 times.

64.	אָבַד	66.	בּוֹשׁ	68.	בִּין	70.	גָּאַל
65.	אָמֵן	67.	בָּטַח	69.	בָּכָה	71.	גָּדַל

257

72.	גּוּר	83.	יָטַב	94.	סָבַב	105.	שָׂרַף
73.	גָּלָה	84.	יָתַר	95.	סָפַר	106.	שָׁאַל
74.	דָּרַשׁ	85.	כָּבֵד	96.	עָזַב	107.	שָׁבַע
75.	הָלַל	86.	כָּסָה	97.	פָּנָה	108.	שָׁבַר
76.	הָרַג	87.	כָּפַר	98.	קָבַר	109.	שָׁחָה
77.	זָבַח	88.	לָבֵשׁ	99.	קָדַשׁ	110.	שָׁחַת
78.	חָלַל	89.	לֶחֶם	100.	קָרַב	111.	שָׁכַן
79.	חָנָה	90.	לָכַד	101.	רָדַף	112.	שָׁלַךְ
80.	חָשַׁב	91.	נָגַע	102.	רוּץ	113.	שָׁלֵם
81.	טָמֵא	92.	נָגַשׁ	103.	רָעָה	114.	שָׁרַת
82.	יָדָה	93.	נָסַע	104.	שָׂנֵא		

LIST IV.

Verbs occurring 50–100 times.

115.	אָבָה	130.	חָדַל	145.	יָרָה	160.	נָחַל
116.	אָחַז	131.	חוּל	146.	כָּבַס	161.	נָטַע
117.	אָסַר	132.	חָלָה	147.	כָּעַס	162.	נָכַר
118.	אָרַר	133.	חָלַק	148.	כָּשַׁל	163.	נָצַב
119.	בָּחַר	134.	חָנַן	149.	לוּן	164.	נָצַח
120.	בָּלַע	135.	חָפֵץ	150.	לָמַד	165.	נָצַר
121.	בָּעַר	136.	חָרָה	151.	מָדַד	166.	נָשַׂג
122.	בָּקַע	137.	חָרַשׁ	152.	מָהַר	167.	סָגַר
123.	בָּרָא	138.	חָתַת	153.	מָכַר	168.	סָתַר
124.	בָּרַח	139.	טָהַר	154.	מָלַט	169.	עוּר
125.	דָּבַק	140.	יָבֵשׁ	155.	מָשַׁח	170.	עָזַר
126.	הָפַךְ	141.	יָכַח	156.	מָשַׁל	171.	עָנָה
127.	זוּר	142.	יָעַץ	157.	נָבַט	172.	עָרַךְ
128.	זָנָה	143.	יָצַק	158.	נָדַח	173.	פָּדָה
129.	זָרַע	144.	יָצַר	159.	נוּחַ	174.	פּוּץ

175.	פָּלָא	184.	קָנָה	193.	רָפָא	201.	שִׁית
176.	פָּלַל	185.	קָרַע	194.	רָצָה	202.	שָׁכַם
177.	פָּעַל	186.	רָחַם	195.	שָׂבַע	203.	שָׁמַד
178.	פָּרַר	187.	רָחַץ	196.	שָׂכַל	204.	שָׁמֵם
179.	פָּרַשׂ	188.	רָחַק	197.	שָׁבַת	205.	שָׁקָה
180.	צָעַק	189.	רִיב	198.	שָׂדַד	206.	תָּמַם
181.	צָפָה	190.	רָכַב	199.	שָׁחַט	207.	תָּפַשׂ
182.	צָרַר	191.	רָנַן	200.	שִׁיר	208.	תָּקַע
183.	קָלַל	192.	רָעַע				

LIST V.

Nouns occurring 500–5000 times.

1.	אָב	11.	בַּיִת	21.	לֵב	31.	קוֹל
2.	אָדָם	12.	בֵּן	22.	מֵאָה	32.	קֹדֶשׁ
3.	אֲדֹנָי	13.	דָּבָר	23.	מַיִם	33.	רֹאשׁ
4.	אָח	14.	דֶּרֶךְ	24.	מֶלֶךְ	34.	שִׁבְעָה
5.	אֶחָד	15.	הַר	25.	נֶפֶשׁ	35.	שֵׁם
6.	אַחַר	16.	חַי	26.	עֶבֶד	36.	שָׁנִים
7.	אִישׁ	17.	טוֹב	27.	עַיִן	37.	שָׁנָה
8.	אֱלֹהִים	18.	יָד	28.	עִיר		
9.	אֱנוֹשׁ	19.	יוֹם	29.	עַם		
10.	אֶרֶץ	20.	כֹּהֵן	30.	פָּנִים		

LIST VI.

Nouns occurring 300–500 times.

38. אָרוֹן	48. זָהָב	58. מָקוֹם	68. פֶּה
39. אֹהֶל	49. חֹדֶשׁ	59. מִשְׁפָּט	69. רַב
40. אֶלֶף	50. חָמֵשׁ	60. נָבִיא	70. רוּחַ
41. אַרְבָּעָה	51. חֶרֶב	61. סָבִיב	71. שָׂדֶה
42. אִשָּׁה	52. יָם	62. עוֹלָה	72. שַׂר
43. בְּהֵמָה	53. כְּלִי	63. עוֹלָם	73. שָׁלוֹשׁ
44. בַּת	54. כֶּסֶף	64. עֵץ	74. שָׁמַיִם
45. גָּדוֹל	55. לֶחֶם	65. עֶשֶׂר	75. שַׂעַר
46. גּוֹי	56. מִזְבֵּחַ	66. עֶשְׂרִים	76. תָּוֶךְ
47. דָּם	57. מִלְחָמָה	67. עֵת	

LIST VII.

Nouns occurring 200–300 times.

77. אֶבֶן	87. בָּשָׂר	97. מְאֹד	107. עָוֺן
78. אֲדָמָה	88. גְּבוּל	98. מוֹעֵד	108. צֹאן
79. אַיִל	89. זֶרַע	99. מַחֲנֶה	109. קְרָב
80. אֵל	90. חַטָּאת	100. מַטֶּה	110. רֶגֶל
81. אַמָּה	91. חַיִל	101. מַלְאָךְ	111. רַע
82. אַף	92. חֶסֶד	102. מִנְחָה	112. רָשָׁע
83. אָרוֹן	93. כָּבוֹד	103. מַעֲשֶׂה	113. שָׁלוֹם
84. בֶּגֶד	94. כַּף	104. מִשְׁפָּחָה	114. שֵׁשׁ
85. בֹּקֶר	95. לֵבָב	105. נַחֲלָה	115. תּוֹרָה
86. בְּרִית	96. לַיְלָה	106. נַעַר	

LIST VIII.

Nouns occurring 100–200 times.

116. אָזֵן	134. יַיִן	152. מִשְׁכָּן	169. צַר
117. אַרְבָּעִים	135. יָמִין	153. נֶגֶב	170. רִאשׁוֹן
118. בְּכוֹר	136. יֵשׁ	154. נַחַל	171. רֹב
119. בָּקָר	137. יָשָׁר	155. נְחֹשֶׁת	172. רֶחֶב
120. גִּבּוֹר	138. כֶּבֶשׂ	156. נָשִׂיא	173. רֶכֶב
121. דּוֹר	139. כֹּחַ	157. סוּס	174. רָעָב
122. זֶבַח	140. כָּנָף	158. סֵפֶר	175. שָׂפָה
123. זָקֵן	141. כִּסֵּא	159. עֲבוֹדָה	176. שֵׁבֶט
124. חוֹמָה	142. כֶּרֶם	160. עֵדָה	177. שַׁבָּת
125. חוּץ	143. לָשׁוֹן	161. עָפָר	178. שְׁלִישִׁי
126. חָכָם	144. מִגְרָשׁ	162. עֶצֶם	179. שֶׁמֶן
127. חָכְמָה	145. מָוֶת	163. עֶרֶב	180. שְׁמֹנָה
128. חֵמָה	146. מְלָאכָה	164. פַּר	181. שֶׁמֶשׁ
129. חֲמִשִּׁים	147. מַמְלָכָה	165. פְּרִי	182. שֵׁנִי
130. חֵצִי	148. מִסְפָּר	166. פֶּתַח	183. שֶׁקֶר
131. חֹק	149. מַעַל	167. צֶדֶק	184. תּוֹעֵבָה
132. חֻקָּה	150. מִצְוָה	168. צְדָקָה	185. תָּמִיד
133. יַחַד	151. מַרְאָה		

LIST IX.

Nouns occurring 50–100 times.

186. אֶבְיוֹן	191. אֲחֻזָּה	196. אַלְמָנָה	201. אֹרַח
187. אֶדֶן	192. אַחֲרוֹן	197. אֱמוּנָה	202. אֲרִי
188. אָוֶן	193. אַחֲרִית	198. אֹמֶר	203. אַרְיֵה
189. אוֹצָר	194. אֱלוֹהַּ	199. אֵפוֹד	204. אֶרֶךְ
190. אוֹת	195. אַלּוּף	200. אֶרֶז	205. אִשָּׁה

№		№		№		№	
206.	בֶּטֶן	234.	חֲמוֹר	262.	מַצָּה	290.	פֵּאָה
207.	בָּמָה	235.	חָמָס	263.	מִקְדָּשׁ	291.	צוּר
208.	בַּעַל	236	חֵן	264.	מִקְנֶה	292.	צָרָה
209.	בַּרְזֶל	237.	חֵץ	265.	מָרוֹם	293.	קֶדֶם
210.	בְּרָכָה	238.	חֶרְפָּה	266.	מַשָּׂא	294.	קָטוֹן
211.	גָּאוֹן	239.	חֹשֶׁךְ	267.	מָשִׁיחַ	295.	קְטֹרֶת
212.	גְבוּרָה	240.	טָהוֹר	268.	מִשְׁמֶרֶת	296.	קִיר
213.	גֶבֶר	241.	טָמֵא	269.	מִשְׁקָל	297.	קָנֶה
214.	גּוֹרָל	242.	יְאוֹר	270.	נֶדֶר	298.	קֵץ
215.	גַּיְא	243.	יוֹמָם	271.	נֶסֶךְ	299.	קָצֶה
216.	גָּמָל	244.	יֶלֶד	272.	נַעֲרָה	300.	קָצִיר
217.	גֶּפֶן	245.	יַעַר	273.	סֶלָה	301.	קָרְבָּן
218.	גֵּר	246.	יְרִיעָה	274.	סֶלַע	302.	קָרוֹב
219.	דֶּבֶר	247.	יְשׁוּעָה	275.	סֹלֶת	303.	קֶרֶן
220.	דְּבַשׁ	248.	כְּסִיל	276.	עֶבֶר	304.	קֶשֶׁת
221.	דֶּלֶת	249.	כְּרוּב	277.	עֵד	305.	רֵאשִׁית
222.	דַּעַת	250.	כָּהֵף	278.	עֵדוּת	306.	רָחַק
223.	הֵיכָל	251.	מִגְדָּל	279.	עוּר	307.	רִיב
224.	הָמוֹן	252.	כָּנָן	280.	עֵז	308.	רֵיחַ
225.	זֵכֶר	253.	מִדָּה	281.	עֹז	309.	רָצוֹן
226.	זְרוֹעַ	254.	מְדִינָה	282.	עֶלְיוֹן	310.	שְׂמֹאל
227.	חֶבֶל	255.	מוּסָר	283.	עָמָל	311.	שִׂמְחָה
228.	חַג	256.	מִזְמוֹר	284.	עֵמֶק	312.	שָׂעִיר
229.	חָדָשׁ	257.	מִזְרָח	285.	עֳנִי	313.	שְׁאוֹל
230.	חִטָּה	258.	מָחָר	286.	עָנָן	314.	שְׁאֵרִית
231.	חֵלֶב	259.	מַחֲשֶׁבֶת	287.	עֵצָה	315.	שְׁבִיעִי
232.	חֲלוֹם	260.	מַלְכוּת	288.	עֲרָבָה	316.	שִׁבְעִים
233.	חָלָק	261.	מְעַט	289.	עֶרְוָה	317.	שׁוֹפָר

318.	שׁוֹר	322.	שְׁמָמָה	326.	שִׁשִּׁים	330.	תִּפְלָה
319.	שִׁיר	323.	שֵׁן	327.	תָּמִים	331.	תְּרוּמָה
320.	שֻׁלְחָן	324.	שִׁפְחָה	328.	תִּפְאָרָה	332.	תִּשְׁעָה
321.	שָׁלֵם	325.	שֶׁקֶל	329.	תִּפְאֶרֶת		

WORD LISTS—TRANSLATION.

LIST I.

Verbs occurring 500—5000 times.

1. Eat
2. Say
3. Go in
4. Speak
5. Be
6. Go
7. Know
8. Bring forth
9. Go out
10. Sit, dwell
11. Take
12. Die
13. Lift up
14. Give
15. Pass over
16. Go up
17. Stand
18. Do, make
19. Command
20. Rise, stand
21. Call, meet
22. See
23. Put
24. Turn
25. Send
26. Hear

LIST II.

Verbs occurring 200—500 times.

27. Love
28. Gather
29. Build
30. Seek
31. Bless
32. Remember
33. Be strong
34. Sin
35. Live
36. Be able
37. Add
38. Be afraid
39. Go down
40. Possess
41. Deliver
42. Prepare
43. Complete
44. Cut
45. Write
46. Be full
47. Be king
48. Find
49. Make known
50. Stretch out
51. Smite
52. Fall
53. Snatch, deliver
54. Turn aside
55. Serve
56. Answer
57. Visit
58. Multiply
59. Be high
60. Lie down
61. Keep
62. Judge
63. Drink

LIST III.

Verbs occurring 100—200 times.

64. Perish
65. Be firm
66. Be ashamed
67. Trust
68. Perceive
69. Weep
70. Redeem
71. Be great
72. Sojourn
73. Reveal
74. Tread, seek
75. Praise
76. Kill
77. Sacrifice
78. Pollute, begin
79. Encamp
80. Impute, think
81. Be unclean

264

82. Thank	93. Depart	104. Hate
83. Be good	94. Surround	105. Burn
84. Be left	95. Number	₊06. Ask
85. Be heavy	96. Abandon	107. Swear
86. Conceal	97. Turn about	108. Break in pieces
87. Cover	98. Bury	109. Do obeisance
88. Put on	99. Be holy	110. Corrupt
89. Fight	100. Draw near	111. Dwell
90. Capture	101. Pursue	112. Cast
91. Touch	102. Run	113. Be whole
92. Approach	103. Feed	114. Minister

LIST IV.

Verbs occurring 50—100 times.

115. Be willing	143. Pour out	171. Be afflicted
116. Seize	144. Form	172. Arrange
117. Bind	145. Cast, instruct	173. Redeem
118. Curse	146. Wash	174. Scatter
119. Choose	147. Be provoked	175. Separate, be won-
120. Swallow	148. Stumble	176. Pray [derful
121. Consume	149. Lodge	177. Do, make
122. Cleave, split	150. Learn	178. Break, fail
123. Create	151. Measure	179. Spread out
124. Flee	152. Hasten	180. Cry out
125. Cleave, cling	153. Sell	181. Watch, cover
126. Turn, overthrow	154. Escape	182. Distress
127. Sojourn [tion	155. Anoint	183. Be light
128. Commit fornica-	156. Rule	184. Get, obtain
129. Sow	157. Look, regard	185. Rend
130. Cease [forth, wait	158. Drive away	186. Have mercy
131. Be pained, bring	159. Rest	187. Wash
132. Be sick	160. Inherit	188. Be far off
133. Distribute	161. Plant	189. Strive
134. Be gracious	162. Know, be ignorant	190. Ride
135. Delight	163. Set	191. Sing, cry aloud
136. Be angry [silent	164. Be pre-eminent	192. Be evil
137. Plow, engrave, be	165. Keep, watch	193. Heal
138. Be dismayed	166. Reach	194. Be pleased
139. Be clean	167. Shut	195. Suffice
140. Be dry	168. Conceal	196. Act wisely, pros-
141. Reprove	169. Awake	197. Cease, rest [per
142. Give counsel	170. Assist	198. Destroy

199. Kill	203. Destroy [tonished	207. Catch, seize
200. Sing	204. Be desolate, as-	208. Strike, blow (a
201. Put	205. Drink	[trumpet)
202. Rise early	206. Finish	

LIST V.

Nouns occurring 500—5000 times.

1. Father	14. Way	26. Servant
2. Man, mankind	15. Mountain	27. Eye, fountain
3. LORD	16. Living, life	28. City
4. Brother	17. Good	29. People
5. One	18. Hand	30. Face
6. After	19. Day	31. Voice
7. Man	20. Priest	32. Holiness
8. God	21. Heart	33. Head
9. Man, mankind	22. Hundred	34. Seven
10. Earth	23. Water	35. Name
11. House	24. King	36. Two
12. Son	25. Soul	37. Year
13. Word, thing		

LIST VI.

Nouns occurring 300—500 times.

38. Master	51. Sword	64. Tree
39. Tent	52. Sea	65. (Ten)-teen
40. Ox, thousand	53. Article, vessel	66. Twenty
41. Four	54. Silver	67. Time
42. Woman	55. Bread	68. Mouth
43. Cattle	56. Altar	69. Many
44. Daughter	57. War	70. Spirit
45. Great	58. Place	71. Field
46. Nation	59. Judgment	72. Prince
47. Blood	60. Prophet	73. Three
48. Gold	61. Around	74. Heavens
49. New, month	62. Burnt-offering	75. Gate
50. Five	63. Age.	76. Midst

LIST VII.

Nouns occurring 200—300 times.

77. Stone	80. Mighty one, God	83. Ark
78. Ground	81. Cubit	84. Garment
79. Ram	82. Nose, anger	85. Morning

86. Covenant	96. Night	106. Boy, servant
87. Flesh	97. Exceedingly	107. Iniquity
88. Boundary	98. Season	108. Flock
89. Seed	99. Camp	109. Midst
90. Sin	100. Rod, tribe	110. Foot
91. Strength	101. Messenger	111. Friend, neigh-
92. Kindness	102. Offering	112. Wicked [bor
93. Honor	103. Work	113. Peace
94. Palm of hand	104. Family	114. Six
95. Heart	105. Inheritance	115. Law

LIST VIII.

Nouns occurring 100—200 times.

116. Ear	140. Wing	164. Bullock
117. Forty	141. Throne	165. Fruit
118. First-born	142. Vineyard	166. Door
119. Herd, cattle	143. Tongue	167. Righteousness
120. Hero	144. Pasture	168. Righteousness
121. Generation	145. Death	169. Adversary
122. Sacrifice	146. Work	170. First
123. Old man, elder	147. Kingdom	171. Abundance
124. Wall	148. Number	172. Breadth
125. Abroad	149. Above	173. Chariot
126. Wise	150. Commandment	174. Famine
127. Wisdom	151. Appearance[nacle	175. Lip, shore
128. Heat, fury	152. Dwelling, [taber-	176. Rod, tribe
129. Fifty	153. South country	177. Rest, sabbath
130. Half	154. Valley, brook	178. Third
131. Statute	155. Bronze, copper	179. Oil, fat
132. Statute	156. Prince	180. Eight
133. Together, alike	157. Horse	181. Sun
134. Wine	158. Book	182. Second
135. Right hand	159. Service	183. Falsehood
136. There is	160. Congregation	184. Abomination
137. Straight, upright	161. Dust	185. Continuity
138. Lamb	162. Bone	
139. Strength	163. Evening	

LIST IX.

Nouns occurring 50—100 times.

186. Needy
187. Socket
188. Iniquity
189. Treasury
190. Sign
191. Possession
192. Last
193. Latter. end
194. God
195. Leader, ox
196. Widow
197. Faithfulness
198. Saying
199. Ephod
200. Cedar
201. Way, path
202. Lion
203. Lion
204. Length
205. Fire-offering
206. Belly
207. High-place
208. Master, Baal
209. Iron
210. Blessing
211. Pride
212. Might
213. Mighty one, man
214. Lot
215. Valley
216. Camel
217. Vine
218. Stranger
219. Pestilence

220. Honey
221. Door
222. Knowledge
223. Temple
224. Multitude
225. Male
226. Arm, strength
227. Line, destruction
228. Festival
229. Fresh, new
230. Wheat
231. Fat
232. Dream
233. Portion
234. He-ass
235. Violence
236. Favor, grace
237. Arrow, handle
238. Reproach
239. Darkness
240. Clean
241. Unclean
242. River, Nile
243. Daily
244. Child, youth
245. Forest
246. Curtain
247. Deliverance
248. Fool
249. Cherub
250. Shoulder
251. Tower
252. Shield
253. Measure

254. Province
255. Chastisement,
256. Psalm [warning
257. East
258. To-morrow
259. Thought
260. Kingdom
261. A little
262. Unleavened food
263. Sanctuary
264. Property
265. High place
266. Burden, tribute
267. Anointed one
268. Observance
269. Weight
270. Vow
271. Libation
272. Maiden
273. Pause
274. Rock
275. Fine flour
276. Over, beyond
277. Witness
278. Testimony
279. Skin, leather
280. Goat
281. Strength
282. High
283. Labor, misery
284. Valley
285. Affliction
286. Cloud
287. Counsel

288. Plain	303. Horn	318. Ox
289. Nakedness	304. Bow	319. Song
290. Side	305. Beginning	320. Table
291. Rock	306. Distant	321. Peace-offering
292. Adversity	307. Strife	322. Desolation, waste
293. Before, east	308. Savor	323. Tooth
294. Small	309. Desire	324. Maid-servant
295. Incense	310. Left hand	325. Shekel
296. Wall	311. Rejoicing	326. Sixty
297. Stalk	312. Hairy, goat	327. Perfect
298. End	313. Underworld	328. Glory
299. End	314. Remnant	329. Glory
300. Harvest	315. Seventh	330. Prayer
301. Offering	316. Seventy	331. Heave-offering
302. Near	317. Trumpet	332. Nine